Psychology in Sports Coaching

es

Have you ever wondered how athletes learn and make use of the feedback they are given by their coach, or how a coach could make his or her feedback more effective for athletes?

Psychology in Sports Coaching has been written specifically for students studying coaching who want to improve their understanding of incorporating psychology into coaching practice. As such, it provides information on how coaches establish the psychological needs of athletes in order for them to provide psychological interventions, such as mental imagery, mental toughness training, and coping effectiveness training.

This book also provides the reader with information on enhancing the awareness of athletes and the relationships that occur between the coach and the athlete. It explains how coaches can coach children, adolescents, adults and athletes with learning disabilities. These groups of athletes have different learning styles, are motivated by different factors and prefer instructions to be administered differently. So, it is important that coaches tailor their coaching based on the athlete they coach, as this has the potential to enhance the performance and enjoyment of the players that are being coached.

Essential reading for all students of sports coaching and sport psychology, and for practising sports coaches, this book will help develop and extend coaching expertise.

Adam R. Nicholls is Lecturer in the Department of Psychology at the University of Hull, UK. He is a Health Professions Council-registered sport and exercise psychologist, who has published over 40 scientific papers on the areas of stress, coping, emotions, and mental toughness. Much of his research has featured international and professional athletes.

Leigh Jones is National Coach Development Manager for the Hong Kong Rugby Football Union and National XV's Head Coach. He is a BASES-accredited sport and exercise scientist with 20 years' applied experience in the UK as a professional coach.

D0322386

Psychology in Sports Coaching

Theory and practice

Adam R. Nicholls and Leigh Jones

Routledge
Taylor & Francis Group

LONDON AND NEW YORK

First published 2013
by Routledge
2 Park Square, Milton Park, Abingdon, Oxon OX14 4RN

Simultaneously published in the USA and Canada
by Routledge
711 Third Avenue, New York, NY 10017

Routledge is an imprint of the Taylor & Francis Group, an informa business

British Library Cataloguing in Publication Data
A catalogue record for this book is available from the British Library

Library of Congress Cataloging in Publication Data
Nicholls, Adam R.
Psychology in sports coaching : theory and practice / by Adam Nicholls and
Leigh Jones.
  p. cm.
Includes bibliographical references and index.
1. Coaching (Athletics) – Psychological aspects. 2. Sports – Psychological
aspects. I. Jones, Leigh. II. Title.
GV711.N54 2013
796.07′7-dc23   2012006093

ISBN: 978-0-415-62598-2 (hbk)
ISBN: 978-0-415-62599-9 (pbk)
ISBN: 978-0-203-10271-8 (ebk)

Typeset in Times New Roman
by HWA Text and Data Management, London

To my lovely niece Daisy, may you always receive excellent coaching!
– Adam

To my son Sam, I hope this in some way inspires you.
– Leigh

Contents

Illustrations

Introduction

This book has specifically been written to help students studying coaching to understand the psychological principles of coaching to maximise coaching effectiveness. The purpose of this introduction is to explain:

- Sports coaching: its purpose, what it is, and how it differs from teaching
- What sport psychology is and isn't and its synergy with coaching
- Contexts in which coaches and sport psychologists work together
- Contexts in which coaches might prefer not to work with a sport psychologist
- The benefits of incorporating psychology within coaching
- Psychology and an athlete's ability
- The structure and contents of this book
- How to get the most out of this book
- Chapter features.

Sports coaching: its purpose, what it is, and how it differs from teaching

According to Lyle (2011), the purpose of sports coaching is to improve the performance of an athlete or sports team. Providing a definition of sports coaching that fully encapsulates what it is, can be somewhat problematic and goes much beyond this introduction. There are a number of extensive commentaries regarding what sport coaching is and how it can be conceptualised (Cushion, 2007a, 2007b; Lyle, 2007).

For the purposes of this book, sport coaching refers to the process in which a person or people attempt to improve the sporting performance of an athlete or team in competition, by manipulating the behaviour and creating practice environments that facilitate improvement. This person or people, are often given the title of 'coach', and perform a multitude of roles (Lyle, 2011). Indeed, Lyle (2011) stated that the coach provides technical advice to his or her athlete or team with the sole purpose of helping an athlete or team achieve better performances and thus results when competing. In addition to providing technical support, Côté and Gilbert (2009) also suggested that sport coaches provide leadership, motivation, and education to their athletes. Although the primary role of coaches who engage in sports coaching is performance enhancement, sport coaching also has the potential to enhance the psychological well-being of athletes by making sport a positive experience for athletes (Côté *et al.*, 2010).

Coaching is different from teaching. Sport coaching refers to the process of preparing an athlete or team to perform within a sports competition, whereas teaching refers to developing a person's skills not for competitive purposes (Lyle, 2011). As such, sport coaching is concerned primarily with performance enhancement within competitive sport.

What sport psychology is and isn't and its synergy with coaching

Psychology refers to the scientific analysis of the way human beings behave, think, and feel. As such, sport psychology refers to the scientific analysis or the way humans behave, think, and feel within sporting contexts, such as training and competition. According to Nicholls and Callard (2012) there are two primary goals of sport psychology: (1) to ensure the psychological well-being of athletes and (2) maximise performance. As such, sport psychology and coaching have a common purpose: performance maximisation of athletes or sports teams. Unlike sport psychology, coaching is not primarily concerned with maximising psychological well-being. However, coaching has the potential to improve well-being by creating positive experiences for athletes (Côté *et al.*, 2010). As such, coaching and sport psychology complement each other nicely, so it could be argued that one of the roles a coach should play should involve an element of psychology, to enhance performance above and beyond what technical training drills may achieve alone.

Some coaches may be sceptical of sport psychology, partly due to the negative attention that this discipline receives or a coach's negative experiences of sport psychology. There are many unqualified individuals working in professional sport who pose as sport psychologists. These individuals will not be sufficiently trained to provide an adequate service and may cause more harm than good. Such individuals may give coaches and athletes unrealistic expectations regarding what sport psychology can achieve.

It is important that coaches realise that sport psychology is not an instant cure for the problems an athlete may be encountering. As stated by Nicholls and Callard (2012), teaching an athlete mental skills is not like waving a magic wand in front of his or her face, that will instantly transform the athlete or team in to world beaters. However, sport psychology involves teaching athletes a variety of mental skills, which when practised can help athletes improve their performance and boost mental well-being.

Contexts in which coaches and sport psychologists work together

Coaches and sport psychologists may work together when athletes from individual sports such as tennis or golf employ both a coach and a sport psychologist. In other circumstances, coaches may employ the sport psychologist to work with his or her team. Generally, a coach would employ a sport psychologist when he or she feels that the athlete or team are suffering from psychological problems (e.g. anxiety) that are having a negative impact on performance. The sport psychologist would work with the athlete or team to help with anxiety, which could then result in performance being increased when the full effects of the sport psychology sessions are observed.

Additionally, coaches might work exclusively with sport psychologists, so the sport psychologist does not have any contact with the athletes, but provides information to the coach who relays that information. For example, the sport psychologist might help with matters such as how to provide more effective instructions, feedback, and communication strategies. There are a number of sport psychologists who work exclusively in this capacity. As such, there are a number of contexts in which coaches and sport psychologists may work alongside one another.

Contexts in which coaches might prefer not to work with a sport psychologist

Although coaches can employ sport psychologists themselves to help their athletes, there may be some instances in which coaches are reluctant to introduce a sport psychologist to his or her team or athlete. For example, a coach may be reticent to hire a sport psychologist if he or she has just started coaching an athlete or team, because the coach may feel that the sport psychologist could in some ways undermine his or her relationship with the team or athletes. Some athletes might not feel comfortable talking about their feelings or problems with sport psychologists who they do not know, and would prefer to speak to their coach. In these instances, coaches might prefer not to employ a sport psychologist, even though the team or athlete could benefit from mental training. In these instances, coaches could provide psychological training themselves and incorporate psychology within their coaching.

The benefits of incorporating psychology within coaching

Coaches invest lots of time learning about how to improve the technical skills of their players or athletes through many different drills, how to improve the fitness or conditioning of their players, and how they can teach different tactics or strategies to enhance performance. Perhaps less time is spent learning and understanding how a coach can apply psychological principles within their coaching. Using psychology in coaching is something that has been, on the whole, ignored in many coaching manuals. This is a shame because there are so many athletes that could benefit from being taught different psychological skills. For example, there are many athletes who perform well in training, but struggle to transfer their performance to competition settings. Physiologically or technically the athlete has not changed, but perhaps these athletes struggle psychologically and could benefit from a coach providing them with some psychological training.

Incorporating psychology within coaching enables the coach to become more effective by improving the quality of his or her coaching, which will have numerous benefits for players including increased enjoyment and performance.

Psychology and an athlete's ability

Psychology is not just for elite athletes, and athletes at all levels ranging from beginners to Olympic champions can potentially benefit from psychology. Therefore, coaches who coach club-level tennis players to those who coach international rugby union teams can help their players by incorporating psychology within their coaching and some of the principles advocated in this book.

The structure and contents of this book

This book has been written for students who study coaching, and who want to learn more about applying sport psychology principles to coaching. This book provides the reader with an understanding of how coaches can apply psychological principles to their coaching to maximise the enjoyment, learning, and performance of the athletes that are coached. The book is presented in six parts:

Part I: Identifying the psychological needs of athletes

This part of the book provides information on the techniques that coaches can use to assess the needs of their athletes, to establish which mental skills training interventions to deliver. As such, Part I provides information on how coaches can conduct interviews (Chapter 1) and use questionnaires (Chapter 2). Some athletes may prefer to talk more than other athletes, whereas others may prefer writing their answers down in the form of questionnaires.

Part II: How to help athletes: mental skills training

Part II describes different mental skill training techniques and provides practical advice on how a coach can deploy a range of psychological skills such as mental imagery (Chapter 3), developing mental toughness (Chapter 4), maximising confidence (Chapter 5), coping effectiveness training (Chapter 6), in addition to choking prevention training (Chapter 7), and helping injured athletes (Chapter 8). These chapters contain scientific evidence that underpins their usefulness and are also supported by sample dialogue to give the coach additional understanding of how to deploy such psychological skills.

Part III: Facilitating awareness

In this part, information is provided on how the coach can assess what the athlete would like to achieve in his or sport through helping the athlete set different goals (Chapter 9) and performance standards that the player wants to achieve through performance profiling (Chapter 10).

Part IV: Coaching different populations

This section of the book provides information on considering the needs of the athlete and how this should influence coaching sessions. There is a chapter on coaching children (Chapter 11), adolescents (Chapter 12), adults (Chapter 13), and athletes with learning disabilities (Chapter 14). These chapters provide information on the different learning styles athletes of different ages have and how this could influence how they are coached. Furthermore, information on how to provide effective feedback, instruction, motivation, reduce dropout rates, and coaching behaviour are other factors that are considered within this part of the book.

Part V: Relationships and support

Part V provides information on the coach–athlete relationship and how the coach can build a strong relationship with the athlete (Chapter 15). This part also contains information on how the coach can build cohesion in team settings (Chapter 16) and can provide social support to athletes (Chapter 17).

Part VI: Concluding thoughts

Chapter 18 considers ethical issues around coaches providing sport psychology, information on the regulation of sport and exercise psychologists, referrals, and practical implications.

Chapter features

Each chapter is set out in same format and includes:

Purpose of the chapter

Every chapter outlines its purposes at the very beginning.

Case studies

All of the chapters, excluding Chapter 18, contain a case study to give the reader a deeper insight and understanding of how coaches can use sport psychology within their coaching. There is also a case study reflection for each case study, that highlights some of the key implications. Thus, this book provides both a theoretical and applied understanding of the psychological principles for coaching.

Summary points

Each chapter contains a series of bullet points that summarise the key points in the chapter.

Practice exam questions

Each chapter contains five practice exam questions, which will allow the student to practise answering questions, and thus will be very helpful for revision.

Critical thinking questions: applying theory to coaching practice

Every chapter concludes with five critical thinking questions. These critical thinking questions will assess how the knowledge gained in the chapter can be transferred to real life coaching scenarios.

Part I

Identifying the psychological needs of athletes

1 Conducting needs analysis interviews

The aim of this chapter is to provide coaches with information regarding how they can establish the psychological needs of an athlete, so that an appropriate intervention can be devised. Information is provided on:

*   the purpose of interviewing athletes;
*   the interview guide;
*   encouraging athletes to open up;
*   listening;
*   avoiding mind reading.

The purpose of interviewing athletes

An interview involves the coach asking a series of questions and listening to the athlete's responses with the aim of trying to gain more knowledge about the needs of the athlete and the problems that he or she is experiencing (Bernstein and Nietzel, 1980). Furthermore, a coach's judgement regarding what psychological training the athlete requires can be gathered from an interview (Bernstein and Nietzel, 1980; Taylor and Schneider, 1992). In order for coaches to attain in-depth information from the athlete, coaches can develop an interview guide.

The interview guide

Taylor and Schneider (1992) developed an interview guide for sport psychologists who want to interview their athletes, which has been adapted in this chapter for coaches to use. This is an excellent guide, although some aspects of their guide (i.e. athletes being asked to describe their athletic status, family, and health) might not be necessary, given that most coaches will generally know more about their athlete than a sport psychologist. The interview is based on the coach asking questions about understanding the problem, building a more detailed understanding, influences and consequences, changes prior to the problem starting, and important life events.

It is important that coaches realise this is just a guide and that the coach does not have to follow the guide regimentally. That is, the coach might want to change the order of the questions, or he or she might not want to ask all of the questions.

Understanding the problem

Before a coach can help an athlete it is important that he or she understands the problem from the athlete's perspective (Petitpas, 2000). Taylor and Schneider (1992) suggested that coaches might want to ask questions such as:

- Please describe the problem.
- How frequently does it (the problem) occur?
- When did it first begin?
- How long has it been going on for?
- Where and when is it most likely to occur?
- What do you think causes it?

Building a more detailed understanding

Once the coach has established what the problem is, he or she can start asking some more probing questions that yield much more information on the problem. This provides the athlete with the opportunity to describe his or her experiences in more detail. Based on the guidelines of Taylor and Schneider (1992), the coach might want to ask the following questions:

- Describe a situation in which the problem occurred. I want you to give me as much detail as possible so I can understand as much as I can.
- Was this the first time that it happened?
- When does it normally occur and is there a consistent pattern?
- What things are going on when the problem is at its worst?
- What things are going on when the problem is at its best?

Influences and consequences

The coach can now ask more probing questions to gather information on the possible influences and consequences (Taylor and Schneider, 1992). As such, the coach might want to ask some of the following questions regarding the athlete's personal influences, social influences, and consequences, which may be related to the problem:

- Who was around you when the situation that you described occurred and what were these people doing? (Social influence question)
- Describe what you were thinking when the incident occurred. (Personal influence question)
- How were you feeling when it happened? (Personal influence question)
- How did you behave? (Personal influence question)
- Please describe what happened after the problem occurred. (Consequence question)
- How did others react? (Consequence question)

Changes prior to the problem starting

Questions relating to factors that might have changed before the problem starting might yield some interesting information. Taylor and Schneider (1992) suggested that questions should be directed towards any physical, mental, technical, and equipment changes that might have occurred. Coaches might want to ask the following questions:

- Please describe the quality and quantity of your training leading up to the problem first occurring. (Physical question)
- Did you have any illness, injury, or fatigue problems prior to the problem starting? (Physical question)
- How did you feel mentally prior to the problem starting? (Mental question)
- Did you notice feeling more worried or less confident? (Mental question)
- Did you make any technical adjustments prior to the problem starting? (Technical question)
- Did you change any equipment prior to the problem starting? (Equipment question)

Important life events

The questions relating to changes in the athlete's physical or mental state, technical adjustments, or equipment might not always yield interesting information and the coach could explore life events that could have contributed to the problem. The coach could ask the following questions:

- Describe some of the most important events in your life.
- Did anything happen in your life away from sport close to the problem occurring?
- Have there been any major changes in your life, such as your family, friends, or relationships?

Encouraging athletes to open up

For an interview to be of use, it is important that the athlete discloses his or her feelings. Andersen (2000) suggested that athletes are encouraged to talk if the interviewer is engaging, genuine, interested in what the athlete is saying, and does not judge the athlete. This may sound an easy task, but Andersen (2000) stated that it is very difficult. It might be more difficult if the coach is responsible for team selection, because the player might not want to disclose things to the coach that might result in him or her being dropped from a team. This is a difficulty of the coach interviewing the athlete. Even though a coach can reassure the athlete that what he or she says will not influence selection the athlete might not believe the coach.

Case study 1.1 Interviewing an athlete

The following case study represents an excerpt of the dialogue between a coach (Darren, a 45-year-old cricket coach) and Matthew (a 21-year-old minor county league player). Darren has seen a deterioration in Matthew's demeanour and performance. This part of the interview focuses on the start of the interview in which Darren asks Matthew to describe the problem.

Darren: Thanks for coming to see me Matthew.

Matthew: I have been wanting to speak to you for a while now, as I have been really struggling this season, and it is not getting any better.

Darren: I would like you to describe all aspects of what is going on. In this chat today, I would like to ask you about what is currently happening, the possible influences, any changes that might have occurred, and even parts of your family life. From what the other lads have said and what you have told me, I know you have been having a few problems there. The purpose of this chat is to help me understand how best I can help you. I want to assure you that what you say in our chat will not influence team selection. I would like you to describe the problem.

Matthew: I can't concentrate when I play. I am playing matches thinking about my dad and wondering how long he has left.

Darren: Does this happen in every match?

Matthew: Yeah, it seems to. Although when we play other teams at the top of the league I seem to be able to concentrate better.

Darren: In the matches you have struggled to concentrate, do you struggle for the whole match?

Matthew: No.

Darren: Could you tell me more about when you concentrate and when your concentration goes?

Matthew: My concentration usually goes when I am fielding. When I am bowling I can usually concentrate, although sometimes I do struggle a bit. When the match is close I don't have any problems.

Darren: When did you notice this starting?

Matthew: It was a month ago, just after my dad first got his diagnosis.

Case study reflection

Some coaches may find interviewing their athletes quite difficult, because it is not an easy process. It may also result in athletes disclosing information that coaches are not comfortable hearing. Coaches may also feel that their skills are not competent to help the athlete. In these instances the coach should refer the athlete to a more suitably qualified individual such as a clinical psychologist or a counsellor.

Listening

Even though the questions asked by coaches are very important, it is also imperative that the coach listens to what the athlete has to say in any interview or conversation. According to Giges (2000), words can be clues to an athlete's inner experiences, which may reveal hidden thoughts, feelings, or wants from the athlete. Coaches should listen to every word the athlete says (see Case study 1.1).

Summary points

•   Interviews can help coaches gain an understanding of problems that may affect their athletes, which then might determine how the coach helps the athlete.
•   Coaches can adapt the interview guide proposed in this chapter.

Practice exam questions

1   What is the purpose of interviewing an athlete?
2   Identify and elaborate on the factors that may influence the extent to which a coach understands an athlete's problem based on an interview.
3   Discuss the importance of asking questions relating to an athlete's life.
4   Discuss the importance of listening to an athlete's response.
5   Describe the importance of identifying problems before providing psychological skills training.

Critical thinking questions: applying theory to practice

1   What can a coach do to encourage an athlete to open up about his or her feelings?
2   Design your own interview schedule and justify each section.
3   What can coaches do if they suspect an athlete is hiding information?
4   What can coaches do if they hear information that goes beyond their own competencies?
5   Discuss the factors that influence how effective an interview will be in providing information to guide any interventions.

2 Using questionnaires to assess the needs of athletes

The purpose of this chapter is to provide information on how coaches can use questionnaires to gather information about their athletes. Information will be provided on:

- defining what a questionnaire is;
- the advantages of questionnaires;
- the disadvantages of questionnaires;
- uses of questionnaires;
- questionnaires that coaches can use.

Definition and advantages of questionnaires

A questionnaire is a series of written questions, which provides the athlete with set choices regarding how he or she will answer each question (i.e. yes or no). An advantage of questionnaires is that they are generally quick to complete (Nicholls *et al.*, 2007), which is important for coaches who have little time. Questionnaires will generate objective scores regarding a psychological quality that an athlete might experience (e.g. anxiety or stress). Additionally, coaches can use these objective scores generated to compare scores with other athletes or data from published research. These comparisons may be useful in providing the coach with objective information.

Disadvantages of questionnaires

A limitation of questionnaires is that they do not allow athletes to explain their answers or document their experiences. Athletes might find the process of completing questionnaires tiresome and pointless. It is important that coaches explain why questionnaires are being completed. Another possible limitation of questionnaires is that they might be subject to athletes over emphasising their abilities, because it might be more socially desirable to do so.

Uses of questionnaires

Coaches can use questionnaires to assess the extent to which an athlete might be afflicted by a condition (e.g. anxiety) and the strategies athletes may use (e.g. coping). Questionnaires can also be used to monitor any changes that occur within an athlete by being completed on a regular basis.

Questionnaires that coaches can use

There is an array of questionnaires, published in peer-reviewed articles and books, which measure a variety of different psychological constructs in the sport literature. There are also a number of questionnaires that are available on the internet. Coaches should consider the quality of the questionnaire that they use and where possible, they should avoid disseminating questionnaires to athletes that are not supported by published research. The list of questionnaires presented in Table 2.1 documents some of the questionnaires that coaches can use. This list is by no means a comprehensive list, but represents questionnaires that are related to some of the psychological constructs that are mentioned in this book, especially the chapters on mental imagery, confidence, and coping.

Case study 2.1 Monitoring change using questionnaires

Paul, a 64-year-old tennis coach, assessed Victoria's mental toughness using the Mental Toughness Questionnaire 48 (MTQ48: Clough *et al.*, 2002) at the end of a season after she complained of not being able to play in pressurised situations, lacking commitment, confidence, and failing to control her emotions during matches. The results were as follows:

Mental Toughness Scores: September

Total Mental Toughness	112
Challenge	24
Commitment	12
Emotional Control	12
Life Control	32
Interpersonal Confidence	22
Ability Confidence	10

Paul developed a mental toughness training programme for Victoria, which lasted an entire season and involved optimism training, coping effectiveness training, goal setting, and sport intelligence training. He also reflected on his own coaching behaviours. He monitored her mental toughness scores every three months.

Continued ...

Mental Toughness Scores: December

Total Mental Toughness	124
Challenge	22
Commitment	14
Emotional Control	14
Life Control	32
Interpersonal Confidence	26
Ability Confidence	16

Mental Toughness Scores: March

Total Mental Toughness	138
Challenge	24
Commitment	24
Emotional Control	16
Life Control	32
Interpersonal Confidence	26
Ability Confidence	16

Mental Toughness Scores: June

Total Mental Toughness	142
Challenge	24
Commitment	24
Emotional Control	16
Life Control	32
Interpersonal Confidence	26
Ability Confidence	20

Victoria's mental toughness increased throughout the season.

Case study reflection

Questionnaires are useful to provide objective measures of the effects of interventions. Sceptics might argue that coaches could just ask an athlete whether he or she feels more mentally tough or not, but questionnaires provide an objective measure.

Table 2.1 A sample of questionnaires from the sport psychology literature

Name of questionnaire	Authors	Construct measured by questionnaire	Brief description
Mental Imagery Questionnaire-Revised (MIQ-R)	Hall and Martin (1997)	Imagery ability	8-item questionnaire that instructs athletes to perform different movements and rate the ease at which the athletes can see or feel themselves perform these movements.
State Sport Confidence Inventory (SSCI)	Vealey (1986)	State sport confidence	13-item questionnaire in which athletes rate how confident they are in competing at a forthcoming competition.
Trait Sport Confidence Inventory (TSCI)	Vealey (1986)	Trait sport confidence	13-item questionnaire in which athletes rate how confident they normally are when playing sport.
Sport Confidence Inventory (SCI)	Vealey and Knight (2002)	Confidence	14-item questionnaire that contains three subscales (physical skills and training, cognitive efficiency, and resilience).
Mental Toughness Questionnaire-48 (MTQ48)	Clough *et al.* (2002)	Mental toughness	48-item questionnaire that contains six subscales: challenge; commitment; personal control; emotional control; ability confidence; and personal confidence.
Australian Football Mental Toughness Inventory (AfMTI).	Gucciardi *et al.* (2009a).	Mental toughness	24-item questionnaire that measures four components: thrive through challenge; sport awareness; tough attitude; and desire success.
Coping Inventory for Competitive Sports	Gaudreau and Blondin (2002)	State coping	36-item questionnaire that measures what an athlete does to cope and includes three dimensions: task-oriented coping; distraction-oriented coping; and disengagement-oriented coping.
Dispositional Coping Inventory for Competitive Sports	Hurst *et al.* (2011)	Dispositional coping	36-item questionnaire that measures what an athlete would usually do to cope and includes three dimensions: task-oriented coping; distraction-oriented coping; and disengagement-oriented coping.

Practice exam questions

1   Discuss the advantages of using questionnaires.
2   Describe the disadvantages of using questionnaires.
3   What are the implications of using questionnaires that do not have research to support them?
4   Compare and contrast the State Sport Confidence Inventory and the Trait Sport Confidence Inventory.
5   To what extent do questionnaires provide reliable information. Discuss.

Critical thinking questions: applying theory to practice

1   Describe why a coach would use a questionnaire to measure traits.
2   Discuss why coaches might use state versions of a questionnaire.
3   Questionnaires are a useful way of measuring psychological constructs. Discuss.
4   Describe how a coach could use interview data along with questionnaire data.
5   Should coaches compare questionnaire results among their athletes? Discuss.

Part II

How to help athletes

Mental skills training

3 Mental imagery

The purpose of this chapter is to provide information on mental imagery so that coaches can provide training in this skill for athletes. This chapter will include information on:

- defining mental imagery;
- the content of mental imagery;
- the 4Ws of mental imagery;
- the benefits of mental imagery;
- theories of mental imagery;
- imagery perspective;
- imagery ability;
- PETTLEP approach;
- different types of imagery content;
- helping athletes do mental imagery;
- optimising imagery training.

Defining mental imagery

Mental imagery has been defined as

> those quasi-sensory and quasi-perceptual experiences of which we are self-consciously aware and which exist for us in the absence of those stimulus conditions that are known to produce their genuine sensory perceptual counterparts.
>
> (Richardson, 1969: 2–3)

That is, mental imagery refers to the process of an athlete using his or her imagination to see himself or herself performing a movement (e.g. running) or a certain skill (e.g. catching a high ball in rugby or heading the ball in soccer).

The content of mental imagery

The title 'mental imagery' might imply that imagery only includes images of what an athlete wants to achieve. This would only be partially correct, as a very important part of mental imagery is the images that athletes create. Coaches should be aware that when they develop mental imagery programmes to also include a number of other elements when asking athletes to engage in mental imagery. Munroe *et al.* (2000) found that in addition to visual images, imagery would be more effective if coaches included:

- feelings of performing a particular skill (e.g. bodily feelings associated with kicking the ball, such as the leg muscles contracting and the feeling in the foot);
- noises associated with the task (e.g. the noise made when a cricketer strikes a ball for six runs);
- smells associated with the image (e.g. the smell of the freshly mown grass on the golf course).

By asking athletes to incorporate visions, feelings, noises, and smells within their mental images, coaches have the potential to make imagery more realistic and thus more beneficial for the athlete.

The 4Ws of mental imagery

Munroe *et al.* (2000) explored where, when, why, and what athletes imagine among a sample of 14 elite sports performers from seven different sports. This information is particularly useful for coaches who wish to design imagery interventions. Athletes engaged in imagery during competition and training, but imaged more prior to competing. The athletes used imagery to help them learn new skills or tactics, regulate their arousal levels, or to improve confidence. Finally, the athletes imaged a variety of different things such as their surroundings and making technical corrections.

The benefits of mental imagery

According to Martin *et al.* (1999) more than 200 studies have been published on the topic of mental imagery. These studies have revealed that mental imagery can influence a variety of constructs.

- *Skill enhancement:* Sport performance in a particular skill can be enhanced by an athlete imaging that same skill being performed (Driskell *et al.*, 1994; Pain *et al.*, 2011).
- *Skill acquisition:* Beauchamp *et al.* (1996) reported that imagery can enhance how people acquire skills. From a coaching perspective, mental imagery may be particularly useful for athletes who are learning new skills.
- *Confidence:* Mental imagery can enhance the confidence of athletes. For example, Callow and Walters (2005) and Nordin and Cumming (2005) found that positive imagery and facilitative imagery, respectively, enhanced self-confidence. That is, imagery associated with athletes being successful helped confidence levels.

- *Flow:* Pain *et al.* (2011) explored the effects of an imagery intervention and music among soccer players and found that both imagery and music helped athletes access the flow state. Flow is associated with enjoyment and fun, and highly regarded as a positive psychological state.
- *Concentration:* A study by Calmels *et al.* (2004) revealed that softball players, who were trained in mental imagery, could make sense of more external stimuli without being overloaded.
- *Injury:* Ievleva and Orlick (1991) found that imagery can help speed up recovery when athletes are injured, reduce the level of skill deterioration, and help them cope with pain.

Mental imagery appears to have a number of benefits, so it is a useful psychological skill that coaches could train their athletes in.

Theoretical models of imagery

It is important that coaches have an understanding regarding how a mental imagery intervention might help an athlete's sporting performance. This is because athletes might ask their coach how mental imagery influences performance. Four different theories have been proposed, which have attempted to explain how mental imagery may influence performance. These are the: (1) psychoneuromuscular theory, (2) symbolic learning theory, (3) bioinformational theory, and (4) triple code model.

1   *Psychoneuromuscular theory:* This theory, which was developed by Carpenter (1894), states that the muscles used in the performance of skills such as goal kicking in soccer, forehand in table tennis, or a putt in golf become innervated when the athlete imagines himself or herself performing the particular skill.
2   *Symbolic learning theory:* The symbolic learning theory was proposed by Sackett (1934), who stated that mental imagery helps athletes' performance by enabling them to understand and acquire the different movement patterns required to execute tasks associated with sports performance (e.g. tennis serve, golf swing, or lay-up in basketball). That is, imagery acts as coding system in which the individual becomes familiar with the sequence of movements that make up skills.
3   *Bioinformational theory:* The bioinformational theory, which was proposed by Lang (1977), indicates that movement patterns are stored in the long-term memory and that engaging in mental imagery strengthens the memory of these movement patterns. Lang suggested that images are stored as stimulus propositions (i.e. relevant stimuli associated with performing a movement, such as spectators being present or the smell of the sporting arena) and response propositions (i.e. the athletes responses to the stimuli, such as the athlete experiencing tension in his stomach when he thinks about the crowd, or the feelings of excitement when the athlete smells the gymnasium in which he or she is used to playing volleyball in).

4   *Triple code model:* Ahsen (1984) proposed the triple code model as an explanation of how imagery facilitates performance. In this model, Ahsen argued that mental imagery provides a sense of reality to the athlete, which enables him or her to interact as though they are interacting with the real world. This then stimulates physiological responses (e.g. increased heart rate), so imagery provides meaning to the athlete so that when they perform the movements for real, they will know what it means. Essentially, this model proposes that imagery prepares the athlete to perform by creating a sense of reality.

There is some evidence to support each of the different theories. From a coaching perspective, most athletes may be more interested in knowing that imagery will enhance their sporting performance or psychological well-being rather than the mechanisms in which imagery works.

Imagery perspective

When a coach asks an athlete to engage in mental imagery, the athlete is likely to have one of two different views in his or her head. These two views are referred to as internal imagery and external imagery.

- *Internal imagery:* Athletes who see their images internally will have images that represent what they would see through their own eyes when they perform a particular skill. For example, a golfer hitting a putt will see the ball and the club head from the same view as though he or she were stood over the ball and about to hit the putt.
- *External imagery:* With external images, the athlete sees himself or herself, through the lens of a camera.

On the whole, athletes tend to have a preference for either internal or external imagery, although some athletes can interchange between internal and external images (Murphy *et al.*, 1990). A coach can find out the imagery perspective of an athlete by simply asking the athlete to describe what he or she sees when he or she images, and whether the images are as though the player was looking through his or her own eyes or whether he or she was looking at himself or herself as though through a camera.

With regard to the effects of internal or external imagery on sporting performance, coaches should be aware that neither internal imagery nor external imagery is more beneficial to the performer than the other. Therefore, coaches should encourage athletes to use the perspective they are comfortable with, even if this means that some athletes will interchange between perspectives, as many Olympic athletes interchange on a very frequent basis (Murphy *et al.*, 1990).

Imagery ability

Imagery ability refers to an athlete's proficiency in engaging in mental imagery. Athletes who are able to create very detailed pictures, smells, noises, and feelings in their mind are regarded as having high imagery ability. Conversely, athletes who struggle to create pictures, smells, noises, and feelings are regarded as having low imagery ability.

Imagery ability is very important because it determines the extent to which an imagery intervention will be effective. For example, Robin *et al.* (2007) found that tennis players with high imagery ability benefited more from imagery training than the players with low imagery ability. As such, coaches need to consider the imagery ability of their athletes and understand that imagery interventions may be more effective for some athletes compared to others. Additionally, the benefits of imagery interventions may take longer to come to fruition for some athletes compared to others.

Sport psychologists have been measuring the imagery ability of athletes for many years. A questionnaire that is frequently used to measure mental imagery is the Movement Imagery Questionnaire-Revised (MIQ-R: Hall and Martin, 1997). The MIQ-R is an eight-item questionnaire that instructs athletes to perform certain movements such as raising their leg or moving their arm and then the athlete rates the ease at which he or she could feel or see himself or herself imagining the movement. Although imagery ability is very important in determining the effectiveness of any intervention (Robin *et al.*, 2007), coaches should understand that imagery ability can be improved with practice. That is, the detail in images and the control an athlete has over his or her images can improve with practice (Rodgers *et al.*, 1991).

The PETTLEP approach

Holmes and Collins (2001) created some guidelines that coaches can use when developing imagery interventions for their athletes, with the view of making these interventions more effective. This approach is grounded in cognitive neuroscience in that the authors believe the brain stores memories that are accessed when: (a) athletes perform different sports and (b) they imagine themselves playing sport. As such the PETTLEP approach indicates that coaches should ensure that their imagery interventions contain key elements, which form the PETTLEP acronym. This stands for physical, environment, task, timing, learning, emotion, and perspective.

- *Physical:* Coaches may have the view that asking athletes to lie on a couch or bed and close their eyes whilst they are engaging in mental imagery is beneficial. However, the PETTLEP approach disagrees with this approach and suggests that the athlete should be physically involved, because this makes mental imagery more realistic. Murphy *et al.* (2008) identified two particular methods by which coaches could include an element of physicality into imagery interventions. First, an athlete could perform the imagery in the kit that he or she normally performs in and hold a piece of equipment. For example, a hooker in rugby union who wants to practise line out throwing, would wear his match kit, hold the ball, stand on the sideline from which throws are taken, and then engage in mental imagery. Athletes may feel self-conscious performing imagery in their kit, but coaches should emphasise the importance of imagery being as realistic as possible. Additionally, athletes could also incorporate movement into their imagery, although coaches should ensure that it is safe for athletes to engage in imagery whilst moving. For example, a tennis player could perform the movements associated with a serve whilst closing his or her eyes and mentally imaging the serve.

- *Environment:* In order to make imagery training more realistic, coaches should ensure that imagery scripts include information regarding details of the environment that their athlete performs in. Furthermore, coaches could provide athletes with photographs or videos of different competition venues which the athlete can look at before engaging in mental imagery. This may be particularly useful for athletes who will be performing at new venues.
- *Task:* Coaches should ask the athlete to describe what they focus on when performing the skill and whether they have any typical thoughts when performing skills. Once these have been collated by the coach, he or she can include these in imagery scripts, so that the athlete thinks about the same things whilst imaging as he or she does when performing the task in real life.
- *Timing:* Athletes should be encouraged by their coach to image in real time, so that the imaging of a task corresponds to the athlete actually performing the task. Therefore, coaches should discourage athletes from engaging in slow-motion imagery or imagery that is speeded up.
- *Learning:* As athletes progress in their chosen sport, they will become more proficient by learning new skills. As athletes learn new skills, their memories will also change over time as function of learning and practice. Coaches should therefore regularly update imagery scripts or imagery training so that it takes into account learning that has taken place by the athlete. That is, imagery scripts should closely reflect the athlete's current stage of learning (Murphy *et al.*, 2008).
- *Emotion:* Participating in sport can evoke a variety of pleasant (e.g. happiness) and unpleasant emotions (e.g. anger: Nicholls *et al.*, 2010), and this should be represented in imagery scripts. This will make imagery scripts more realistic and has the potential to strengthen the memory of athletes. However, Murphy *et al.* (2008) suggested that emotions that associated with successful performances should be included in imagery scripts, whereas inappropriate emotions should not be included as they may negatively influence performance. One might assume that pleasant emotions such as happiness may have a positive influence on performance, whereas unpleasant emotions negatively influence performance. However, this is not always the case as unpleasant emotions might have a positive effect on performance (Hanin, 2010). Coaches could therefore speak to athletes prior to designing the imagery intervention to identify emotions that the athlete perceives as being facilitative to performance. This may vary dramatically across different athletes, which is why imagery scripts should be individualised.

- *Perspective:* Coaches should not prescribe either the internal or external imagery perspective, but merely allow the athlete to use the perspective or perspectives that they feel comfortable with. It is important that coaches encourage athletes to imagine the feelings that they normally experience when performing the task. Although not specifically stated by Holmes and Collins (2001), coaches could also encourage athletes to imagine noises and smells to increase the reality of the mental imagery even further.

The PETTLEP approach to mental imagery training is a useful guide for coaches, which has been supported in recent research. Smith *et al.* (2007) found support for many aspects of the PETTLEP model. Indeed, Smith and colleagues found that athletes who imagined in the clothes they wear when competing, whilst at the competition venue, performed better in comparison to athletes who imagined in non-sport clothing or at their home wearing non-sport clothes.

Different types of imagery content

In addition to the guidelines presented in the PETTLEP approach (Holmes and Collins, 2001), coaches should also consider the needs of the athlete and devise the imagery intervention based on those needs. Martin *et al.* (1999) proposed an applied imagery model that contained five types of imagery, along with explanations regarding when coaches could train their athletes in each specific form of imagery.

1　*Cognitive specific (CS):* Imagery that includes an athlete rehearsing different skills such as goal kick in rugby union, a forehand in tennis, or a short-corner push in hockey is regarded as cognitive-specific imagery. Coaches can use CS imagery to help athletes learn new skills and enhance the performance of skills such as a backhand in tennis. Additionally, Martin *et al.* (1999) suggested that CS imagery can be used by athletes when they are in rehabilitation to help them maintain their skill level prior to sustaining their injury.
2　*Cognitive general (CG):* CG imagery includes imagery that relates to strategies an athlete might engage when playing sport. This would include a rugby player imaging himself or herself lining up in a defensive formation to defend an opponents' attacking lineout or a hockey player imaging his or her tactics for an attacking short corner. CG imagery training can be given by coaches who want to help their athletes learn new tactics and enhance the performance of athletes when performing certain tactics.
3　*Motivational specific (MS):* Images that involve athletes seeing themselves winning important competitions, receiving a trophy from an official, or standing on a podium with a medal around their neck are classified as MS imagery. This type of imagery can be used by coaches to help athletes formulate goals relating to outcomes (e.g. results of competitions), performance (e.g. specific standards of performance), and processes (e.g. technical components associated with different skills).

4   *Motivational general-arousal (MG-A):* Imagery that includes how an athlete feels is considered MG-A imagery. As such, images that involve athletes with an increased heart-rate, sweaty hands, a nervous stomach, worry, and even being relaxed are considered MG-A images. This type of imagery will be useful for athletes who want to regulate their arousal levels. The coach would speak to the athlete to discover whether the athlete needs help in regulating his or her arousal, such as psyching the athlete up prior to competition or calming the athlete down before competition.

5   *Motivational general-mastery (MG-M):* Images of athletes coping effectively, feeling confident, and mentally tough are classified as MG-M images. If a coach thinks an athlete lacks confidence, he or she could provide the athlete with MG-M imagery training. This form of imagery might also be useful for athletes who struggle to maintain a positive attitude during competition.

Empirical evidence in the sport psychology literature has provided varying amounts of support for the applied model proposed by Martin *et al.* (1999). For instance, in the model proposed by Martin and colleagues, only MG-M should be related to confidence. However, other studies have found that more than one imagery type is related to confidence (Callow and Hardy, 2001). From a coaching perspective, this is not a damning finding, and means that although an imagery intervention may be geared towards helping an athlete learn a new skill, it is likely the intervention will improve the athlete's confidence level. As such, the model proposed by Martin *et al.* provides a useful framework for coaches when they design individualised imagery interventions.

Providing athletes with mental imagery training

The easiest way for a coach to help his or her athlete engage in mental imagery is to provide him or her with an imagery audio-file or an imagery script so that the athlete can create his or her own audio-file. Athletes can record the script onto a mobile phone or a voice recorder and then transfer it onto an MP3 player.

The imagery script provided in this chapter is generic, and is for an athlete who wants to improve his or her confidence. It is important that athletes have individualised imagery scripts depending on their needs. However, coaches could adapt and modify the imagery script based on the needs of their player. For instance, if a coach is working with an athlete who has problems controlling his or her anger, images relating to the player controlling his or anger could be included in the script, where the current script is focused on confidence and mental toughness.

Instructions

Before athletes start imaging, athletes should be made aware from the coach that they should be wearing the clothes they compete in, and hold a piece of equipment associated with their sport (e.g. basketball, golf club, or tennis racquet etc).

Ideally, they should be at a training venue or competition venue when engaging in the script. If a footballer is imaging himself or herself taking penalties he or she should be stood by the penalty spot in front of the goal.

Generic imagery script

Imagine that you are about to perform a skill that is associated with your sport such as [insert skill here]. As you partially exhale see yourself performing a [insert skill here]. When you have exhaled to the point where you feel comfortable, perform your skill again in your mind, feeling confident and mentally tough as you do so. Focus your thoughts on the things that you normally think about when performing your skill. Notice how you feel what you would normally feel when performing this skill. Feel the confidence in your body and the excitement about the challenge of performing. Notice the sense of ease and lightness whilst you are performing this skill. Almost as if performing [insert skill] is effortless. Practise [insert your skill] several more times.

30 second pause in script

Good, now rehearse [insert your skill] in different scenarios in competitions and in environments that are realistic of where you perform. Make the skills you rehearse relevant to when you perform these skills in matches. See and feel yourself performing successfully [insert your skill]. As in competitions, there will be other people around such as coaches or other competitors. Imagine these others present, but don't let them rush you. Notice how the focus of your concentration shifts from a broad focus as you are looking around to a very narrow focus, as you prepare to execute [insert your skill]. Imagine feeling that you have the ability to meet any challenges you are faced with during your competition. Practice [insert your skill] now making it as realistic as possible. Notice the sounds, smells, and feelings in your body as you mentally image the skill. Take some time to mentally practise these skills.

2 minute pause in script

That's fine. Now imagine you are about to perform [insert your skill] and you are feeling a little nervous, because you want to perform well. You can stop your worrying by taking a breath and imagine yourself performing with confidence and mental toughness.

30 second pause in script

Imagine yourself feeling confident in your preparation and focused on your next competition.

20 second pause in script

You imagine that your pre-competition warm-up goes very well and you remind yourself that you are ready to face the challenge of unexpected obstacles. You notice how confident you feel in your ability to re-focus after any distractions and remind yourself that you are mentally tough. You feel energized and ready to compete.

End of script

Optimising mental imagery training

- It is important that athletes realise that mental imagery is a skill. Like all skills, athletes should be told that good quality imagery practice will help them improve their imagery ability and thus the impact this has on their sports performance.
- The generic imagery script provided in this chapter will last around eight minutes, if it is unaltered. Coaches should ask athletes to listen to the script twice a day for the first week and then once a day for the following week. After this period, coaches could ask their athletes to use the script prior to competition.
- Athletes should be told and encouraged to listen to the imagery script before training sessions.

Summary

- Mental imagery refers to the process of an athlete using his or her imagination to see himself or herself performing a movement or a certain skill.
- Mental imagery includes visions, feelings, noises, and smells associated with executing a skill.
- There are numerous benefits associated with mental imagery, which include increased performance, confidence, and concentration.
- It does not matter whether an athlete engages in internal or external imagery.
- It is important that coaches consider the imagery ability of an athlete before initiating imagery training.
- The PETTLEP (Holmes and Collins, 2001) and the applied model of mental imagery (Martin *et al.*, 1999) are useful guidelines for coaches who want to develop an imagery intervention for their athletes.

Practice exam questions

1   Compare and contrast the different theories of mental imagery.
2   Describe the 4Ws of mental imagery, as proposed by Munroe *et al.* (2000) and their implications for sports performance.
3   Discuss the potential benefits of providing imagery training for athletes.
4   Imagery perspective matters. Discuss.
5   To what extent is imagery ability important? Discuss.

Case study 3.1 Helping a badminton player manage his anxiety

Christine is a 45-year-old badminton coach who has been coaching badminton players for almost 20 years. She is currently coaching a club-level player called George, who is keen to play in competitions. George is a 51-year-old accounts executive, who has recently complained to Christine that he suffers with anxiety during competitions. George's symptoms are manifested as worry, sweaty palms, increased heart-rate, tension in his stomach, and his muscles feel heavy. When hearing this information, Christine asked some questions regarding George's feelings, such as instances that trigger these feelings. George said that he experienced those negative feelings when he wanted to win an important point or in matches that were very tight.

Christine told George that a mental imagery intervention was something that could benefit him. She explained what would be involved and asked for George's feelings and he was keen to receive some imagery training. Prior to the training starting, Christine asked George to complete the MIQ-R (Hall and Martin, 1997) and found that George had moderate imagery ability, so could benefit from the intervention.

The imagery intervention was guided by the PETTLEP principles, so when George received the imagery audio-file, he was asked to listen to it in his match kit, at match venues, whilst holding his badminton racquet. At first, George felt self-conscious doing this, so he arranged to arrive at match venues early so no one could see him engaging in the imagery.

George's intervention involved MG-A images, as George imagined controlling his emotions and successfully recovering. George listened to the script before matches and training sessions for over a month and commented that he really benefited to the extent that he no longer needed to listen to the audio-file as he naturally engaged in imagery. With regards to his performance, George felt that he had made small improvements, but the biggest and most welcome improvement was how he felt.

Case study reflection

In this instance, the intervention had a positive effect on the negative emotions and the symptoms that George experienced, but less impact on George's performance. Sometimes psychological interventions, such as imagery, may have little or no impact on performance. Just because an intervention may not influence sport performance, it does not mean it has been ineffective. Indeed, interventions that improve the psychological well-being of athletes, regardless of how they affect sport performance should be considered successful.

Critical thinking questions: applying theory to practice

1   Describe the imagery training you would provide for a golfer who is new to the sport and justify your choice with evidence.
2   One of your players has experienced a drop in confidence. Describe what you would do and how you would help the player with mental imagery.
3   Critically evaluate the PETTLEP (Holmes and Collins, 2001) approach to imagery in relation to developing imagery interventions.
4   Discuss the importance of matching the imagery type with an athlete's needs.
5   How would you describe to an athlete how mental imagery improves performance if they ask you to do so?

4   Mental toughness training

This chapter provides coaches with information regarding how they can develop the mental toughness of their athletes. In particular, this chapter will provide:

- a definition of mental toughness;
- conceptual models of mental toughness;
- the development of mental toughness;
- overview of mental toughness interventions;
- mental toughness training.

Definition of mental toughness

Mental toughness has been rated, by a group of wrestling coaches, as the most important construct that determines success in wrestling (Gould *et al.*, 1987). However, researchers within the sport literature have not agreed upon a common definition of this construct. For example, Clough *et al.* (2002) defined mental toughness as athletes having 'a high sense of self-belief and an unshakable faith that they control their own destiny, these individuals can remain relatively unaffected by competition and adversity' (p. 38). Alternatively, Jones *et al.* (2002) stated that:

> Mental toughness is having the natural or developed psychological edge that enables you to general lycope better than your opponents with the main demands (competition, training, and lifestyle) that sport places on a performer and specifically, be more consistent and better than your opponents in remaining determined, focused, confident, and in control under pressure.
>
> (Jones *et al.*, 2002: 209)

Andersen (2011) criticised this definition of mental toughness because he stated that the opponents of the athlete are too pivotal. An athlete can't be considered mentally tough if his or her opponents are more mentally tough according to the definition of Jones *et al,* (2002). Additionally, Nicholls (2011) suggested that there is no published evidence that documents athletes generally coping better than their opponents, because coping effectiveness fluctuates.

Another definition was proposed by Coulter *et al.* (2010), who defined mental toughness as:

> Mental toughness is the presence of some or the entire collection of experientially developed and inherent values, attitudes, emotions, cognitions, and behaviours that influence the way in which an individual approaches, responds to, and appraises both negatively and positively construed pressures, challenges, and adversities to consistently achieve his or her goals.
>
> (Coulter *et al.*, 2010: 715)

This definition of mental toughness was also critiqued by Andersen (2011), who stated that Coulter *et al.* (2010) use the word 'inherent' for characteristics such as values, attitudes, cognitions, emotions and behaviours. Andersen stated that these characteristics are gained from experience. Indeed, Andersen stated that 'such imprecise and incorrect use of language does not give one much faith in this definition of the construct' (p. 74). It would appear that more work is required to produce a more precise definition of mental toughness. Nevertheless, there appear to be some commonalities in the definitions provided by Clough *et al.* (2002), Jones *et al.* (2002), and Coulter *et al.* (2010).

Conceptual models of mental toughness

There are three main conceptual models of mental toughness within the sport psychology literature, which are the: (1) 4Cs model of mental toughness (Clough *et al.* 2002), (2) the Jones and colleagues model (2002; 2007), and (3) the model proposed by Gucciardi *et al.* (2008).

The 4Cs model of mental toughness (Clough et al., 2002)

According to Gucciardi *et al.* (2011) the 4Cs model of mental toughness is the most dominant in terms of peer-reviewed research. This model, which is grounded in Kobasa's (1979) theory of hardiness, suggests that mental toughness consists of challenge, commitment, control, and confidence.

- *Challenge:* refers to athletes viewing sporting situations (e.g. being 1–0 down in a soccer match) as being changeable. Athletes high in challenge would perceive competitive events as an opportunity rather than a threat. As such, athletes would focus on what can be gained from competitions or training sessions (e.g. place in starting line-up) as opposed to what can be lost (e.g. losing place in starting line-up).
- *Commitment:* athletes who score highly on this quality have a tendency to involve themselves in sporting situations, rather than alienate themselves from an encounter.
- *Control:* relates to athletes feeling and acting as if they are in control of the sporting situation. Furthermore, athletes who are high in this quality plan for

stressful events by using their knowledge, choice, and skill regarding how they will combat potentially stressful incidences.

- *Confidence*: an athlete who scores highly on this construct will have a strong sense of self-belief and an unshakeable faith concerning his or her ability to achieve success.

This model has received criticism from sport psychology researchers, who have suggested that the model represents hardiness, with the addition of confidence. As such, Connaughton *et al.* (2008a) argued that it does not encapsulate mental toughness. More recently, however, Weinberg and Butt (2011) suggested that mental toughness and hardiness share a common thread. That is, they influence how individuals evaluate and handle stressful sporting situations.

Jones et al.'s model of mental toughness (2002; 2007)

Jones *et al.* (2002) identified 12 key attributes associated with mentally tough individuals:

1 having an unshakeable self-belief in your ability;
2 having an unshakeable self-belief that you possess unique qualities and abilities;
3 having an insatiable desire and internalised motives to succeed;
4 bouncing back from performance setbacks;
5 thriving on the pressure of competition;
6 accepting that competition anxiety is inevitable and knowing you can cope with it;
7 not being adversely affected by others' performances;
8 remaining fully-focused in the face of personal life distractions;
9 switching a sport focus on and off as required;
10 remaining fully-focused on the task at hand in the face of competition-specific distractions;
11 pushing back the boundaries of physical and emotional pain; and
12 regaining psychological control following unexpected, uncontrollable events.

In their next study, Jones *et al.* (2007) reported 30 qualities associated with mental toughness, within the four dimensions of :

1 *attitude/mindset* (e.g. belief and focus);
2 *training* (e.g. using long-term goals for motivation and pushing oneself to the limit);
3 *competition* (e.g. handling pressure, creating belief, and regulating performance etc);
4 *post-competition* (e.g. handling failure and handling success).

There are several limitations regarding the models of Jones *et al.* (2002; 2007), which have been highlighted by Crust (2008) and Gucciardi *et al.* (2009a). For example, Crust pointed out that the Jones *et al.* (2002) study was methodologically flawed, because they had inappropriate numbers of athletes in their focus groups. Furthermore, Gucciardi *et al.* (2009a) stated the Jones *et al.*'s (2002; 2007) models are not grounded in existing psychological theory. It could also be argued that there is a large discrepancy between the 12 attributes identified by Jones *et al.* (2002) and the 30 qualities in Jones *et al.* (2007). This large discrepancy may be a reflection of the methodology used, because identifying an extra 18 attributes indicates that many qualities were missed in the Jones *et al.* (2002) paper and one would have to wonder why this happened.

Gucciardi et al.'s (2008) model of mental toughness among Australian footballers

The model proposed by Gucciardi *et al.* (2008) is grounded in Kelly's (1991 [1955]) Personal Construct Theory (PCT). PCT indicates that individuals try to make sense of themselves and their environment by developing theories about the world. These theories differ from person to person, because individuals differ regarding how they perceive situations and interpret them. Gucciardi identified three dimensions of mental toughness, which included:

1   *Characteristics:* 11 characteristics of mental toughness were identified (self-belief, work ethic, personal values, self-motivation, tough attitude, concentration and focus, resilience, handling pressure, emotional resilience, sport intelligence, and physical toughness.
2   *Behaviours*: athletes who are mentally tough prepare well for competitions, recover well from injuries, and perform consistently at sport.
3   *Situations*: within Australian Rules football there are (a) general and (b) competition situations in which athletes demonstrate mental toughness. The general situations included athletes being mentally tough when going through their rehabilitation programme and when they prepare for sport. Athletes also demonstrated mental toughness in dealing with competition pressures (e.g. match environment, competing whilst fatigued, and experiencing decreases in confidence).

A possible limitation of this model of mental toughness relates to the participant sample, given that it is relatively homogenous. As such, female athletes were not used to develop this model. Furthermore, another issue raised by Andersen (2011) concerned the behavioural component of their model. He suggested that it is very difficult, if not impossible, to measure mentally tough behaviour.

The development of mental toughness

Researchers have also examined how athletes become more mentally tough throughout their career. It is important that coaches have an understanding of how mental toughness develops, so that mental toughness training can be shaped more effectively. Bull *et al.* (2005) were among the first to reveal that mental toughness could be developed, but Bull and colleagues did not explore how mental toughness developed in an athlete's career (Connaughton *et al.*, 2011). Nevertheless, the Bull *et al.* study paved the way for more rigorous studies that have explored how mental toughness develops.

Connaughton *et al.* (2008b) interviewed seven athletes regarding how the 12 attributes, proposed by Jones *et al.* (2002), developed in the early, middle, and later years of an athlete's career. They found that during the early years an unshakeable self-belief to achieve goals, unshakeable belief that the athlete possesses the unique qualities and abilities to make him or her better than opponents, and insatiable desire to succeed were developed. The attributes were influenced by effective leadership that the athletes received, advice from parents and coaches, and observing elite performers. Three more attributes developed during the middle phases of an athlete's career (e.g. bouncing back from performance setbacks, pushing back the boundaries of physical and emotional pain, and accepting that competition anxiety is inevitable and knowing you can cope with it). Support from significant others, such as parents, coaches, or peers, was crucial in the development of these qualities. In an athlete's later years, switching sport focus on and off as required, remaining fully-focused on the task at hand in the face of competition-specific distractions, not being adversely affected by others' performances, and remaining fully-focused in the face of personal life distractions developed.

The next study to explore how mental toughness developed was by Gucciardi *et al.* (2009b), who took a different perspective to Connaughton *et al.* (2008b), by asking Australian football coaches for their perceptions regarding the development of mental toughness. The coaches said that early childhood experiences, football experiences, coach–athlete relationships, coaching philosophy, training environment, and specific strategies influenced the development of mental toughness. Interestingly, Gucciardi and colleagues found that coaches could hinder the development of mental toughness of their players. This could happen if the coach let their desire for success, rather than the development of the athlete, overrule what they did. Other coach behaviours that could hinder mental toughness development were coaches over emphasising athletes' weaknesses, imposing low or unrealistic expectations, or creating a training environment that did not push the players. It is important that coaches are aware of their role in helping athletes develop mental toughness.

Thelwell *et al.* (2010), who reverted to the strategy adopted by Connaughton *et al.* (2008b), asked the athletes to provide information on how they felt their mental toughness developed. Thelwell and colleagues interviewed 10 gymnasts and created four dimensions regarding how mental toughness is developed:

1   *sport process* (e.g. training, competition, and club);
2   *sporting personnel* (e.g. coach, team-mates, competitors, and sport psychologists);

3   *non-sporting personnel* (e.g. parents, siblings, and significant others);
4   *environmental influences* (e.g. training environment, family environment, modelling, and the country the gymnast was from).

Connaughton *et al.* (2010) further advanced our understanding regarding how mental toughness develops by examining the perceptions of athletes, coaches, and sport psychologists within one study, across three specific career phases (1) initial involvement to intermediate level, (2) intermediate level to elite level, and (3) elite to Olympic/world champion level, based upon the four dimensions proposed by Jones *et al.* (2007). Similar to Connaughton *et al.* (2008b), each phase was associated with the development of different characteristics. For example, in the initial involvement to intermediate level the attitude/mindset of the athlete and training dimension (e.g. using long-term goals for motivation) developed. The environment, parents, coaches, enjoyment of activities, and competitive training were all crucial in helping athletes develop mental toughness. With regards to the intermediate level to elite level, characteristics from the training, competition dimension, and post-competition dimension developed during this stage of the athlete's career. However, the development of mental toughness was completed in the elite to Olympic/world champion level, when these qualities were at their strongest.

Overview of mental toughness interventions

At the present time two interventions have been published, which aimed to enhance mental toughness among athletes. The first study to attempt to enhance mental toughness was by Sheard and Golby (2006). They explored the effects of a seven-week psychological skills programme on swimming performance and positive psychological development, including mental toughness among 36 national swimmers. The intervention included goal setting, mental imagery, relaxation, concentration, and thought-stopping training. The authors reported some increases in swimming performance at competitive meets and a significant increase in mental toughness scores.

More recently Gucciardi *et al.* (2009c) explored the effects of a specific mental toughness training intervention and a general psychological skills training programme on mental toughness, in comparison to a control group. The mental toughness training intervention comprised of seven sessions and included an introduction (Session 1), training in personal and team values (Session 2), work ethic, attitude, and self-motivation (Session 3), self-belief, concentration, and focus (Session 4), resilience (Session 5), emotional intelligence (Session 6), and sport intelligence and physical toughness (Session 7).

The general psychological skills training included the following seven sessions: information evening (Session 1), self-regulation (Session 2), arousal regulation (Session 3), attentional control (Session 4), self-efficacy (Session 5), mental rehearsal (Session 6), and ideal performance state (Session 7). Gucciardi and colleagues found that athletes in the mental toughness training group and the psychological skills training group experienced an increase in mental toughness after their respective training programmes.

These mental toughness interventions (e.g. Gucciardi *et al.*, 2009c; Sheard and Golby, 2006) could be criticised for excluding training in qualities that have previously been associated with mental toughness. For example, Jones *et al.* (2002) stated that mental toughness is related to coping, whereas Nicholls *et al.* (2008) found that mental toughness was associated with optimism, and Gucciardi *et al.* (2009b) reported that mental toughness was influenced by coach behaviour. However, training in these constructs or indeed training the coaches was not included in these two interventions. By including training in psychological constructs that have been found to be related to mental toughness, coaches could make mental toughness interventions more effective.

Mental toughness training

This section provides information on how coaches can help improve their athletes' level of mental toughness. The information is not presented as a session by session content, more an ongoing process regarding what coaches can do to help their athletes. Given the number and varied psychological constructs that are associated with mental toughness, it could be argued that helping an athlete reach his or her full potential in mental toughness will be a long process that requires time and training. Furthermore, as more research emerges on mental toughness, coaches might want to supplement the mental toughness training guidelines provided in this chapter. These guidelines are based upon models of mental toughness (e.g. Jones *et al.*, 2007), research that has examined mental toughness (Nicholls *et al.*, 2008), and existing mental toughness interventions (e.g. Gucciardi *et al.*, 2009c). Some of the mental toughness training procedures (e.g. coping effectiveness training, confidence, and goal setting) are covered in more detail elsewhere in this book, so will only be briefly mentioned in this section. For more information on these topics, please see the relevant chapters in this book.

Coach behaviour

Before engaging athletes in different psychological interventions to help them build their mental toughness levels, it is important that the coach considers his or her behaviour and the training environment. Previous research by Gucciardi *et al.* (2009b) found that coaches play a pivotal role in the development of an athlete's level of mental toughness. As such coaches should carefully consider their behaviour and ensure that:

- More emphasis is placed on players improving as opposed to the outcome of competitions. This refers to the motivational climate, which is discussed in detail in Chapter 11 of this book. Essentially, coaches should attempt to develop a mastery climate as opposed to a performance climate, so the role of the coach is to provide the athletes with tasks that focus on self-improvement and refrain from comparing athletes with other athletes (Amorose, 2007). If less emphasis is placed on results athletes should be able to adjust to either winning or losing better, because outcomes are less important in a mastery motivational climate.

- Athletes' weaknesses are not over exposed by the coach. Research has indicated that athletes prefer positive feedback rather than negative feedback (Chiviacowsky *et al.*, 2008a). However, if athletes do not know what their weaknesses are they may never work on any shortcomings and thus reach their full potential. Therefore, coaches have to be very careful how they present criticism to athletes and could present criticism in a positive manner that motivates the athlete to work on his or her weaknesses.
- The training environment challenges athletes. It is also crucial that coaches create an environment that pushes players to try their hardest, so when they play competitive matches they will be used to performing in challenging situations.

Sport intelligence

Gucciardi *et al.* (2008) found that sport intelligence, refers to how athletes perceive training and understand competition processes such as tactics, which are crucial factors in mental toughness. Coaches can play a strong role in helping athletes increase their sport intelligence. With regards to training, coaches can explain why certain training principles are important and relevant to matches. Sport intelligence in competition can be increased by coaches providing more detailed information on individual roles within a team, team tactics, and other processes that are related to competition, which will be sport specific.

Coping effectiveness training

Qualitative research by Jones *et al.* (2002) and quantitative research by Nicholls *et al.* (2008) reported that coping was highly associated with mental toughness. Despite this strong association, coping training has not featured in the only two interventions on mental toughness (e.g. Sheard and Golby, 2006; Gucciardi *et al.*, 2009c). Furthermore, in Weinberg and Butt's (2011) chapter on how mental toughness can be developed, they only advocated the use of one coping strategy (i.e. cognitive restructuring). This strategy was not associated with mental toughness in the Nicholls *et al.* paper. However, coping is a crucial aspect of mental toughness, which has been overlooked in mental toughness interventions. It is important coaches incorporate coping within mental toughness training. Information on coping effectiveness training is outlined in Chapter 6, so it will not be mentioned here in great detail. This form of training was developed by Chesney *et al.* (2003), and has three central themes: (1) athletes are taught to recognise if they can control the stressor or not, (2) deploy appropriate strategies depending on whether the stressor is controllable or not, and (3) seek social support from the appropriate person.

Appraisal training

Clough *et al.* (2002) stated that mentally tough athletes view sport as a challenge (i.e. focus on what can be gained) as opposed to a threat (i.e. focus on what can be lost). Therefore, coaches can provide athletes with appraisal training, and teach athletes to perceive situations as a challenge rather than a threat. Coaches can do this by encouraging athletes to focus exclusively on what can be gained from challenging situations. More information on how coaches can teach athletes to appraise stress more effectively is presented in Session 2 of coping effectiveness training in Chapter 6.

Enhancing optimism and reducing pessimism

Research has suggested that mental toughness is positively related to optimism, but negatively related to pessimism (Nicholls *et al.*, 2008). Seligman (2006) suggested that coaches could teach their athletes to be more optimistic by applying the ABCDE acronym of learned optimism to their coaching. This acronym stands for:

- *Adversity*: During times of stress, such as when an athlete makes a mistake (e.g. missing a tackle, dropping a ball, or missing a penalty), the athlete has encountered difficulty or adversity.
- *Beliefs:* It is likely that the athlete will dwell on the mistake that he or she has just made, which can shape his or her beliefs. For example, if an athlete has dropped a ball, they might believe that they are not very good at catching.
- *Consequences:* All beliefs have consequences. For example, if an athlete believes he or she is poor at catching he or she might try and avoid situations in which they have to catch, such as having a preference to stand where the ball is less likely to go to.
- *Disputation:* In order to help athletes remain optimistic during adversity, it is important that coaches dispute any negative beliefs that might occur. First, the coach has got to identify negative beliefs among athletes and can do this by speaking to athletes to find their views on different matters.
- *Evidence:* Coaches can dispute negative beliefs by using evidence. If an athlete drops a catch, the coach could say 'Unlucky with the catch, you've caught some great catches this year and I am sure you will get the next one'.

In addition to maximising optimism, it is also important that coaches reduce pessimism. Seligman (2006) also provided useful information regarding how coaches can reduce this, using the 3 Ps: personal, permanent, and pervasive:

- *Personal:* An athlete who is a pessimist believes that his or her misfortune (e.g. not being selected for a team or dropping a high catch) lies within himself or herself rather than being external. Therefore, misfortune is thought to be personal. As such, athletes should be encouraged to attribute their misfortune to external sources (e.g. dropped the ball because of the wind or moisture on the ball).

- *Permanent:* Pessimistic athletes also believe that their misfortune is permanent (e.g. I am never going to be selected for the team). Coaches should encourage athletes to view all setbacks as being temporary and state that with practice to improve techniques setbacks will not regularly occur.
- *Pervasive*: Pessimists also believe that their misfortune is pervasive to all parts of their life and expect to experience misfortune in all parts of their

---

Case study 4.1 Mental toughness in swimming

Linda is a 57-year-old swimming coach, who has coached Janine for the last nine years, which included Janine competing at two Olympic games. Janine is now 26 years old and wants to compete at one more Olympic games in four years time, before pursuing a career in banking. Linda has suspected that Janine lacks mental toughness as she tends to focus on the negatives, lack confidence, and struggles to cope among other things. As Janine knows that she is attempting to swim at one more Olympics, she wants to give everything and is dedicated to improving psychologically as well as technically.

Linda recently assessed Janine's level of mental toughness using a mental toughness questionnaire, to see if she had low levels of mental toughness. Linda spoke to Janine about what she felt she needed and they planned a mental toughness training programme. This included coping effectiveness training, confidence, and optimism training. This was because Janine had always used goal setting very effectively and did not have problems concentrating, so they did not need to include this in the training programme. However, they did spend one session discussing Janine's long-term, medium-term, and short-term goals.

As Janine felt her ability to cope with stress needed more urgent work, they started the coping effectiveness training first. This involved Linda working with Janine, to help her understand more about stress, how to cope, and who to turn to for support. For the most part, they had weekly sessions. Linda felt that Janine struggled with certain concepts of coping effectiveness training because they had less time in some weeks, so they spent more time working on parts she did not understand as well. Once Janine had finished the coping effectiveness training, she felt she needed a break before starting the optimism and confidence training.

Case study reflection

As mental toughness encapsulates a broad range of characteristics (e.g. coping, confidence, concentration etc), helping an athlete become more mentally tough is something that could take time, so coaches should be patient.

life (e.g. sport, education, and relationships etc). Coaches should encourage athletes to think positively and rationally – just because one area of an athlete's life is not going to plan, other parts of his or her life should not be affected.

Confidence

Clough *et al.* (2002) and Jones *et al.* (2002) stated that confidence is crucial. Observational learning and mental imagery are crucial in helping athletes build their confidence. Information regarding how coaches can enhance the confidence of their athletes is presented in Chapter 5 of this book.

Concentration

Coaches can enhance the concentration of their athletes, which has been identified by Clough *et al.* (2002), Gucciardi *et al.* (2008), and Jones *et al.* (2002) as being an important mental toughness characteristic, by encouraging athletes to use cue words (Miller and Donohue, 2003). The coach could ask the athlete to focus on technical cue words (e.g. follow through, body position, watch ball) or motivational (e.g. confident) when they are performing. Coaches could also encourage athletes to develop routines, which should be learned in practice and then transferred to competition (Schack *et al.*, 2005). It is also important that the routines are individualised for the performer (Cotteril *et al.*, 2010).

Goal setting

Jones *et al.* (2007) found that athletes use goals for a source of motivation. A goal refers to an objective, target, or desired standard that an athlete wants to achieve in relation to a specific task or sport, and within a specific time limit (Locke and Latham, 2002). Information regarding how coaches can help athletes set goals is provided in Chapter 9.

Summary points

- Establishing an agreed definition of mental toughness has proved troublesome in the sport psychology literature.
- There are three main models of mental toughness, which were proposed by Clough *et al.* (2002), Jones *et al.* (2002; 2007), and Gucciardi *et al.* (2008), with these models having many similarities.
- Mental toughness appears to develop through an athlete's career.
- Coaches play a vital role in the development of an athlete's mental toughness.
- Current mental toughness interventions have not included some key qualities that contribute to mental toughness such as coach behaviour, coping, and optimism training.

Practice exam questions

1 What are the strengths and weaknesses of the 4Cs model of mental toughness.
2 Critically evaluate Jones *et al*'s (2002; 2007) model of mental toughness.
3 Discuss the strengths and limitations of Gucciardi *et al.*'s (2008) model of mental toughness.
4 What similarities exist between the models of mental toughness proposed by Clough *et al.* (2002), Jones *et al.* (2002; 2007), and Gucciardi *et al.* (2008)?
5 Mental toughness changes across an athlete's career. Discuss.

Critical thinking questions: applying theory to practice

1 Discuss the role of the coach in shaping an athlete's mental toughness.
2 From a coaching perspective, what are the strengths and limitations of the mental toughness guidelines proposed in this chapter?
3 What challenges may coaches face when they try and implement optimism training? Discuss.
4 Devise your own mental toughness intervention for an athlete you have coached in the past that you feel lacked mental toughness.
5 What are the implications of a coach who never points out his athlete's weaknesses? Discuss.

5   Maximising sport confidence

The purpose of this chapter is to provide information on the factors that coaches should consider when they coach athletes who lack confidence. Specifically, in this chapter information is provided in relation to:

* a definition of sport confidence;
* conceptual model of sport confidence;
* benefits of sport confidence;
* sources of sport confidence;
* sport confidence profiling;
* developing sport confidence.

A definition of sport confidence

Vealey and Chase (2008) defined sport confidence as 'an athlete's belief or degree of certainty that she or he has the abilities to perform successfully in sport' (p. 71). This definition is grounded in self-efficacy theory (Bandura, 1977), so it is similar in some ways to self-efficacy, but different in that sport confidence is related exclusively to competitive sport.

Conceptual model of sport confidence

Vealey (2001) created an integrative model of sport confidence, stating that the culture of a sports organisation and individual differences among athletes (e.g. personality characteristics, attitudes, and values) influence confidence levels. The level of sport confidence an athlete possesses influences how an athlete will behave, think, and feel. This then influences how the athlete will perform. As such, sport confidence is critical to how athletes perform; even when factors that are uncontrollable (e.g. weather or opponents) and the physical capabilities of the athlete are accounted for (Hays *et al.*, 2009).

The benefits of sport confidence

It is important that coaches understand the benefits of sport confidence, because this may provide them with extra motivation to ensure their athletes are confident. The benefits of athletes with high sport confidence include:

- *Enhanced sporting performance:* a meta-analysis by Woodman and Hardy (2003) revealed that there was a significant relationship between sport performance and confidence ($r = 0.24$).
- *Emotions:* research by Jones and Swain (1995) has found that athletes who are highly confident are more likely to interpret anxiety as being positive compared to athletes who are low in confidence.
- *Effort:* Weinberg *et al.* (1980) revealed that confident athletes are more likely to exert effort than athletes who are not confident. In addition to highly confident athletes exerting more effort to pursue their goals, they will also persist longer at trying to achieve their goals. This is important from a coaching perspective, especially if an athlete is making technical changes to their game, because these may take time. A confident athlete is more likely to complete any technical changes, whereas an unconfident athlete might give up.
- *Psychological momentum:* Psychological momentum refers to an athlete's perception regarding whether a goal is being achieved (Vallerand *et al.*, 1988). Being confident influences momentum, and momentum influences the likelihood of an athlete winning or losing (Miller and Weinberg, 1991). The most confident players are able to reverse negative momentum. This is because they have a never say die attitude and refuse to give up.

Sources of sport confidence

Once coaches understand how athletes derive their sport confidence, they can help shape an athlete's sport confidence. A study by Hays *et al.* (2007) examined the sources of sport confidence among a sample of 14 world-class athletes, and identified nine sources. These included:

1   *Coaching:* The coach played two pivotal roles in determining how confident an athlete was. For example, some athletes gained confidence from the advice that their coach had given them, whereas others found confidence from receiving social support. As such, coaches should be aware of their role in influencing confidence levels among athletes. Coaches should ensure that their instruction is appropriate and that they are also supportive to maximise confidence levels among athletes.

2   *Preparation:* Athletes felt confident when they were physically and mentally prepared for competing in their sport. For instance, athletes who felt they were able to perform at their best when their physical preparation in training had gone well. Mental preparation, which included the athletes setting themselves goals, mental imagery, and developing strategies were also important.

3 *Performance accomplishments:* Performing well in previous competitions was a source of confidence for the athletes, with one of the athletes being highly confident because he had not lost to a particular team in four years.

4 *Social support:* Athletes rated the support they received from their family, partners, or friends, especially during competitive periods, as a source of confidence.

5 *Innate factors:* Some athletes believed they had a genetic advantage that made them resilient to the effects of stress, which gave them an inner belief and acted as a source of confidence.

6 *Competitive advantage:* Athletes also gained confidence from seeing their opponents perform poorly in other competitions.

7 *Experience:* Using one's previous experience was an important source of confidence for some athletes, because they knew what to expect and gained confidence from it.

8 *Trust:* Trust was an important source of confidence for some athletes and involved the athletes trusting other teammates or support teams.

9 *Self-awareness:* Being aware of one's self was an important source of confidence for some athletes, because they knew exactly what they wanted.

In addition to these nine global themes, Hays *et al.* (2007) also identified a number of individual differences among the athletes that could not be classified within the dimensions. These included enjoyment, commitment of team-mates, and whether the athletes felt that it was meant to be that they would do well, which Hays *et al.* referred to as omens.

Coaches also need to consider the age of their athletes when considering the sources of their confidence. This is because Wilson *et al.* (2004) found some subtle differences to Hays *et al.* (2007), with a sample of masters athletes, aged between 50 and 96 years (the sample in the Hays *et al.* study was aged between 21 and 48 years). Although there were some similarities between the two studies such as preparation, coaching, and social support, the masters athletes rated physical self-presentation, watching others perform, and mastery as sources of confidence. Although it should be noted that physical self-presentation and vicarious experience were reported as additional sources among the Hays *et al.* study. It was apparent from the Hays *et al.* (2007) study that there are individual differences in sources of confidence. Coaches need to investigate and harness these differences to make confidence training more effective. One such method of assessing sport confidence and sources of sport confidence among athletes is called confidence profiling (Hays *et al.*, 2010a).

Confidence profiling

Confidence profiling (Hays *et al.*, 2010a) has recently been introduced to the psychology literature. The confidence profile originates from Butler's (1989) performance profile, which is grounded in Kelly's (1991 [1955]) Personal Construct Theory (PCT). Information on performance profiling and Kelly's PCT is presented in Chapter 10, so will only be discussed briefly here. PCT suggests that an athlete will attempt to make sense of himself or herself and his or her environment by developing theories about the world. These theories vary from person to person, because individuals differ regarding how they perceive situations and interpret them. Confidence profiling was designed to be an applied method of assessing confidence, so it is very appropriate for coaches to use. Research that has used the confidence profile (Hays *et al.*, 2010b) found that this instrument increased the athlete's awareness of the factors that enhanced and decreased confidence.

The processes involved in confidence profiling by Hays *et al.* (2010a) have been adapted in this chapter and involve four stages:

Stage 1

During this initial stage, after explaining the concept of confidence profiling, the coach asks the athlete to 'write down what you need to be confident about to be successful in your sport'. The example of a completed list is presented in Table 5.1 and relates to what a soccer player might think is important to be confident about to be successful in soccer.

Stage 2

In Stage 2, the coach then asks the athlete to identify the 12 most important characteristics it is important to be confident in, and asks the athlete to provide a meaning. As such, the coach would ask the player to 'rank the 12 most important qualities it is important to be confident in, with 1 being the most important and 12 being the least important of the list'. The coach would then ask the athlete to 'describe what each item on the list means by completing the table'. An example of a completed table that identifies the 12 most important characteristics it is important to be confident in, is presented in Table 5.2.

Stage 3

The athlete is then asked to rate where the sources of confidence come from for each of the 12 most important characteristics, which have previously been identified by the athlete. The coach would ask the athlete to 'write down where being confident in the important qualities comes from'. An example of a completed source of confidence sheet is presented in Table 5.3.

Stage 4

Finally, the athlete is asked to plot: (a) the 12 most important factors to be confident in, (b) their current ratings between 1 and 10, with 10 being the most confident they could be and 1 being the least confident they could be, and (c) the sources of sport confidence for each category in the specified box. Figure 5.1 represents a completed confidence profile for the soccer player.

Table 5.1 A soccer player's view about what he or she needs to be confident about to be successful in soccer

Having a good first touch

Stamina

Trust from coach

Speed

Skill

Good training sessions

Get on well with teammates

Enjoy matches

Good at defending

Able to pass well

Can play when things get tight

Not afraid to take chances

Feel mentally good

Don't have aches or pains during matches

Comments from coach during matches

Table 5.2 Ranking and meaning of the 12 most important qualities to be confident in

Rank order	Qualities an athlete needs to be confident in to be successful at sport	Meaning
1	Speed	Being able to run really fast
2	Stamina	Being able to run for the whole match at a good level
3	Good training sessions	Things go well in training, which makes you feel good going into matches.
4	Trust from coach	Knowing that the coach believes in you
5	Comments from coach during matches	What the coach says or shouts during matches or half-time break
6	Not afraid to take chances	Even though a game is close, doing what it takes to win a match
7	Get on well with teammates	Being friendly with other teammates
8	Enjoy matches	Like the feeling of playing in matches
9	First touch	Being able to control the ball well when I first get it, which gives me time
10	Good at defending	Not letting other players get past
11	Able to pass well	Passes go to right player
12	Feel mentally good	In right frame of mind to play well

Table 5.3 Completed sources of confidence table for a soccer player

Qualities an athlete needs to be confident in to be successful at sport	Sources of confidence
Speed	Amount of training, effort in training, Legs feeling good
Stamina	Performance in fitness tests, time spent in training working on endurance
Good training sessions	Coach comments, what other teammates say
Trust from coach	Selection for team, extra responsibilities
Comments from coach during matches	Coach told me I was doing well
Not afraid to take chances	Feedback from coach during matches, praise from teammates
Get on well with teammates	Spending time together away from soccer
Enjoy matches	Positive comments from coach during matches, parents being positive
First touch	Coach feedback, comments from other players, more time in matches
Good at defending	Time spent practising defensive formations
Able to pass well	What other players say, coach comments during matches, parents' comments during matches
Feel mentally good	Getting support from parents

As with normal performance profiling (Butler, 1989), the confidence profiling (Hays *et al.* 2010a) should be conducted on a regular basis. This helps athletes and coaches monitor the effects of any confidence training that a coach may provide, as in accordance with Hays *et al.* (2010b).

Developing sport confidence

Once a coach has established that his or her athlete could benefit from a sports confidence training programme, an intervention can be developed. Feltz *et al.* (2008) provided an excellent framework that coaches can adopt, although coaches should adapt the guidelines based upon the needs of their athlete and the ability of the athlete.

Instructional strategies

A coach can enhance the sport confidence of the athletes he or she coaches by the way instruction is provided and the drills that are used within training sessions (Hays *et al.*, 2007; Vargas-Tonsing *et al.*, 2004). Normally, a coach would give athletes instructions to help athletes master specific techniques or tactics (i.e. putting in golf or attacking formations in basketball). Coaches should also try and

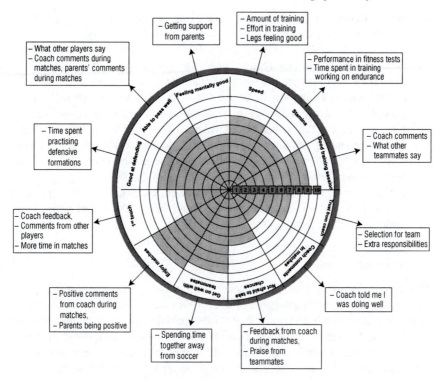

Figure 5.1 Completed confidence profile for a soccer player

build confidence in athletes' ability to complete tasks. Feltz (1994) suggested that coaches must take a methodical approach and go through each component of a skill. In putting, the coach could break the skill into its component parts: stance, spine angle, position of ball in the stance, grip, ball strike, and follow through. The coach should be enthusiastic about the athlete's ability.

Feedback

The feedback an athlete receives from his or her coach is important in building an athlete's sport confidence levels, especially when athletes learn new skills, as they are likely to make mistakes (Feltz *et al.*, 2008). A coach who encourages his or her athlete, by providing positive feedback, may enhance his or her sport confidence during what can be a difficult time. Jourden *et al.* (1991) suggested that positive feedback involves the coach focusing on the positive aspects of a skill being performed, but it also involves illustrating any mistakes the athlete has made. It is important that coaches provide information regarding how athletes can reduce the mistakes they typically make. The coach should also inform the athlete that mistakes are a normal part of the learning process. Based on the guidelines proposed by Jourden *et al.* (1991), Feltz (1994) suggested that coaches should:

1   Acknowledge the athlete's distress (e.g. 'I can see that you are very upset and frustrated about the ball not going into the correct service box').
2   Tell the athlete what aspect of the skill he or she performed correctly (e.g. 'The acceleration of the racquet head was excellent, as was your follow-through. You are generating some excellent power in your serve').
3   Let the athlete know how he or she can correct the mistake (e.g. 'You just need to get more consistency in your ball toss, because it is making you hit the ball from the wrong place, which is why your serve is inconsistent. This is something that many beginners struggle with. Once you get this more consistent your serve will be excellent because all the other parts of your serve are very good').
4   Finish by providing positive feedback to the athlete (e.g. 'With more practice you will get the ball toss more consistent and then you will start hitting more powerful and accurate serves!').

Observational learning

Observational learning involves the coach demonstrating a particular skill (e.g. set shot in basketball) or asks another athlete to perform the skill in front of other athletes so they can see how it is performed. Feltz (1980) provided specific recommendations on what coaches can do when they conduct observational learning demonstrations. The coach should verbally explain the skill in the first instance. He or she should give a demonstration and then ask the athlete to repeat the verbal instructions he or she has just heard. Following this procedure, the coach then asks the athlete if he or she is comfortable performing the task unassisted or whether assistance is required. If assistance is required the coach can physically guide the athlete through the movement, but if no assistance is required the athlete performs by himself or herself. Guidance is removed once the athlete can perform the task consistently.

For observational learning to be effective, Bandura (1997) stated that four conditions need to be accomplished: attention, retention, production, and motivation.

1   *Attention:* For observational learning to be effective, the coach needs to ensure that the athlete or athletes are paying attention. This may be more difficult when the coach is providing the demonstration to larger groups, so this is something that needs to be considered.
2   *Retention:* The athlete must be able to remember the skill that he or she has observed in the demonstration. Therefore, if the skills are very complex, the coach could break the skill into several demonstrations to help the athlete remember what he or she has observed.
3   *Production:* It is important that coaches ensure that the athlete has the ability to re-produce the skill that he or she has observed. If athletes do not possess the ability, observational learning will not be effective.
4   *Motivation:* Athletes need to be motivated to perform the skill they have observed. If the athlete is not motivated towards performing a skill, observational learning will be of limited benefit to the athlete. Coaches can

enhance motivation by manipulating the sport environment, by rewarding athletes who try hard and make the most improvement, which is referred to as a mastery oriented climate. Manipulating the motivational climate has resulted in sport being more enjoyable, increased perceived competence, intrinsic motivation, and improved motor performance (Theeboom *et al.*, 1995). Information regarding how coaches can enhance the motivation of different athletic populations is presented for children (see Chapter 11), adolescents (Chapter 12), and adults (Chapter 13).

Mental imagery

Mental imagery refers to the process of an athlete using his or her imagination to see himself or herself performing a movement (e.g. running) or a certain skill (e.g. catching a high ball in rugby or heading the ball in soccer: Richardson, 1969). A motivational general-mastery intervention in which the athlete imagines himself or herself successfully mastering a skill may be help in enhancing confidence (Martin *et al.*, 1999). For more information regarding how coaches can develop an imagery intervention, please read Chapter 3.

Summary points

- Sport confidence refers to an athlete's view about whether he or she has the skill to be able to perform successfully in his or her sport (Vealey and Chase, 2008).
- Sport confidence is associated with a variety of benefits, including enhanced sports performance.
- Research indicates that there are nine sources that athletes derive their confidence from, such as coaches, preparation, and the social support they receive.
- Coaches can assess and monitor an athlete's confidence by using confidence profiling.
- Confidence in athletes can be developed by coaches behaving correctly, using observational learning, and mental imagery.

Practice exam questions

1   Describe Vealey's (2001) model of confidence.
2   Being confident benefits athletes. Discuss.
3   Discuss the extent to which coach behaviour influences sport confidence.
4   Compare and contrast confidence profiling (Hays *et al.*, 2010a) with performance profiling (Butler, 1989).
5   Confidence is affected by age. Discuss.

Case study 5.1 How to help an athlete when the fire goes out

Vicky, a county tennis player who is 31 years old, was absolutely flying. She had just received a promotion at work and achieved selection for her county team, which was a remarkable achievement, given she had only been playing the sport for three and a half years. She played against a national player in her first match and suffered a heavy defeat (6–2, 6–1). She lost all of her confidence.

Christopher, who was Vicky's county coach, could see a change in Vicky's demeanour, energy levels, and desire to train at the training session following Vicky's first match. She seemed a shadow of her former self, previously bubbly and inquisitive. After the session, Christopher took Vicky to one side and spoke to her about what had happened. Vicky said that she felt horrible, because she had let her team-mates down and everything she tried on the court no longer worked. She said that she felt helpless.

Due to time pressures after the coaching session, Christopher asked to speak to Vicky before the next session and they arranged a time to speak. During this second conversation Christopher explained how confidence is like a fire – it can be burning strong one minute and the next it can have disappeared. Christopher was keen to listen to Vicky's concerns that included doubts about whether she deserved a place on the county squad, and whether she was good enough to play county tennis. Once he listened to these concerns, Christopher provided reassurance, support, and advice regarding what Vicky could do to improve. He also asked Vicky if she was keen to try an imagery intervention, which she was, so Christopher developed an MG-M imagery training programme.

Christopher knew that it was a delicate time for Vicky, so he ensured his behaviour was always very positive and encouraging around Vicky, to help her get through the sticky patch.

Case study reflection

It is important that coaches consider the needs of the athlete when providing confidence training. In this case study, it is apparent that Vicky is a talented tennis player because she is already playing for her county team. As such, players of a higher ability may require less information on their technique given that it will already be strong, so techniques such as observational learning and instructional strategies that coaches can employ will not be as relevant as they would be for a beginner athlete who is having confidence problems.

Critical thinking questions: applying theory to practice

1 Feltz (1980) stated that a coach could physically help an athlete if he or she cannot perform a skill unassisted. Critically evaluate this instruction.
2 Discuss how coaches can have a positive influence regarding the sources of sport confidence outlined by Hays *et al.* (2007).
3 From the guidelines provided by Feltz *et al.* (2008), state which training procedures would benefit elite athletes, and which would be more suitable for beginners.
4 How can coaches make observational learning more effective?
5 Describe how coaches can provide feedback to maximise the confidence of their athletes.

6   Coping effectiveness training

The purpose of this chapter is to provide information on coping effectiveness training for athletes and understanding the principles behind this training. More specifically, this chapter will contain information on:

*   defining stress;
*   neuroendocrine responses to stress;
*   defining coping;
*   the functions of coping;
*   coping interventions;
*   defining coping effectiveness;
*   coping effectiveness training theory;
*   developing a coping effectiveness training programme.

Defining stress

Defining stress is a very contentious issue, with researchers struggling to agree on a common definition (Lazarus, 1999). Within the sport psychology literature, Lazarus and Folkman's (1984) definition of stress is still widely used. They defined stress as 'a particular relationship between the person and the environment that is appraised by the person as taxing or exceeding his or her resources and endangering his or her well-being' (p. 19). This definition is relational, because it assumes that stress is a product of the person who is interacting with his or her environment, who evaluates whether he or she has the resources to deal with the environment. A person experiences stress when he or she evaluates that he or she has insufficient resources to manage the situation.

Neuroendocrine responses to stress

Experiencing stress can cause parts of the brain to interact with the pituitary glands and adrenal glands, which produces a variety of hormonal responses (Aldwin, 2007). As such, when an athlete perceives threat (e.g. he or she might lose), the part of the brain known as the hypothalamus is activated, which stimulates the pituitary gland to release hormones that activate the adrenal glands. It is the activation of adrenal glands that stimulate the sympathetic nervous system (Cannon, 1915). According to Aldwin (2007), the results of the sympathetic nervous system being stimulated include:

- increased blood pressure, heart rate, respiration rate, and perspiration;
- increased blood sugar levels;
- increased blood clotting;
- dilated pupils;
- piloerections (goose bumps);
- decreased saliva and mucus;
- gastro-intestinal disturbances;
- blood is diverted from the intestines to the brain and muscles that are being used.

Essentially, these responses to stress prepare athletes to mobilise their efforts to effectively manage the situation they are in, which is known as the fight–flight reaction (Cannon, 1915). The athlete is ready to confront the source of stress (fight) or run away (flight). As such, it is important that coaches understand that stress is not just a figment of an athlete's imagination. When athletes experience stress they will experience an array of physiological symptoms that might not necessarily be conducive to successful performance. Indeed, two meta-analyses (e.g. Craft *et al.,* 2003; Woodman and Hardy, 2003) explored the relationship between pre-competitive anxiety, which is a stress emotion (Lazarus, 1999), and performance. Both sets of authors found a negative relationship between these two variables. As such, it is important that coaches help their athletes manage stress. One way athletes attempt to manage stress is through coping.

Defining coping

Coping has been defined as 'constantly changing cognitive and behavioural efforts to manage specific external and/or internal demands that are appraised as taxing or exceeding the resources of the person' (Lazarus and Folkman, 1984: 141). That is, coping refers to the thoughts and behaviours that an athlete engages in, aimed at reducing the stress he or she is experiencing. This definition and conceptualisation of coping has been adopted by over 80 per cent of the coping research articles published in the sport psychology literature (Nicholls and Polman, 2007).

The coping functions

Researchers have classified coping in many different ways. For a review of the different ways coping has been classified, see the chapter by Nicholls and Thelwell (2010). Within the sport psychology literature, researchers have, on the whole classified all coping strategies within one of three dimensions: problem-focused coping, emotion-focused coping, or avoidance coping.

Problem-focused coping refers to coping strategies that are aimed directly at the problem which causes the person to experience stress (Lazarus and Folkman, 1984). Coping strategies that have been classified as problem-focused coping in the sport psychology literature include: increased effort (e.g. Reeves *et al.*, 2009), remaining on the task (e.g. Anshel, 2001), time management planning (e.g. Gould *et al.*, 1993), and problem solving (e.g. Holt and Hogg, 2002).

Emotion-focused coping refers to strategies that regulate the emotional responses to stress. Coping strategies that have been classified within the emotion-focused dimension include: seeking support from others (e.g. Poczwardowski and Conroy, 2002), humour (e.g. Crocker and Graham, 1995), prayer (Gould *et al.*, 1993), and thought control (e.g. Holt and Mandigo, 2004).

Based on the recommendations of Kowalski and Crocker (2001), the researchers have also added a third dimension, called avoidance coping. Avoidance coping refers to strategies that consist of cognitive and behavioural attempts to disengage from a stressful encounter (Krohne, 1993). Strategies that have been cited as avoidance coping include: blocking (e.g. Nicholls, 2007a), walking away (e.g.,Nicholls *et al.*, 2009), and ignoring other people (e.g., Nicholls *et al.* 2005a).

Coping interventions

Sport psychology researchers have developed three types of coping interventions, with the aim of reducing stress, through teaching athletes to cope. These were:

1   *Cognitive-affective stress management training (SMT)* (Smith, 1980): The SMT program consists of the athletes learning behavioural relaxation strategies in addition to cognitive strategies to reduce emotional arousal. Furthermore, the SMT also involves specific phases known as conceptualisation (i.e. the athlete identifying how he or she currently copes), skill acquisition rehearsal (i.e. the athlete being taught new coping strategies), and skill application (i.e. the athlete using the strategies he or she has been taught). However, support for SMT programs is somewhat mixed. Crocker *et al.* (1988) found that the SMT had a limited effect in reducing the anxiety experienced by athletes, although SMT appears to have more positive influence on athletic performance (e.g. Crocker *et al.*, 1988; Smith, 1980).

2   *The COPE intervention* (Anshel *et al.*,1990): In this coping programme athletes are taught to *control* emotions, *organise* the most important information to attend to, *plan* how they will respond to stressful encounters, and *execute* their responses. This intervention appears to help athletes manage negative feedback; maintain self-esteem, and self-confidence levels.

3   *Coping skills programme* (Nicholls, 2007b): Based on recommendations from recent coping studies among golfers (e.g. Nicholls, 2007a; Nicholls *et al.*, 2005a, 2005b) Nicholls (2007b) developed a coping skills programme. As such, the golfer was encouraged to use coping strategies that had been deemed effective (e.g. rationalisation and re-appraisal), whilst refraining from using ineffective coping strategies (e.g. speeding up between shots

and making routine changes). Results revealed the participant 'benefited a lot' from knowing why certain stressors were effective and others were not. This study was limited by the absence of any baseline measurements, so the impact this intervention had on the golfer cannot be deduced.

Although these three coping interventions have yielded some positive results, none of these studies have included coping effectiveness training. That is, participants in these studies were not specifically taught to assess stress controllability and then direct coping strategies accordingly depending on whether the athlete felt that he or she can control the stress. Further, these interventions did instruct participants to elicit social support. Therefore, coaches could improve the effectiveness of coping interventions by including elements of coping effectiveness training.

Definition of coping effectiveness

Coping effectiveness has recently been defined as the 'degree in which a coping strategy or combination of strategies is or are successful in alleviating stress' (Nicholls, 2010: 264). It is important that athletes cope effectively, especially when they experience immense stress, so that their performance does not deteriorate (e.g. Haney and Long, 1995; Lazarus, 2000a).

Coping effectiveness training theory

Coping effectiveness training (CET) (Chesney *et al.*, 1996) is underpinned by the transactional-theoretical perspective of stress and coping (Lazarus and Folkman, 1984) and in particular the goodness-of-fit model (Folkman, 1984). The goodness-of-fit approach states that when an individual can control a stressful situation problem-focused coping strategies are the most effective (e.g. planning, time management, and information seeking). Conversely, when situations are uncontrollable emotion-focused and avoidance coping strategies will be more effective (e.g. deep breathing, physical relaxation, and acceptance). CET is different from the three coping interventions developed by Smith (1980), Anshel *et al.* (1990), or Nicholls (2007b). In addition to being taught how to cope, athletes would also be taught to assess stress controllability and then direct coping strategies accordingly depending on whether the athlete felt that he or she can control the stress. Athletes are also taught how to make the most of social support. The goal of coping effectiveness training is to reduce stress, enhance emotional well-being, and maximise sporting performance. Furthermore, the literature also indicates that coping is particularly useful in generating both positive and optimal performance states (Hanin, 2004, 2007; Nicholls *et al.*, 2010). As such, coping effectiveness training should help athletes maintain optimal performance states.

Coping effectiveness training was originally designed as a group-based intervention, directed to the needs of the target population, with sessions being based around elements of cognitive and behavioural stress management interventions (e.g., cognitive therapy, relaxation, and problem-solving). However, when Reeves *et al.* (2011) developed their intervention for academy soccer players, each soccer player received his training individually.

A number of studies from the mainstream and sport psychology literature have provided supporting evidence for the CET. For instance, Chesney *et al.* (1996) conducted a randomised control trial among male patients diagnosed with HIV. The recipients of the CET intervention significantly increased coping self-efficacy (CSE) and significantly decreased perceived stress and burnout. More recently, Chesney *et al.* (2003) found that CET was also effective in reducing anxiety, perceived stress, and burnout among 128 men diagnosed with HIV. Regression analyses also indicated higher levels of CSE-mediated improvements in perceived stress and burnout, meaning that self-efficacy is an important variable to consider in coping interventions. CSE has been defined as 'a person's confidence in his or her ability to cope effectively' (Chesney *et al.*, 2006: 422). Reeves *et al.* (2011) examined the effects of a Coping Effectiveness Training for Adolescent Soccer Players (CETASP) intervention on coping self-efficacy (CSE), coping effectiveness (CE), and subjective performance among five participants. The participants played for an English Premier League Soccer Academy. A single-subject multiple-baseline, across individuals design was employed. Each participant spent a different amount of time in the baseline and intervention phase of the study. The intervention appeared successful in enhancing coping effectiveness, coping self-efficacy, and subjective performance among the players.

Developing a CET intervention

To help athletes cope more effectively, coaches can devise a CET programme, based on the guidelines proposed in this chapter. As such, information is provided on what coaches should do in each session. The sessions are primarily designed for individual athletes, but can easily be adapted for team settings. The guidelines are based on the study by Reeves *et al.* (2011), which were developed in accordance with Chesney *et al.* (2003). A session on stress appraisals has been included in these guidelines. This is because emerging research by Nicholls *et al.* (2011), who has revealed how elite rugby union players' appraisal of stressful environment stimuli (e.g. dropping a ball, opponents scoring a try, being criticised by a coach) shaped emotional reactions. As such, teaching athletes to appraise stress more favourably may generate more positive emotions. More recent research (Nicholls *et al.*, 2012) revealed that appraisals are related to perceived stress and how athletes cope, so shaping appraisals could be very important in helping athletes combat stress. As such, information has been provided on how coaches can train athletes in appraisal.

CET training programmes usually contain seven sessions. It is recommended that coaches conduct one session per week, with each session lasting around 60 minutes. If coaches conduct any more than one session per week, athletes might not have time to grasp each concept before moving onto the next. It is important to note that the guidelines presented merely serve as a reference for coaches who may wish to adapt elements of the programme.

Before starting the programme, and after the coach has assessed the needs of the athlete, it is important that the coach describes the nature of CET and the level of commitment that will be required from the athlete or the team. This is so the individual or individuals can decide whether they would like to receive CET. It is very important that the athlete is keen to take part in CET.

Coping Effectiveness Training intervention guidelines

Session 1: Understanding stress and coping

The aim of an introductory session is to help develop the athlete's self-awareness of stress and coping. First, the coach provides the athlete with a description of what stress is, such as 'stress is when you feel that situation you are in exceeds your resources and reduces your well-being and is associated with symptoms such as increased heart rate, worrying and muscle tension' (Nicholls *et al.*, 2011: 81). The athlete is then presented with a figure that contains some of the symptoms associated with stress (Figure 6.1), so they are aware that the symptoms they experience are normal.

The coach then asks the athlete to describe and write down several sporting situations in which he or she has experienced stress and the symptoms that were

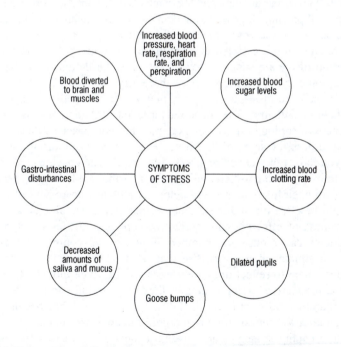

Figure 6.1 The symptoms of stress

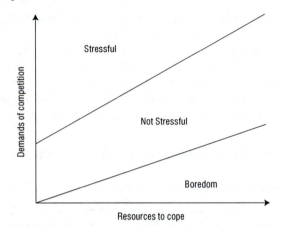

Figure 6.2 Why athletes experience stress: demands vs. resources to cope

experienced. This is so the coach and the athlete generate an understanding of the stress symptoms the athlete experiences and whether there are any common symptoms or experiences that lead to the athlete experiencing stress. The coach then presents the athlete with a figure that depicts why athletes experience stress. As indicated in Figure 6.2, when the demands of the situation (e.g. taking a penalty) are equal to the athlete's resources stress will not be experienced. When the athlete's resources are high and the demands of the sporting situation are low, boredom will prevail. Only when the demands of the situation are much greater than the person's resources to cope will the athlete experience stress.

The remainder of Session 1 is spent discussing coping. The coach provides a definition of coping such as 'coping refers to the thoughts and behaviours that you make to reduce the stress or the worry that you experience. Coping comes in many forms, and the key is that you purposefully engage in those thoughts or behaviours'. The coach then asks the athlete to describe his or her experiences of coping in sport. For example, the sport coach could say 'I would like you to describe some of the strategies you have used during instances in which you have felt worried or stressed in sport'. The coach can also ask the athlete to distinguish between coping strategies that are helpful and those that have been unhelpful. This process helps the athlete's awareness of strategies that might be effective and those that are ineffective. Helping an athlete gain an awareness of effective and ineffective coping strategies is important, so that athletes can reduce the number of ineffective coping strategies they use. Some athletes may not realise that what they are doing is ineffective, and require help to reflect upon their experiences. Even though athletes have identified ineffective coping strategies they may continue to use them, as did the international golfer in Nicholls (2007b), because they had become a habit. Although after awareness training the golfer knew it was unhelpful to use the ineffective coping strategies and made a concerted effort to stop using such strategies, but that took time.

Session 2: Appraisal training

Appraisal refers to an evaluative process in which the athlete appraises what is going on in the environment (i.e. competition or training session) in relation to his or her goals or values (Lazarus, 1999). Appraisal might be a very important construct in shaping emotional well-being given that the emotion a person experiences is shaped by appraisal (Lazarus, 1991; 1999). Lazarus (1991, 1999, 2000a, 2000b) proposed a two-factor schematisation of appraisals, or as he also termed them relational meanings that comprised of losses and gains. Loss appraisals comprise of: (a) anticipated losses and thus the threat of a loss occurring such as an opponent scoring a goal in addition to (b) losses that have already occurred such as a team scoring. Gain appraisals referred to gains that a person anticipates and gains that have already occurred.

A recent study by Nicholls *et al.* (2011), with a sample of 11 professional rugby players, found that loss evaluations generate predominantly negative emotions (e.g. anxiety, anger, and shame). Gain appraisals generated mainly positive emotions (e.g. happiness, relief, and pride). As such, the coach would ask the athlete to describe instances in which he has experienced stress and then ask the player to 'please describe how you evaluated that stressor. Were you focused on what could be gained or what could be lost?' This will allow the coach to assess appraisal patterns of the athlete. The coach can then explain the differences between the different types of appraisals and teach the athlete how appraise stressors as gains, rather than losses. For example, instead of the athlete appraising playing an opponent with a superior ranking as a loss (i.e. anticipating that he or she will lose the match), the athlete could be encouraged to focus on what can be gained from the situation (e.g. ranking points by beating a higher-ranked athlete, a chance to monitor progress, a chance to impress coaches with improvements made etc) and to view the situation as a challenge.

The coach would also present the athlete with a range of sport scenarios (e.g. you are about to play a number 1 ranked player, who you have a losing record against, in the presence of national selectors) and asked how he or she would appraise each situation. Once each scenario has been evaluated, the coach would go through each in turn, especially the negatively appraised events, to ask how they could be appraised differently with an emphasis focusing on what could be gained from a situation. When athletes focus on gains, they will make positive appraisals.

Session 3: Problem-focused coping

The goodness-of-fit approach, proposed by Folkman (1984) suggested that athletes should deploy problem-focused coping strategies in relation to stressors or stressful situations that they can control. In this session the coach helps the athlete distinguish between controllable stressors (e.g. lack of fitness) and uncontrollable stressors (e.g. not being selected by a coach). In order for the

Table 6.1 Controllable versus uncontrollable stressor checklist

Stressor	Controllable	Uncontrollable
Making a mental error (e.g. wrong choice)		
Making a physical error (e.g. poor execution of pass)		
Opponents playing well		
Sustaining an injury		
Opponents cheating		
Receiving a poor call from an official		
Weather conditions		
Receiving coach criticism		
Not being selected for the team		
Arguing with teammates		
Being substituted		
Fatigue		
Letting teammates down		

coach to ensure that the athlete has a good grasp of stressor controllability, the athlete should be tested with a range of different stressors before being taught problem-focused coping strategies. That is, the coach will present the athlete with a variety of stressors that have been found among athletes in the sport literature and ask the athlete to denote whether the stressor is controllable or uncontrollable (Table 6.1).

The coach then explains the concept of problem-focused coping strategies by saying something such as 'problem-focused coping strategies involve you using strategies that help you solve the problem that is causing you stress and thus reduce the amount of stress you are experiencing, because the problem is gone'. Once the definition has been read out, the coach can teach the athlete a variety of different problem-focused coping strategies such as planning a strategy, increasing concentration, creating a performance routine, and thought stopping. Once the athlete has an understanding of the coping strategies, the coach can ask the athlete to try using them in training sessions, before progressing to matches when the athlete is competent to do so.

Session 4: Emotion-focused coping

When an athlete experiences a stressor that he or she cannot control, it has the potential to be one of the most distressing experiences in sport. This is because the athlete may feel a sense of powerlessness. Folkman (1984), in her goodness-of-fit approach, suggested that in such stressful situations athletes should use emotion-focused coping strategies. The coach explains the concept of emotion-focused coping, by saying something along the lines of 'when you experience stress that you can't do anything about, you might feel very distressed, upset, or even angry. When you experience these types of stressors you can use emotion-focused coping strategies. These strategies are aimed at reducing your emotional reactions to the stress you are feeling'. As such, the athlete is attempting to take control of his or her emotional reactions to the source of stress. The coach then describes the different emotion-focused coping strategies such as breathing techniques, how to accept mistakes, and positive self-talk. As with the problem-focused coping strategies, the coach should encourage the athlete to practise these strategies in training, before attempting the coping strategies in competitions.

Session 5: Avoidance and ineffective coping

Coaches can also teach athletes to use avoidance coping strategies when athletes cannot control the stressor. The coach could explain avoidance coping by saying 'avoidance coping is when you try to not think about a stressful situation or you physically remove yourself from the stressor such as walking away'. Avoidance coping comprises of cognitive avoidance such as attempts to mentally withdraw from a stressor and behavioural avoidance, such as physically removing oneself from a stressor. Following the definition, the coach can teach the athlete avoidance coping strategies, such as blocking negative thoughts and walking away from stressful incidents. In Session 1 the coach asked the athlete to identify the coping strategies that he or she found ineffective. The coach can ask the athlete to refrain from using these strategies along with those that have been identified in previous research, such as forcing play, speeding up, focusing on outcome and not attempting to cope. The coach could emphasise that the athlete might find it difficult not using the ineffective strategies he or she has previously been using, if any, and that it will take time and practice.

Session 6: Social support

All athletes need a support network, because they might not be able to manage some stressors themselves and thus need to rely on significant others such as the coach, parents, spouse, siblings, or peers. In this session, the coach asks the athlete to identify the people he or she relies on for social support. Following this process the coach asks the athlete to distinguish between the people who are excellent at providing technical support and those who can provide emotional support. The athlete would then be encouraged to speak to those who are good at providing technical support with technical problems, and those who are good at providing emotional support when they worry. The coach then presents the athlete with several stressful situations and asks the athlete to identify who he or she would speak to when seeking support, with an emphasis on matching the problem with the person he or she speaks to. The athlete is encouraged to speak to members of his or her support network in the following week and let them know he or she will be asking them for their advice in the future.

Session 7: Summary

In the seventh, and final session, the coach summarises the sessions and answers any questions. This session is very useful to monitor the progress of the athlete, who will be seven weeks into the intervention. The coach could ask the athlete to complete a variety of questionnaires at the start of the intervention relating to constructs such as anxiety, coping, or coping self-efficacy and have the athlete complete the same questionnaires during Session 7 to monitor the progress of the athlete. The coach could also monitor the effects of the intervention long after the seven week programme and conduct recap sessions if they are needed.

Case study 6.1 Helping a shot-putter cope more effectively

Tom, who is a 48-year-old part-time athletics coach, started coaching Karen towards the end of the season. In training, Karen regularly throws over 16 metres, but seems to crumble in competition settings. Tom asked Karen what she felt the reasons for this were and she said that she was just too anxious to perform and did not know how to manage her stress. Tom suggested that a coping effectiveness training programme could be useful and explained what this would involve. Karen decided to take part in the programme during her close season. Tom conducted seven sessions, which included a session on understanding stress and coping, appraisal training, problem-focused coping, emotion-focused coping, avoidance coping, seeking social support and a summary. At first, Karen tended to concentrate too much on what she was doing to cope to the detriment of her technique and her performance deteriorated slightly in training. What she was doing to cope was actually becoming a source of concern to her. Tom asked her to spend more time learning and reviewing the coping strategies and practise these away from training such as when she was driving or working, so that they became second nature to her. After a few weeks, Karen became much more comfortable with using the coping strategies and spent less time thinking about them, which enabled her to perform better. Karen practised using the principles she had used over the close season and felt more than ready to use the strategies when she entered competition again.

Case study reflection

If possible, athletes should receive psychological training programmes during their off season, so that they get time to work on the different techniques they learn. Sometimes, athletes might struggle to learn new psychological techniques, whereas others will immediately flourish. It is important that coaches are aware of this and allow athletes time to adapt to using the new psychological strategies they have acquired.

Summary points

- Defining stress is a very contentious issue, with researchers struggling to agree on a common definition.
- Stress is associated with a variety of symptoms such as increased blood pressure, heart rate, respiration rate, and perspiration.
- Coping refers to the thoughts and behaviours that an athlete engages in to manage stress.
- Coping can be classified as problem-focused, emotion-focused, or avoidance coping.
- CET has the potential to improve how an athlete copes with stress, and involves athletes being taught how to use different coping strategies, appraisal training, and seeking social support.

Practice exam questions

1 Describe the symptoms associated with stress and the implications for sport performance.
2 Compare and contrast the different coping functions.
3 Discuss how coping effectiveness may influence performance and the emotional well-being of athletes.
4 Outline how coping effectiveness training is different to other coping interventions that have been used with athletes.
5 Critically evaluate the goodness-of-fit approach.

Critical thinking questions: applying theory to practice

1 Will all athletes experience the same symptoms of stress? Discuss the implications.
2 With reference to the fight–flight explanation of stress, discuss whether stress is inherently bad for athletes.
3 A player struggles to cope with stress. How could a coach help this player?
4 Discuss the practical strengths and limitations of coping effectiveness training.
5 What could a coach do if an athlete continues to use ineffective coping strategies, despite coping effectiveness training?

7 Choking prevention training

The purpose of this chapter is to provide coaches with information on choking under pressure in sport, so they can help their athletes to prevent this from occurring in pressurised situations. As such, information will be provided on:

- a definition of choking under pressure in sport;
- physiological and psychological feelings associated with choking;
- theoretical explanations of why athletes choke;
- choking prevention training.

Definition of choking under pressure in sport

An athlete's desire to perform at his or her best, or very close to his or her best, in a competition or match that is deemed to be very important creates performance pressure (Baumeister, 1984; Hardy *et al.*, 1996). It is the will of the athlete to perform at his or her very best that causes choking under pressure in sport, which will be referred to as choking in the remainder of this chapter.

Choking, defined as 'performing more poorly than expected given one's skill level, is thought to occur across diverse task domains where incentives for optimal performance are at a maximum' (Beilock *et al.*, 2004: 584). According to Beilock *et al.* there are a number of terms that are often used in sport to denote choking in sport, which include the yips (i.e. when an athlete misses a putt from two feet) and the bricks in basketball (i.e. when a basketball player misses easy shots that they would normally make).

Beilock and Gray (2007) suggested that instances of choking have a clear beginning and end, so a coach would be able to distinguish the period in which an athlete is choking and when they have finished choking. This is because an athlete's performance will dip below his or her normal level during choking, but will return to the expected level after the choking episode has concluded. Furthermore, Beilock and Gray argued that choking normally occurs across short periods of time, such as a soccer player hitting a very poor penalty or a hockey player performing poorly for an entire match.

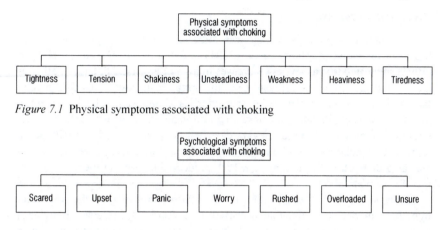

Figure 7.1 Physical symptoms associated with choking

Figure 7.2 Psychological symptoms associated with choking

Physical and psychological feelings associated with choking

When athletes choke, they experience a variety of physical and psychological symptoms. Nideffer (1992) outlined some of the physical symptoms, which are presented in Figure 7.1. The psychological symptoms are presented in Figure 7.2.

Theoretical explanations of why athletes choke

Two main explanations have been developed by researchers to explain why athletes' skills can sometimes fail under pressurised conditions. These are the self-focus or the explicit monitoring hypothesis and the distraction hypothesis.

The self-focus or explicit monitoring hypothesis

The self-focus or explicit monitoring hypothesis, which was initially proposed by Baumeister (1984) and expanded by Masters (1992), suggests that performance pressure increases: (a) the amount of anxiety an athlete will experience and (b) his or her self-consciousness about the skill being performed. The desire to perform at a high level and the athlete being more self-conscious about performing certain movements (e.g. putt in golf or a serve in tennis) results in the athlete focusing on the sequence of movements that make the entire skill. This is similar to what an athlete would have done when he or she first learned the movement. As the pressure to perform increases, the athlete tries even harder to control the sequence of movements that make up an entire skill in the hope that the performance of the skill will be more accurate through being more controlled. When athletes attempt to consciously monitor or control the movements they are performing, the automated processes that athletes usually engage in are disrupted, which is why performance suffers (Beilock *et al.*, 2004).

Distraction hypothesis

The distraction hypothesis, which was initially proposed by Nideffer (1992), has been extended by Hardy *et al*. (2001) and Mullen *et al*. (2005). Nideffer (1992) suggested that as anxiety increases in high pressurised situations, athletes' attention shifts from task-relevant (e.g. thoughts about how to execute specific tactics) to task-irrelevant thoughts (e.g. worries about team selection in future matches). As such, the athlete whose attention is diverted towards task-irrelevant cues no longer attends to the relevant cues that he or she would normally attend to, which are conducive to higher levels of sport performance. Therefore, anxiety acts as a distraction to the athlete, which reduces the working memory and the task-focused attention.

Hardy *et al*. (2001) and Mullen *et al*. (2005) supplemented the distraction hypothesis theory by arguing that increased anxiety and task-irrelevant thoughts do not result automatically in choking. They cause choking when they simultaneously compete with the attention an athlete usually allocates to performing the task. That is, an athlete chokes when his or her attentional threshold to maintain performance is exceeded.

According to Mesagno and Mullane-Grant (2010) the distraction hypothesis is the most widely supported model, but that these models may co-exist. Regardless of why choking occurs, it is apparent that choking could be a very unpleasant experience for athletes. This is because when an athlete really wants to perform at his or best, the athlete fails to do so.

Choking prevention training

Researchers in sport psychology have conducted studies that provide some useful guidelines for how coaches can help their athletes avoid choking. The first step involves coaches reducing the stigma associated with choking by informing their athletes that this is something that has happened to many athletes and will happen to lots more athletes in the future. Once the coach has attempted to reduce the stigma associated with choking, he or she can provide choking prevention training.

Pre-performance routine

A pre-performance routine, according to Moran (1996), is a sequence of task-relevant thoughts and behaviours that an athlete engages in before performing in a sports skill. A pre-performance routine may be more suitable in sports that are self-paced, such as golf, tennis, or for regular free-kick takers in soccer. This is because the athlete will have an appropriate time to conduct his or her pre-performance routine. A pre-performance routine can help reduce the likelihood of choking, because it helps focus an athlete's attention on task-related cues as opposed to task-irrelevant cues (Mesagno and Mullane-Grant, 2010). Research has found that a pre-performance routine can improve performance, within high pressure situations, by as much as 29 per cent compared to when athletes were not provided with a pre-performance routine (Mesagno *et al.*, 2008). The pre-performance routine by Mesagno *et al.* involved deep breathing, using task-relevant cue words, in addition to the participants spending a consistent amount of time on each pre-performance routine.

Mesagno and Mullane-Grant (2010) extended the findings of Mesagno *et al.* (2008) by exploring whether specific elements of the pre-performance routine were more effective than a combined pre-performance routine that involved deep breaths, cue words, and consistent timing. They found that a pre-performance routine that included all the elements (e.g. timing consistency training, deep breathing, and cue words) enabled athletes to perform the most successfully under pressurised situations.

Coaches can help their athletes perform in pressurised sporting events by providing training on pre-performance routines. This training should involve:

- *Cue words:* The coach could ask the athlete to consider some task-relevant cue words, which he or she thinks are important for performing in his or her sport. For example, a rugby union goal kicker may choose the words 'coil' and 'follow through', whereas a golfer might use the words 'hands' and 'spine' to denote where and how he wants to position his hands and the angle of his spine. Once the athlete has identified two or three keywords the athlete can say these keywords prior to performing, as a part of a pre-performance routine.
- *Deep breathing*: An athlete can be taught to take two deep breaths prior to performing, whereby the athlete is instructed to inhale deeply through his or her nose and exhale through the mouth.
- *Timing:* Whilst the athlete practises his or her pre-performance routine in training, the coach can ask the athlete to try and spend the same amount of time each time he or she engages in the routine. The coach could time the athlete and let him or her know how consistently the pre-performance routine has been performed.

With regards to helping an athlete develop a pre-performance routine, the routine should be individualised (Mesagno and Mullane-Grant, 2010). That is, the keywords should be chosen by the athlete. Some athletes might prefer to say their keywords whilst they are taking their deep breaths, others might want to say their keywords before taking the breaths, whereas other athletes might want to say their keywords after taking their breaths. There is no wrong or right approach, but it is important that once the athletes have tried different pre-performance routines that they establish their own routine, which they consistently perform. This is because athletes perform better when they stick to their established pre-performance routine compared to when they deviate away from it (Lonsdale and Tam, 2008). As such, coaches should state the importance of always using established pre-performance routines to their athletes.

Pressure acclimatisation training

Oudejans and Pijpers (2010) have found evidence to suggest that training with anxiety present may reduce choking. When athletes train whilst feeling anxious they learn to perform their skill in conditions that promote self-conscious behaviour (Jordet, 2010). Coaches can create situations that promote anxiety in training among athletes by:

- *Stating the importance of training*: Prior to the training session starting, the coach can tell his or her players that he or she is going to rate the performance of each player in terms of the effort exerted, skills executed, and impact on other players (if in a team sport). The coach could then inform the players that this information will help him or her decide team selection.
- *Encouraging athletes to set their own performance targets:* Nicholls and Callard (2012) suggested that players should set themselves targets in training sessions and play competitive games among themselves. For instance, a player might set himself or herself the target of catching 50 high balls in a row. Once the player drops a ball, he or she starts again from the beginning so by the time the player gets to around 40 he or she might start feeling anxious. Coaches can use their imagination to create sport-specific challenges such as this.
- *Mimic anxiety symptoms:* Coaches can develop drills that mimic the symptoms of stress and anxiety and ask athletes to perform drills whilst experiencing similar symptoms (Nicholls and Callard, 2012). For example, stress is associated with symptoms such as an increased heart-rate, breathing rate, and perspiration rate, so a coach could have athletes do some sprints before conducting penalty practice in soccer. As such, the athletes would be taking a penalty whilst experiencing some of the symptoms they would when they take a penalty in competitions.

Although inducing anxiety among athletes has the potential to help athletes become accustomed to playing in high pressured situations (e.g. Oudejans and Pijpers, 2010), coaches have to be careful regarding how they create this anxiety and ensure that it does not have detrimental effects.

Movement acclimatisation training

Another technique, which was advocated by Beilock and Carr (2001), involves the athlete being encouraged by the coach to focus on his or her movements whilst performing. Athletes will become used to performing whilst feeling self-conscious. As such, when athletes perform in important competitions and start becoming self-conscious about their movements, they will be acclimatised to this level of consciousness. Therefore, sporting performance should remain unaffected.

Case study 7.1 Choking in professional rugby union

James is a 54-year-old professional rugby union coach, who coaches attacking play and has recently taken an interest in coaching the kickers in his team. His team's leading kicker, Dave, is a 19-year-old player who is playing his first season as a professional player. Dave made his first team debut as an 18-year-old and made a good start playing the last four games of the previous season. Dave played the first two games of the present season, but had a poor game in which he missed four goal kicks and was dropped from the team.

As the kicking coach, James was keen to speak to Dave to try and help establish what went wrong and develop a plan regarding what they could work on. First, James spoke to Dave about the match prior to him being dropped, to try and explain Dave's performance. In particular, James asked Dave how he felt during the match. Dave said that he started the match feeling fine, successfully kicking his first kick, but after missing his next kick he felt more worried. This worry increased with each kick that was missed, especially when he had a kick with four minutes from the end of the match to lead by a point, which he missed. James also watched Dave's performance on video and timed his pre-performance kicking routine. As the match went on Dave's routine became much quicker, until the last kick where he spent much longer stood over the ball. James also noticed that the behaviours in James' pre-performance routine were also inconsistent. He would look at the posts three times prior to some kicks, but would only look at the posts once prior to taking other kicks.

James suggested to Dave that he should develop a more consistent pre-performance routine that he uses before every kick, regardless of how easy or difficult the kick is. Dave agreed with this, and they developed an ideal pre-performance kicking routine which involved task-relevant thoughts (e.g. keywords) and behaviours (e.g. looking at posts), by writing this down. They then took the piece of paper with them onto the training pitch and experimented with the routine and made some minor tweaks to the routine.

Dave was asked to engage in his pre-performance routine before every kick that he took, whether that was in training, warming up for matches, or in the match.

Case study reflection

There are a number of things a coach can do to help athletes who are prone to choking. It is important that the coach is supportive of the athlete, because choking can be a very distressing experience. Athletes are likely to respond differently to forms of training to prevent choking, so coaches might have to try a number of techniques before finding what works best for the athlete.

Compassion

Jordet (2010) stated that athletes can be very hard on themselves, especially when they have made a mistake. As such, coaches can provide support to athletes and tell them that they are not perfect and that mistakes will occur when athletes try to win matches or competitions (Leary, 2004).

Summary

- Choking is when an athlete performs worse than would be expected in an important competition.
- Choking is associated with a variety of physical and psychological symptoms.
- Two theoretical models have attempted to explain why athletes choke in sport – the self-focus or explicit monitoring hypothesis theory and the distraction hypothesis theory.
- Coaches can help athletes who choke by providing choking prevention training, which may include developing a pre-performance routine, pressure acclimatisation training, movement acclimatisation training, and encouraging and athlete to be more compassionate towards himself or herself.

Practice exam questions

1 Why do athletes choke? Discuss.
2 Describe the physical and psychological symptoms associated with choking.
3 Describe the explicit monitoringhypothesis theory of choking and research that has supported this theory.
4 Critically evaluate the distraction hypothesis of choking.
5 Compare and contrast the explicit monitoring hypothesis theory of choking and the distraction hypothesis of choking.

Critical thinking questions: applying theory to practice

1 Describe the circumstances that may contribute to athletes feeling performance pressure.
2 Discuss the advantages and disadvantages of performance pressure.
3 What key characteristics should be included in a pre-performance routine? Discuss.
4 Critically evaluate the process of increasing anxiety within training sessions.
5 Discuss the potential positive and negative implications of teaching athletes to be more compassionate towards themselves.

8 The injured athlete

The purpose of this chapter is to provide the coach with information on how he or she can help athletes whilst they are injured and when returning to sport after injury. As such, this chapter contains information regarding:

- a definition of an injury;
- psychological response to injuries;
- role of the coach;
- rehabilitation;
- strategies that can be used during rehabilitation;
- competitive return to sport after injury;
- preventing a fear of re-injury.

A definition of an injury

An injury has been defined as any incident that happens during training or competition, which requires help from a medical professional, and prevents the athlete from training or competing in his or her sport for a period of up to one day after the injury happened (Kerr *et al.*, 2008). Injuries can be common in sport, so it is important that coaches understand how athletes respond to injuries in order to help athletes through the challenging period in which they are injured.

Psychological responses to injury

Athletes who sustain an injury are likely to experience stress, anger, depression, anxiety, tension, fear, and even mood disturbances (Nippert and Smith, 2008; Smith, 1996; Udry *et al.*, 1997). The severity of the injury is likely to influence the psychological responses, with less severe injuries being associated with less psychological disturbances (Nippert and Smith, 2008).

Udry (1997) stated that there are three phases that an injured athlete will pass through (1) information-processing, (2) emotional upheaval, and (3) the positive outlook phase.

1. Injury information processing

As soon as the injury has happened the athletes tend to focus on:

- pain caused by the injury;
- the amount of time the athlete will be unable to play for;
- how the injury occurred;
- what the athlete could have done differently to prevent the injury from occurring in the first place.

During this phase, the athlete might also start thinking about the consequences of being injured, such as the competitive events or matches that the athlete will not be able to play in.

2. Emotion upheaval

When the athlete has received information from medical professionals regarding the length of time the athlete will be unable to play sport for, a variety of negative emotions including anger, agitation, and frustration might be experienced. Athletes may also feel emotionally depleted, isolated from their team-mates, and self-pity. Some athletes may be in denial about the injury and think they will be able to return much quicker than the medical professionals have stated.

3. Positive outlook

During this phase the athlete accepts that he or she is injured. The mood of the athlete starts to improve once he or she starts to see progress in his or her injured body part in rehabilitation.

According to Udry (1997), the rate at which an athlete passes through each phase is dependent on the severity of the injury, the personality of the athlete, and the progress an athlete makes in rehabilitation.

The role of the coach

Although some coaches may only be tempted to concentrate on the players who are un-injured, the coach has a very important role in helping athletes who have sustained an injury. Several studies have found that the social support a coach provides injured athletes may facilitate recovery from an injury, reduce stress, and improve motivation. More specifically, Bianco (2001) found the social support that injured national skiers received from their coach was very important in reassuring the athletes that they would get better, helping the athletes maintain a perspective about the injury, encouraging the skiers to focus on future opportunities, and adhere to their rehabilitation programme. Other studies by Gould *et al.* (1997) and Johnston and Carroll (1998) found that athletes believed the social support they received from their coach was instrumental in their recovery.

Information regarding how coaches can provide social support to athletes is covered in Chapter 17 of this book. It is important that coaches spend time with injured athletes and reassure them throughout their time being injured. This period involves the rehabilitation period and when the athlete returns to his or her sport. The rehabilitation period can be a very difficult time for athletes, especially if they have a serious injury.

Rehabilitation

The rehabilitation process

When an athlete's injury has been diagnosed and the correct medical treatment (e.g. surgery) has been conducted, the athlete will start his or her rehabilitation. The length of the time the athlete will spend in rehabilitation is dependent upon the injury, with this phase varying from a week and to several years in extreme cases. The aim of rehabilitation is to help the injured body part heal, so the athlete can return to sport. As such, the athlete may spend long periods of time working on restoring his or her injured body parts.

Taylor and Taylor (1997) stated that in addition to athletes engaging in physical exercises to heal injured parts of their body, athletes should also take part in mental rehabilitation training. Mental training for injured athletes has the potential to increase an athlete's emotional well-being during the rehabilitation phase to prevent psychological problems when athletes return to their sport.

Before the psychological training strategies are taught to athletes, coaches should first provide assurance and information to the athlete about how he or she may feel during rehabilitation and the processes an athlete is likely to go through during his or her rehabilitation. Taylor and Taylor (1997) identified four stages of the rehabilitation process:

- *Stage 1 – Range of motion*: During the initial rehabilitation sessions, the primary aim is to increase and athlete's range of motion within the injured body part. The coach should reassure the athlete that he or she is likely to experience pain during this phase, because he or she will be performing movements that are unfamiliar and under the control of the physiotherapist. It is therefore essential that coaches encourage athletes to engage in pain management strategies (information regarding how athletes can deploy pain management strategies is presented in this chapter).
- *Stage 2 – Strength:* When an athlete has achieved an 80 per cent range of motion in his or her injured body part, the athlete is considered as being in Stage 2 of the rehabilitation process. The athlete will be asked by his or her physiotherapist to start testing the injured body part for the first time since the injury occurred to increase its strength. It is likely that the athlete may experience some doubt and apprehension about his or her ability of the injured area to manage these demands. The coach should reassure his or her athletes that they may experience worry and negative emotions during this

phase, but that this is completely normal. Coaches could provide coping training to the athletes.

- *Stage 3 – Coordination:* Once an athlete's strength has improved, he or she will be in Stage 3 of rehabilitation. During this phase, the athlete will be instructed by his or her physiotherapist to continue strengthening the injured body part. When the injured body part is strengthened to a sufficient level, he or she will be instructed to engage in more specialised exercises (e.g. balance, agility, acceleration, and speed exercises). It is important that coaches help athletes maintain a positive focus during this phase, because as athletes are asked to perform sport specific exercises they are likely to make comparisons with their pre-injury performances. The coach should provide reassurance that performance will get better with time and hard work.
- *Stage 4 – Return to sport:* The final phase of the rehabilitation process is when the athlete returns to sport. Once an athlete's injured body part is able to perform at its pre-injury level, the athlete is physically ready to resume training. An athlete's return to competition can be difficult, so the coach has an important role to play.

Problems in rehabilitation

Coaches should be aware that athletes may experience setbacks in rehabilitation, whereas other athletes may become fearful of resting when they are rehabilitating their injured body part.

Setbacks during rehabilitation

When an athlete receives information about the four stages of the rehabilitation process, he or she may perceive that his or her rehabilitation will be very straightforward. That is, the athlete may feel that he or she will make steady progress and then return to sport within the time-frame provided by medical professionals.

In an ideal world the rehabilitation would run smoothly, but Taylor and Taylor (1997) suggested that most athletes experience a setback along the way. An athlete's injured body part might initially respond very well to treatment, but then he or she might not make further improvements for a number of weeks. When an athlete's progress is slower than anticipated or a setback has occurred (e.g. the athlete regressing from Stage 2 to Stage 1 after too much pain and soreness), it is paramount that the coach provides encouragement and assurance to the athlete. They can do this by telling the athlete about other athletes, who had the same injury and went on to make a full recovery despite having setbacks. Additionally, Podlog and Dionigi (2010) suggested that coaches could arrange for injured athletes to speak to athletes who had previously had the same injury and discuss their worries.

The fear of rest during rehabilitation

Taylor and Taylor (1997) stated that athletes who are especially motivated and disciplined, may have a tendency to spend too much time doing rehabilitation exercises, because of feelings of guilt. The coach should regularly speak to the athlete and the medical professional to check whether this is happening. When this occurs, the coach should speak to the athlete about the importance of rest within the rehabilitation process. The coach can tell the athlete about the importance of rest in boosting recovery (Kindermann, 1988) and that feeling guilty is normal, but that there is nothing to be guilty about.

Psychological strategies during the rehabilitation process

Coaches can provide training in a variety of strategies to help athletes manage the feelings they are likely to encounter during their rehabilitation. Some of these strategies (e.g. goal setting, mental imagery, and coping training) have been mentioned in other chapters in this book, so won't be mentioned in as much detail in this chapter. However, information will be provided on how coaches can adopt these strategies so that they can be used with injured athletes.

Goal setting for injured athletes

Setting goals whilst injured involves the athlete being asked by the coach to consider objectives, targets, or a desired standard for their injured body part. The goals an athlete sets should be influenced by the extent of the injury, so the coach could involve the medical professionals within the goal-setting process to ensure the goals set are realistic. Goal setting may be especially beneficial for injured athletes, because Locke and Latham (2002) found that goals have an energising influence that may result in athletes sticking to programmes, such as their rehabilitation programme.

When helping athletes set goals, coaches should apply the SMARTS goal principles (Smith, 1994), which are covered in depth in Chapter 9 of this book. As such, athletes should be encouraged to set goals that are specific (e.g. return back to sport stronger than pre-injury level), measurable (e.g. improve quadriceps strength by five per cent), action-oriented (e.g. goals should incorporate plans regarding how they can be achieved), realistic (e.g. improving quadriceps strength by five per cent of pre-injury level is realistic, but to improve the strength in these muscles by 25 per cent would not be realistic), time (e.g. return to training by the 22 July), and self-determined (i.e. the athlete sets his or her own goals, with little help from the coach; the coach only supports the athlete).

Mental imagery

Mental imagery, which is outlined in depth in Chapter 3 of this book, refers to the process of an athlete using his or her imagination to see himself or herself performing a movement (e.g. moving injured body part) or a certain skill (e.g.

serve in tennis that the athlete wants to perform when he or she returns to sport). Coaches should encourage athletes to engage in mental imagery during their rehabilitation, because there is evidence that mental imagery can aid recovery (Durso-Cupal, 1996). Mental imagery can enhance recovery during rehabilitation by increasing the amount of blood and warmth that flows to the injured body part (Blakeslee, 1980). In order to promote healing, Taylor and Taylor (1997) suggested that coaches could ask athletes to imagine images associated with the healing process or even create imagery scripts that are associated with healing. Such imagery scripts could encourage athletes to imagine blood flowing to the injured area or ice on the injured area, which will block the pain.

In addition to imagery being useful in aiding injury, Martin *et al.* (1999) argued that mental imagery also serves a number of other purposes such as:

- replacing the physical practice that the athlete can no longer do with mental practice, so the athlete can mentally practise skills he or she had learned prior to being injured;
- allowing an athlete to see himself or herself in a recovered state;
- controlling negative disturbances that can occur among injured athletes.

Coping

Coping refers to thoughts and behaviours that an athlete engages in to manage the stress they are encountering. Being injured and going through a rehabilitation programme can be very stressful (e.g. Nippert and Smith, 2008; Smith, 1996; Udry *et al.*, 1997), so it is essential that coaches reassure their athletes that it is normal to experience stress and teach their athletes how to cope. Information on coping and how coaches can teach their athletes to cope is presented in Chapter 6 of this book.

In addition to the strategies recommended in Chapter 6, research with a sample of injured athletes found that avoidance coping may be a particularly effective coping strategy that coaches can teach injured athletes, especially those athletes who have a long-term injury (Carson and Polman, 2010). There are two forms of avoidance coping (1) behavioural and (2) cognitive avoidance.

- *Behavioural avoidance:* Coping strategies that are classified as behavioural avoidance involve athletes physically removing themselves from stressful situations, such as walking away from another athlete that is frustrating them. The behavioural coping strategies in the Carson and Polman (2010) study included the players taking up a new hobby (e.g. learning a new language), involving themselves around the team (e.g. doing match analysis), continuing outside interests (e.g. learning new recipes), and organising coaching sessions for younger players within the club. Coaches could therefore encourage injured athletes to engage in these behavioural avoidance strategies.

- *Cognitive avoidance:* Coping strategies classed as cognitive avoidance involve attempts to mentally disengage from thoughts surrounding a stressor, such as blocking out the pain of an injury. The cognitive avoidance strategies used by the players included denial (e.g. the players denied that they were experiencing pain during rehabilitation sessions by blocking out thoughts of pain) and players not speaking about their injury (e.g. players would change the conversation so they were not chatting about their injury all of the time). Coaches should be aware that some athletes might want to speak about their injury, whereas others will not.

Pain management strategies for rehabilitation

Rehabilitation sessions can be extremely painful for athletes (Carson and Polman, 2010). Coaches can also teach their athletes a variety of pain management strategies, such as abdominal breathing and dissociation (Taylor and Taylor, 1997).

1 *Abdominal breathing:* According to Taylor and Taylor (1997), abdominal breathing is one of the simplest and yet most neglected methods of reducing pain within rehabilitation sessions. Coaches can help athletes heal more effectively by training athletes in deep breathing techniques, which provide the body with more oxygen than normal. Athletes need more oxygen when they are in pain. As such, coaches could encourage their athletes to inhale through their nose to the count of five and exhale slowly to the count of 10 whilst in rehabilitation sessions.
2 *Dissociation:* Dissociation training involves the athlete being taught to focus his or her attention away from the pain by distracting himself or herself (Taylor and Taylor, 1997). As such, the coach could ask the athlete to count, hum a song, listen to music, or imagine himself or herself in a favourite location (e.g. beach).

Coaches can encourage athletes to use abdominal breathing simultaneously with dissociation during rehabilitation sessions.

Positive focus

To help athletes maintain a positive attitude during their rehabilitation period, Taylor and Taylor (1997) argued that coaches could ask their athletes to focus on the four Ps:

- positive – the coach could ask the athlete to think about the positive aspects of his or her rehabilitation (e.g. gains made to injured body part);
- present – coaches could ask athletes to think about the present and not to think a long way ahead, nor dwell on the past;
- process – athletes could be asked by the coach to think about what they need to do daily in order to enhance their recovery so that the athletes can take confidence that they are doing the right thing;

- progress – finally, the athlete should be encouraged to write down and then think about the gains that have been made.

Returning to play

Once the athlete has completed his or her physical rehabilitation programme and the injured area has returned to the same level as it was prior to injury, the athlete will be ready to return to full training and then competition. However, the role of the coach in supporting the injured athlete should not be over. This is because athletes may experience a variety of fears about getting re-injured (Kvist *et al.*, 2005), concerns about whether they will be able to perform at the same level before they sustained the injury (Crossman, 1997), and anxiety (Rotella, 1985). Furthermore, athletes may spend too much time focusing on their injured area, which contributes to them struggling to regain their pre-injury form (Williams and Roepke, 1993).

Coaches can help returning athletes by providing information on the five stages that Taylor and Taylor (1997) identified, which should help reassure the athlete. Taylor and Taylor (1997) stated that returning athletes go through five stages: (1) initial return, (2) recovery confirmation, (3) return of physical and technical abilities, (4) high intensity training, and (5) return to competition. Providing athletes with an understanding of these stages should make the transition to competing more manageable and less stressful.

1   *Initial return:* The athlete returns to full training, which is potentially very stressful because the athlete will find out whether his rehabilitation programme was successful or not. The athlete will also be excited, because it will be his or her first time playing their sport for a while. The coach should encourage the athlete not to set performance expectations that are too high, as this could lead to disappointment if expectations are not fulfilled.

2   *Recovery confirmation:* During the second stage the athlete receives confirmation that his or her injury has healed or that there are complications. Some athletes will return with few or no problems, but other athletes may experience unexpected pain, swelling, decreased strength, and compensation injuries to other parts of their body. Athletes that experience complications during this phase of their return might experience psychological difficulties, because they may think that all of their efforts in rehabilitation were wasted. The coach should support the athlete and state this happens and that a full recovery will be made.

3   *Return of physical and technical abilities:* In Stage 3, the athlete increases his or her intensity of training. The athlete improves his or her conditioning and spends time practising the technical skills associated with his or sport, that he or she could not do whilst injured.

4   *High intensity training:* By the time the athlete is ready to take part in high intensity training, he or she is in Stage 4, and can focus on improving his or

her conditioning. The injured area will be better or the same level as it was prior to being injured.

5   *Return to competition:* When the physical conditioning has been completed, the athlete is ready to compete. He or she may feel both excited and nervous. The coach should state that is to be expected and encourage them to use coping strategies to manage any stress encountered (see Chapter 6).

Fear of re-injury

Even though an athlete may have physically healed when he or she returns to competition, it does not mean that he or she will not experience any psychological stress from the injury (Taylor and Taylor, 1997). Indeed, Heil (1993) argued that athletes might experience the most stress when they return to their sport, due to fears about re-injury. A fear of being re-injured can cause psychological difficulties such as reduced focus and decreased confidence, in addition to physical difficulties such as muscle tension, which actually increases the likelihood that the athlete will become injured again.

Preventing a fear of re-injury

Some athletes may develop a fear of being re-injured when they return to sport (Kvist *et al.*, 2005). This fear can be related to athletes spending a long time away from their sport, which may involve being isolated from team-mates (Taylor and Taylor, 1997). Coaches should therefore try and foster continual involvement among injured athletes by asking them to analyse matches, scout opposition, get involved in coaching, and attend social functions.

Summary points

- An injury prevents an athlete from training or competing in his or her sport for a period of at least one day after the injury occurred.
- Stress, anger, depression, anxiety, tension, fear, and even mood disturbances may be experienced by the athlete after an injury.
- There are three phases that an injured athlete will pass through (1) information-processing, (2) emotional upheaval, and (3) the positive outlook phase.
- The coach has an important role to play in helping an injured athlete make a successful return to sport.
- Many setbacks can occur during an athlete's rehabilitation.
- Coaches can make an athlete's rehabilitation more manageable by providing information on how they are likely to feel and teach them a range of strategies that can be used.
- An athlete may find returning to sport very stressful and be fearful of re-injuring himself or herself, so the coach should continue the support provided to the player during this phase.

Case study 8.1 Supporting an athlete with an anterior cruciate ligament injury

George is a 59-year-old coach who has been coaching soccer professionally for 25 years and is now the head coach of a semi-professional side which play in the sixth-tier of English football. One of his senior players, Maurice a 32-year-old centre back, has suffered an anterior cruciate ligament injury and is expected to be out injured for at least nine months. As soon as Maurice suffered the injury, George spoke to him and reassured him that whatever the injury was, he would be back playing and that it was not the end of his soccer career. George stayed in regular contact with Maurice and even before Maurice's operation, George asked him to set some goals. Maurice wanted to return to the first team and play at this level until he was 35 years old.

Maurice had a particularly painful rehabilitation, due to a previous injury, so George taught Maurice a variety of psychological skills such as coping strategies, mental imagery, and pain management skills. Maurice found these really helpful. George did not explain the psychological responses to injury phases to Maurice, because Maurice had suffered this type of injury in the past and was aware of how he would feel.

George encouraged Maurice to maintain his involvement in the team. He asked him to scout opponents and provide feedback to the team. Maurice was also asked to attend training sessions, when he could, and attend matches so he could keep up to date with team tactics.

Additionally, George also encouraged Maurice to spend time thinking about what he was going to do after his soccer career had finished and he encouraged Maurice to speak to a careers advisor, which he found useful.

Above all, George maintained regular contact with Maurice throughout his injury period and provided continual reassurance that George had a part to play in his team when he recovered from injury.

Case study reflection

Coaches should base the psychological support to injured athletes upon his or her individual needs. In this example, Maurice had previously suffered other serious injuries so did not need information on how he might feel at different stages, because he will have experienced all of these feelings before.

Practice exam questions

1   Describe the psychological responses an athlete may have and what are their implications?
2   Discuss the role that the coach plays in an athlete's recovery.
3   Outline the four stages an athlete goes through in the recovery and describe what a coach can do to make the progression from one stage to another smoother.
4   All rehabilitations will be straightforward. Discuss.
5   An athlete's rehabilitation is complete when their injured body part has healed. Discuss.

Critical thinking questions: applying theory to practice

1   Discuss the factors that may influence how an athlete responds to an injury.
2   It is commonly thought that keeping an athlete involved whilst they are injured will be very beneficial. Describe the activities a coach can set an injured player to foster involvement.
3   Critically evaluate whether a coach should spend a large amount of time with injured athletes.
4   How can a coach make an athlete's return to sport smoother?
5   Discuss the role that psychological skills may have in an athlete's rehabilitation programme.

Part III
Facilitating awareness

9 Goal setting

The purpose of this chapter is to provide information on how coaches can set both individual and team goals for their athletes. In particular, information is provided on:

- defining goals;
- the benefits of goal setting;
- types of goals;
- short-term, medium-term, and long-term goals;
- helping athletes set SMARTS goals;
- goal-setting styles;
- individual goals;
- team goals;
- problems that may be encountered when goal setting.

Defining goals

A goal refers to an objective that an athlete may have, a target of an athlete in relation to sport, or even a desired standard that an athlete wants to achieve in relation to a specific task or sport, and within a specific time limit (Locke and Latham, 2002).

The benefits of goal setting

Locke and Latham (1990; 2002) conducted a review that included 35 years' worth of research regarding the effects of goal setting. They found that:

- Specific goals were consistently associated with enhanced performance on more than 100 different tasks, which involved over 40,000 participants from more than eight countries. Goals enhanced performance by directing the attention and effort of athletes towards goal relevant activities. As such, a coach who asks his or her athletes to do their best will not get the best performance from his or her athletes. Locke and Latham argued that giving people goals 'to do their best' allows for a wide range of acceptable performance levels.

This is not the case when a goal level, such as performance standard (e.g. percentage of successful fairways hit in golf), is specified.
- Goals have an energising influence, and may result in athletes exerting more effort compared to those who do not have goals.
- Goals encourage people to plan strategies to enable them to achieve their goals.
- Goals ensure that athletes remain persistent during times of adversity (e.g. being dropped from a team or losing two matches in a row), because the athlete has something he or she wants to achieve.

Other researchers such as Martin *et al.* (2009) and Kingston and Hardy (1997) have also found that:

- Goal setting has a positive impact on teams. Indeed, goal-setting interventions have been shown to have a positive impact on both team performance and how cohesive a team is.
- Goal-setting programmes have been found to have a positive impact on different psychological constructs. For example, Kingston and Hardy (1997) found that self-efficacy, cognitive anxiety, and confidence levels were all improved among a sample of golfers.

Types of goals

Burton *et al.* (2001) suggested that there are three different types of goals, which are related to the outcome of competitions, the standard of performance, and the actions athletes must engage in to perform well. These goals are referred to as outcome goals, performance goals, and process goals.

- *Outcome goals:* Outcome goals are related to the result or outcome of a particular match or competition, and may include the position an athlete finishes in a competition, whether he or she wins, or even whether an athlete earns a professional contract. Although it is important that coaches set outcome goals, because sporting success is often determined by winning or losing, it is also crucial that coaches understand some of the possible disadvantages of outcome goals. For instance, outcome goals are only partially controllable by an athlete or a team, because the outcome of a match is determined by factors that an athlete or team cannot control, such as the performance of the opponents or the decision making of an official. As such, a cross-country runner may finish seventh in a race, and has performed to his or her potential in that race and would not have been fast enough to win at his current fitness level, so an outcome goal of winning would result in the athlete feeling disappointed. As such, coaches should not rely too heavily on outcome goals, because they can negatively affect motivation. Indeed, coaches are encouraged to use outcome goals in combination with performance and process goals.
- *Performance goals:* Performance goals are related to athletes achieving specific standards of performance, usually in relation to an athlete's previous

levels of performance such as their personal best. Performance goals are not concerned with outcomes or results, only standards of performance. For example, a golfer might want to improve the number of fairways he or she hits by 10 per cent in a season, from 35 per cent to 45 per cent.

* *Process goals:* Goals that focus on the actions an athlete needs to perform to be successful are known as process goals. For example, a soccer player who takes free kicks for his or her team could have a goal of wanting to improve his follow-through with his leg when striking the ball. As such, process goals enable athletes to improve their performance by focusing on improving techniques that are associated with enhanced performance.

Goal-setting styles

Burton and Naylor (2002) found that athletes have goal-setting styles. That is, athletes will set particular types of goals depending on their personality without any help from their coach. Therefore, athletes have a predisposition to set certain types of goals. According to Burton and Naylor there are two types of goal-setting styles, which are performance- and success-oriented goal-setting styles.

* *Performance-oriented:* Athletes who have a tendency to set goals that are related to their own self improvement, rather than to demonstrating their ability in comparison with other athletes, are said to have a performance-oriented goal-setting style. Athletes with this goal-setting style tend to focus on improving their performance and are less concerned with results. Athletes with performance-oriented goal-setting styles are likely to set goals that are difficult and challenging, and are not concerned about making mistakes or failing. This is because their main motivation is to improve as an athlete. As such, athletes with a performance-oriented goal-setting style are comfortable about playing opponents who have more skill, because they judge success on their own performance and any improvements they have made, as opposed to the outcome of a match or competition.
* *Success-oriented:* Athletes who have a tendency to set goals that involve social comparisons with their competitors or team-mates (e.g. beat a specific opponent) are classified as having a success-oriented approach to goal setting. Coaches should be aware that athletes who have a tendency to set success-oriented goals may avoid setting themselves challenging goals, because they are worried about the humiliation they might experience when failing to achieve their goals and what other people will think about them if they fail to achieve their goals. Therefore, athletes with this goal-setting style will only set goals they know they can achieve.

Short-term, medium-term, and long-term goals

Coaches should be aware that goals can be short-term, medium-term, or long-term:

- Short-term goals refer to achievements that will happen shortly after a goal is set, usually within a week of the goal being set, such as an athlete winning his or her next match the following day or the following week.
- Medium-term goals refer to goals set from a week to several months, such as an athlete wanting to make a set number of appearances during a season or winning a specific number of races within a season.
- Long-term goals relate to desired achievements that may happen a few months up to 50 years after a goal is set. For instance, a long-term goal of a 15-year-old golfer might be to win a major before his or her 40th birthday.

It is very important that coaches help their athletes set a variety of short-term, medium-term, and long-term goals. Long-term goals are crucial for helping athletes develop a sense of purpose regarding what they do. This should also make sacrifices they have to make more bearable, because they know the sacrifices are being made for the good of their goal. Additionally, medium-term and short-term goals can make longer-term goals seem more achievable to athletes. The coach can tell his or her athletes that they will eventually succeed in achieving their long-term goals, if they regularly achieve their short- and medium-term goals.

Helping athletes set SMARTS goals

Smith (1994) developed a guide for helping coaches to set effective goals, by using the acronym SMARTS, which refers to specific, measurable, action-orientated, realistic, timed, and self-determined:

- *Specific:* Coaches could help their athletes set goals that are clear. That is, the athlete states exactly what he or she wants to happen (e.g. improve pass success by 10 per cent from 65 per cent to 75 per cent by the end of the season). Locke and Latham (2002) found that specific goals result in enhanced performance.
- *Measurable:* Goals should be measurable, so athletes will know whether they have been successful in achieving their goal. When athletes can see that they have improved, their motivation levels may also increase. This can, in turn, result in athletes making even more improvements.
- *Action-oriented:* In addition to helping athletes set goals, coaches should facilitate a discussion regarding how an athlete can achieve his or her goals and what he or she will have to do to achieve these goals.
- *Realistic:* When helping athletes set goals, coaches must ensure that the goals athletes set are realistic and encourage them to modify their goals if they are not realistic. If a goal is not realistic and an athlete has little or no chance of achieving his or her goal the athlete may become very frustrated and de-motivated. Conversely, if athletes set goals that are too easy they may become very bored. As such, goals should be achievable, but should push the athlete to work hard to achieve the goal.

- *Timely:* All goals should involve a specified time period in which the athlete wants to achieve the particular goal. This may involve a goal being set for the next match or a goal that might not be achieved for many years, but there is still a time limit set.
- *Self-determined:* Goals should be set by the athlete or by the team, rather than by a coach. Coaches can have an input into the goals, but Locke and Latham (2002) found that goals are more effective when the individual is committed to his or her goal.

Setting individual goals

Coaches can work with athletes to set individual goals or to help teams set goals. Coaches working with athletes from individual sports may find setting goals more straightforward because there is only one athlete to work with and it is more likely that the athlete will be committed to the goals he or she sets. Conversely, it might be more difficult to ensure an entire team agree with, and are committed to, the team goals. However, regardless of whether an athlete plays an individual sport (e.g. tennis) or team sport (e.g. soccer) he or she should have individual goals.

Coaches can help and encourage their athletes to set their own goals, by adopting the SMARTS goal-setting principle, as proposed by Smith (1994). Coaches should also encourage athletes to set a variety of short-, medium- and long-term goals. It is important that coaches do not set their athletes' goals, because they will not be committed to achieving these goals. Research by Shilts *et al.* (2004) found that if people are provided with information to set their own goals they are more committed. Furthermore, coaches could also support their athletes regarding the goals they set. This could involve coaches being supportive and encouraging about their athletes achieving their goals.

Setting team goals

As previously mentioned in the section on the benefits of goal setting, the meta-analysis by Martin *et al.* (2009) indicated that team goal-setting programmes have a positive impact on team cohesion and team performance. It is therefore important that coaches have understanding of team goal setting and encourage their teams to set team goals. A team's goal can be defined as 'the future state of affairs desired by enough members of a group to work towards its achievement' (Johnson and Johnson, 1987: 132).

Widmeyer and Ducharme (1997) provided information on how coaches can set team goals more effectively. In particular, they outlined six key principles for effective team goal setting and a rationale for each principle:

1 *Establish long-term goals first:* Although short-term goals are those that are achieved first and are likely to be more realistic, athletes are more likely to agree with the long-term goals that they want to achieve whilst playing for a team. Coaches should still apply the SMARTS principle to setting long-term

goals, and all goals for that matter, with these long-term goals being specific and realistic.

2   *Establish clear paths to long-term goals:* Coaches should help athletes establish clear paths regarding how their teams can reach their long-term goals. This can be achieved by encouraging athletes to set short-term team outcome, performance, and process goals. For example, a team's long-term goal could be to finish at least second in the league, so the coach could encourage the players to split the league into 10 segments containing three games. The short-term outcome goal could be to win at least two games per segment, which if achieved would allow the team to achieve their long-term goal. In order for the team to achieve their outcome goals, they could be encouraged to set performance goals that will make the outcome goal realistic, such as not conceding more than five goals in any three segments and taking at least 40 shots per segment. Short-term team process goals would focus on the processes that determine successful performances, which will vary from sport to sport. This might include reducing the number of two-on-ones when defending in rugby to zero per match, but increasing the number of two-on-ones when attacking by 10 per cent.

3   *Involve all team members when developing team goals:* It is important that all team members have an input in developing their team goals. This could potentially be quite challenging for a coach who coaches a team with many athletes such as rugby union or American football. Asking athletes to publicly provide input into a team's goal might not be a wise decision by coaches, because athletes will be concerned about what other team-mates think when they set team goals. As such, coaches could ask their players to anonymously write down their goals for the team on a piece of paper and collect these ideal goals for the team. The coach could then collate and present these to the team to discuss which goals are realistic, with the view of developing team goals that all athletes are committed to achieving.

4   *Monitor the progress of team goals:* Coaches should monitor and record the progress of their teams in achieving their short-, medium- and long-term goals. This information should be presented to players, which might facilitate discussion if teams are not performing as well as they like, regarding what they could do differently to get back on track. Monitoring goals provides motivation to athletes and encourages athletes to focus on their team goals (Weldon and Weingart, 1988).

5   *Reward team progress in achieving team goals:* It is important that coaches reward players when they make progress in achieving their team goals. This could be in the form of praise or have a social activity that the players will enjoy, which may foster even more team spirit.

6   *Foster collective efficacy regarding team goals:* Teams with athletes who are more confident in achieving their goals will perform better. As such, a coach can enhance his or her team's belief in their ability to be successful by employing techniques that maximise the chances of team success, such

as ensuring optimal preparation. Other techniques could include the coach providing information regarding how goals can be achieved and practising relevant drills in training sessions. For example, if a team has a process goal of limiting the opposition to zero two-on-ones when defending per rugby match, the coach could have players practise defensive drills that make this more likely, and thus enhance players' confidence regarding achieving their team goal.

Problems that may prevent effective goal setting

Although goal-setting seems a relatively straightforward process, some common problems may arise:

- Some athletes may not want to set themselves goals, because they feel that goal setting takes up too much time. Other athletes might not want their goals to become public knowledge (Murphy, 1996). Coaches can inform athletes that goal setting is an important process that will remain confidential.
- Athletes might fail to adjust their goals if they struggle to accomplish their targets (Burton, 1989). If an athlete is halfway through his or her season and will not achieve the seasonal goal of finishing in the top five of the rankings, he or she may experience a decline in motivation. Coaches can help monitor an athlete's progress in achieving his or her goal and then encourage them to adjust their goals if they are not going to achieve their goals.
- Athletes might not be motivated by their goals. As such, coaches should work with athletes and monitor the effects of goals on motivation levels of athletes by chatting to athletes or administering motivation questionnaires. Coaches should regularly monitor the impact that goals have on athletes.
- Coaches should encourage athletes not to set too many goals. If athletes set too many goals their attention will not be focused on achieving specific goals because they have too many things to think about. As Locke and Latham (2002) pointed out, goals work because they focus the mind. Although athletes may set a few goals, coaches could encourage athletes to focus on two or three goals at a time. Once athletes have achieved these goals they could work towards achieving their other goals or set new goals.
- One factor that may prevent athletes from achieving their goals is barriers. Helping athletes remove these barriers may be pivotal in helping athletes succeed and experience higher levels of motivation. As such, the coach could work with the athlete to identify the barriers that may prevent his or her athlete from achieving his or her goals, by discussing barriers and their impact. These barriers might include other commitments that prevent athletes from doing the necessary practice needed to reach their goals (e.g. education, work, or family). If the barriers cannot be overcome, coaches should encourage athletes to adjust their goals accordingly.

Case study 9.1 Working with an adolescent basketball player to develop goals

Dave is a 59-year-old coach, who has been coaching basketball at national level for over 25 years. One of his players is Michael, a 14-year-old player who is already playing under-18 national basketball. Although Michael is highly motivated, Dave feels Michael should set some goals. After an individual training session, Dave asks Michael to arrive 30 minutes early for the next session, so they can set some goals. Dave started the goal-setting session by explaining what goals are and the potential benefits of setting goals. He then asked Michael whether he set goals for himself and what those goals were, to see if Michael was likely to set performance-oriented or success-oriented. It turned out that Michael did not really set any goals for himself, other than to play for his country at the Olympics. Dave told Michael that this goal was a good starting point. He also explained the concept of setting short-term and medium-term goals that were related to outcomes, performance, and processes to help Michael achieve his ultimate aim of playing for his country at the Olympics.

Dave was conscious of the fact that he wanted Michael's goals to be his own goals and did not want to force his own goals on Michael. After explaining the different types of goals, he asked Michael to pick several outcome, performance, and process goals. Although Dave wanted Michael to choose his own goals, he provided guidance for Michael using the SMARTS principles of goal setting. For instance, Dave suggested that Michael's goals should be specific because these would focus his attention, measurable so they could monitor his progress, realistic, and set within specific time frames. Michael had set several goals, such as playing for his national under-16 team at the world championships and starting all of the matches. He also wanted to improve his shooting accuracy, and in particular his follow-through when shooting. Dave encouraged him to focus on three specific goals, and asked Michael what he thought he had to do to achieve his goals. They then developed a two-month training programme to work on Michael's acceleration, shooting, and passing. They planned to review Michael's progress after two months and adapt the programme if necessary.

Case study reflection

Goal setting is a power tool that coaches can use to maximise the performance of their athletes in addition to the well-being of athletes (i.e. reduced cognitive anxiety, and enhanced confidence). It is important that coaches regularly monitor the progress of their athletes and support them in achieving their goals. If a coach feels his athlete is struggling to achieve his or her goals, the coach should encourage the player to adjust his or her goals.

Summary

- A goal refers to an objective, target, or a desired standard that an athlete wants to achieve in relation to a specific task or sport.
- Goal setting is associated with numerous benefits such as enhanced performance, team cohesion, and they also have a motivating effect on athletes.
- There are three types of goals: (1) outcome goals, (2) performance goals, and (3) process goals.
- Coaches should help athletes set effective goals by adhering to the SMARTS principle of goal setting.
- Athletes should be encouraged by their coach to monitor their progress in attaining their goals, and adjustments should be made if necessary.
- It is important that athletes do not set too many goals.

Practice exam questions

1 Compare and contrast the advantages and disadvantages of goal setting.
2 Discuss the implications of coaches who set too many outcome goals.
3 Athletes are predisposed to set certain types of goals. Discuss.
4 Critically examine the relationship between goal setting and performance.
5 Discuss the implications of coaches who set team goals without consulting their athletes.

Critical thinking questions: applying theory to practice

1 Discuss the importance of setting short-, medium- and long-term goals.
2 Design a goal-setting intervention, adhering to the SMARTS principles.
3 Discuss the implications of players who focus too much on long-term goals.
4 Coaches can alter an athlete's predisposition to set certain types of goals. Discuss.
5 How can coaches prevent problems occurring when their athletes engage in goal-setting interventions?

10 Performance profiling

The purpose of this chapter is to provide information on how coaches can use performance profiling with individual athletes and in team settings. As such, information will be provided on:

- defining the performance profile;
- the benefits of performance profiling;
- teaching athletes to complete their own individual performance profile;
- team performance profiling;
- coach performance profiling.

Defining performance profiling

The performance profile was developed to enhance an athlete's self-awareness regarding the characteristics that facilitate successful performance and to enhance the coach's understanding of the athlete's viewpoint (Butler, 1989; Butler *et al.*, 1993). As such, performance profiling is a method of allowing coaches to understand how athletes rate themselves in the qualities that are needed to be successful in their sport. Coaches can use this information to help develop training schedules in the areas in which players feel they could improve (Butler, 1996a).

Performance profiling is embedded in Kelly's (1991 [1955]) Personal Construct Theory (PCT). The major tenet of the PCT is that individuals continually strive to make sense of the world that they are in, and themselves, by constructing personal theories. This leads individuals to anticipate what will happen in given situations (e.g. playing a highly ranked player at tennis) and these theories are either validated when the match is played or are revised (Butler and Hardy, 1992). As such, PCT is concerned with the athlete's view or perception. The PCT has two fundamental principles according to Butler (Butler, 1996a; Butler *et al.*, 1993):

1 Each athlete has a unique way of making sense of his or her experiences in sport, which might otherwise remain at a low level of consciousness if he or she does not engage in performance profiling.

2 In order to understand an athlete's point of view, it is essential that the coach sees things from the athlete's perspective. Coaches and athletes may have a

tendency to see things from their own perspective, because they both have a unique set of experiences (e.g. playing vs. coaching).

The benefits of performance profiling

Sport psychology scholars (e.g. Dale and Wrisberg, 1996; D'Urso *et al.*, 2002; Jones, 1993; Weston *et al.*, 2011) have found that the performance profile has a number of benefits that include:

1 helping athletes identify the qualities that are associated with successful performances in their chosen sport;
2 helping athletes identify their own strengths and weaknesses;
3 fostering an athlete's understanding of his or her abilities and what is required to be successful in his or her chosen sport;
4 enhancing an athlete's motivation if a performance profile is completed at least three times in a six-week period;
5 allowing athletes to monitor their own progress;
6 facilitating a discussion between the coach and athlete;
7 enhancing communication between athletes in team settings.

How does the performance profile work?

Traditional methods of providing psychological support would involve a coach deciding what an athlete needs and then delivering an intervention to help the athlete's psychological needs (Jones, 1993). However, in this process the athlete is relatively passive and has little say regarding what psychological skills he or she receives. This may reduce an athlete's motivation to engage in and adhere to any psychological intervention (Butler and Hardy, 1992). The performance profile eradicates athletes being passive, because he or she is instrumental in the performance profile procedure.

The performance profiling procedure involves three main stages:

Stage 1

The coach asks the athlete to list the qualities that the athlete feels are the most important for success in their sport. As such, the athlete would list a variety of qualities that the best players in his or her sport possess, which will include:

- physical (e.g. stamina, acceleration, agility etc);
- technical (e.g. serve in tennis, shooting in soccer, or passing in rugby etc);
- tactical (e.g. understanding of sport specific tactics etc);
- psychological (e.g. ability to cope with stress, confidence, or mental toughness).

Players would write this information down in a table. An example of a completed table is presented in Table 10.1. This table represents a soccer player's

Table 10.1 An example of the qualities a soccer player identified as being important in his or her sport

Physical	Technical	Tactical	Psychological
Acceleration	1st touch	Positional play	Manage stress
Speed	Passing	Set play defensive formations	Mental toughness
Stamina	Shooting		Motivation
Agility	Heading		Concentration
Explosive strength			Managing anger
Flexibility			
Core strength			

performance profile. It is important that coaches encourage their athletes to complete the table honestly and it should reflect their own opinions.

Stage 2

Stage 2 involves two distinct processes. First, the coach asks the athlete to rank the 12 most important qualities that he or she has identified in Stage 1. Quality 1 is the most important, whereas quality 12 is the least important quality of those that the athlete has listed. Sometimes athletes may struggle to think of more than 12 qualities, but they still rank the qualities in order of importance, whether they have identified 10 qualities or only five qualities. The second process involves the athlete writing down what each quality means. Some athletes might find this difficult, but it is important that they write down the meaning of the quality so that there is no confusion regarding the meaning of each quality at a later date. Players would list this information in a table, with Table 10.2 being an example of a completed table by the same soccer player who completed Table 10.1.

Stage 3

Stage 3 also contains two processes. First, the coach asks the athlete to write down the qualities the athlete has listed in the performance profile and then rate his or her current ability out of 10. A score of 10 indicates that the athlete cannot improve in a particular area, whereas a score of 1 suggests that the athlete has much room for improvement. Second, the coach asks the player to write down action points which represent what the player feels he or she needs to do. See Figure 10.1 for an example of a completed performance profile.

Assessing athlete and coach discrepancies

Once the player has completed his or her performance profile, Butler (1996a) suggested that the coach should rate the athlete in each characteristic to assess

Table 10.2 Ranking the qualities and providing a meaning

Rank order	Quality	Meaning
1	First touch	Being able to control the ball well when I first get it, which gives me time
2	Acceleration	Being quick over the first five metres
3	Stamina	Being able to run for the whole 90 minutes
4	Positional play	Knowing where to be at the right time
5	Managing stress	Not letting my nerves get the better of me
6	Shooting	Accurate and powerful shots at goal
7	Passing	Making sure passes are hit with the right pace and in the right direction
8	Agility	Being able to change direction quickly
9	Concentration	Not letting unrelated thoughts affect me
10	Speed	Running as fast as I can
11	Flexibility	Range of movement in my joints to prevent injury
12	Managing anger	Not letting anger get the better of me

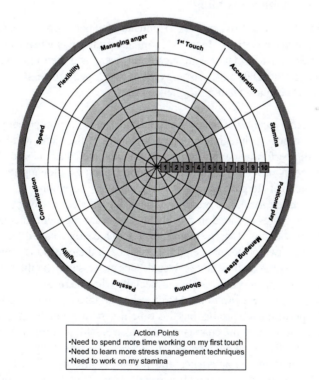

Figure 10.1 Example of a completed performance profile

the discrepancy between the coach and the athlete. Ideally, the coach would rate the athlete on the qualities without knowing how the player rated himself or herself. Large discrepancies between the coach and the player require discussion between the coach and the player in which the two parties discuss their reasons for awarding the score they awarded. Butler argued that it is often the areas of mismatch between the coach and the athlete that contribute to tension between the two people and even to a lack of progress. If the coach and athlete still disagree after a discussion, they could ask the opinion of another coach or use video feedback, so that the athlete can see the coach's perspective.

Monitoring progress

Coaches can monitor their athlete's level of improvement by asking the athlete to complete a performance profile on a regular basis, such as once a month. Improvements in qualities that athletes are working towards can instil confidence and also illustrate to the coach that their training programme is effective, or whether it needs altering (Butler, 1996b).

Team performance profiling

Research by Dale and Wrisberg (1996) indicates that performance profiling can be very useful in team settings. Team performance profiling is when a team identify the characteristics associated with successful teams and then rate themselves in each characteristic. Dale and Wrisberg (1996) developed a three-step procedure in which coaches can use team performance profiling.

1   *Initial team meeting:* The coach should call a team meeting, ideally at the start of the season, to integrate any new members of the team, and then explain what the performance profile is. Additionally, the coach should also explain the benefits of team performance profiling, such as allowing the coach and team members to gain an insight into each other's opinions.
2   *Individual performance profiling:* The coach asks each player to go through the three stages outlined in this chapter, in order for them to complete their own individualised performance profile. Once the player has completed his or her own performance profile, the coach then rates the athletes on the characteristics that they have selected. This process may facilitate discussions between the players and coaches, especially when there are any discrepancies.
3   *Team performance profiling:* Athletes then go through the same three stages of the performance profile, but this time it is related to a team. So instead of athletes describing the characteristics of successful performers in their sport, they identify the characteristics of successful teams (Stage 1), rank the 12 most important characteristics and provide a meaning for each (Stage 2), and then individually rate their current scores out of 10. Each athlete's score contributes to the overall team average, which is plotted on the performance profile (Stage 3).

Coach performance profiling

Dale and Wrisberg (1996) also suggested that coaches could ask their teams to profile their ideal coach behaviour, with the view of allowing coaches to maximise their behaviour. The coach would ask his or her team to collectively identify ideal coach behaviours (Stage 1), rank the 12 most important characteristics and define their meaning (Stage 2), and individually rate their coach on each characteristic which contributes to a mean score, which is plotted on the performance profile (Stage 3).

Case study 10.1 A season-long performance profiling intervention in professional rugby union

Ian is a 45-year-old professional soccer coach, who has previously used the performance profile to good effect with injured players during their rehabilitation, but not in a team setting. In the close season a number of players have left his club and the team recruited 12 new players. As such, Ian thought it could be useful to conduct a performance profiling session to help integrate his new players. Ian also planned to have a performance profiling session once every two months to allow his players to monitor their progress. In the initial meeting, Ian explained what performance profiling was and how it could benefit his players. In particular he emphasised that if all his players could make small improvements in many areas then their overall performance would improve. Once the players had completed their own performance profile, Ian asked them to consider the characteristics of successful teams in a brainstorming session. The players identified 27 different characteristics, and they decided that some characteristics were quite similar. By consensus, the players picked the 12 most important characteristics and spent 20 minutes or so describing each characteristic, before rating themselves. The performance profile presented in Figure 10.2 below, is the outcome of this meeting.

Ian held meetings every two months with his players in which they completed a team performance profile. The team performance profile from April is presented in Figure 10.3. The team improved in a number of areas by putting in lots of hard work on different elements throughout the season. The team also established action points for the following season.

Case study reflection

The performance profile can be an excellent tool in both individual and team sport settings if used correctly. It is essential that coaches are not prescriptive when conducting performance profile sessions, and allow athletes to complete their own performance profile. The benefits of the performance profile will be much greater if it is completed on multiple occasions.

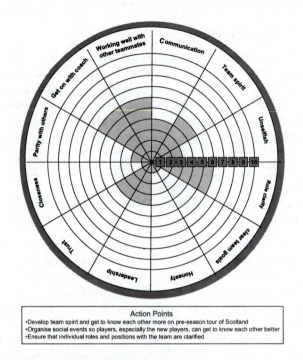

Action Points
•Develop team spirit and get to know each other more on pre-season tour of Scotland
•Organise social events so players, especially the new players, can get to know each other better
•Ensure that individual roles and positions with the team are clarified

Figure 10.2 Team performance profile for June

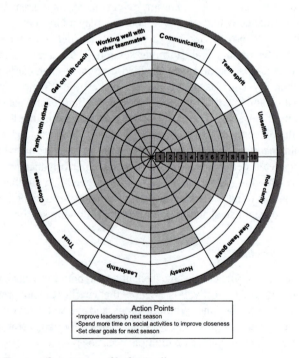

Action Points
•Improve leadership next season
•Spend more time on social activities to improve closeness
•Set clear goals for next season

Figure 10.3 Team performance profile for April

Summary

- Performance profiling is based upon Kelly's (1991 [1955]) Personal Construct Theory.
- Performance profiling is a method of allowing coaches to understand how athletes rate themselves in the qualities that are needed to be successful in their sport.
- Performance can be beneficial to athletes, and is associated with enhancing athletes' motivation.
- Performance profiling can be conducted with individual athletes or with teams.

Practice exam questions

1 Discuss the origins of the performance profile.
2 Performance profiling can enhance motivation. Discuss.
3 Describe the benefits of performance profiling.
4 What are the benefits and possible negative effects of coach performance profiling?
5 Critically evaluate the advantages of team performance profiling.

Critical thinking questions: applying theory to practice

1 Describe how performance profiling may cause conflict between the coach and the athlete.
2 Describe how a coach would plan a performance profiling intervention over a season for an elite athlete.
3 Discuss why some coaches may be reluctant to conduct coach performance profiling with their team.
4 What are the implications of coaches who play too vocal a part when athletes create their own performance profile?
5 What difficulties may coaches encounter when conducting team performance profiling sessions? Discuss.

Part IV

Coaching different populations

11   Coaching children

The purpose of this chapter is to provide information on the factors that coaches could consider when they coach children. Children are classified as athletes aged between four and eleven years of age. Specifically, in this chapter information is provided in relation to children and:

*   motivation and creating the optimal motivational climate;
*   enhancing learning;
*   self-awareness of coaching behaviour;
*   enhancing positive experiences: fun and enjoyment.

Motivation

Sport England (2007) revealed that there has been a rise in the number of children who are involved in sport. In 2003/2004 22 per cent of children were actively involved in sport and this number increased to 27 per cent by 2005 to 2006. Indeed, a number of scholars have suggested that participating in sport has numerous benefits for children such as the development of movement skills, social skills, and self-esteem (Stryer *et al.*, 1998), health benefits (Zaff *et al.*, 2003), and improved motor abilities (Loko *et al.*, 2000). It is therefore important to consider motivation among children, because if more children are to participate in sport, it is essential that coaches have an understanding of motivation among the athletes that they coach, so they can maximise motivation among their athletes (Keegan *et al.*, 2009).

According to Conroy *et al.* (2007) motivation refers to 'the process of initiating, directing, and sustaining behaviour' (p. 182). Essentially, motivation is concerned with the *why* people conduct certain behaviours (Deci and Ryan, 2000). Indeed, Keegan *et al.* (2009) found that coaches can influence motivation through their instruction and assessment among child athletes by creating a motivational climate. A motivational climate refers to the way in which coaches influence motivation through their coaching practices (e.g. providing feedback, structuring practices, and providing recognition: Ames, 1992).

It is therefore essential that coaches develop the optimal motivational environment when coaching all athletes, but especially children. According to McArdle and Duda (2002) and Treasure (2001) the way in which the coach emphasises or determines success versus failure determines the motivational climate and there are two main types of motivational climates (Amorose, 2007):

1   *Mastery motivational climates:* In a mastery motivational climate the coach focuses on encouraging the athletes to learn, make personal improvements in the activities they are undertaking, and exert maximal effort in all activities. In this coaching environment, the coach provides tasks that challenge the athlete towards self-improvement, but these tasks are not unrealistic in the level of challenge that is set. The coach also rewards the athlete or athletes based on progress and improvement. Athletes are evaluated based on the amount of effort that they put into a task and are praised for trying as hard as they can. Finally, in mastery motivational climates, the coach develops activities that promote maximal co-operation among athletes.
2   *Performance motivational climates*: Performance motivational climates are sport settings in which the coach emphasises and rewards winning. As such, coaches in this environment only praise the athletes that win in both training and competition. Within this environment there is also an emphasis on players outperforming other players, so a coach would set tasks that encourage competition between players and allows players to be ranked. An example of this type of task would be a sprint task in which the coach keeps all of the times and produces a rank order. In addition to rewarding winning, Amorose (2007) also reported that coaches in this environment punish mistakes by shouting at athletes or giving them physical tasks such as press-ups and promote rivalries between athletes.

Scholars have found that the climate a coach develops influences motivation. Athletes in a mastery motivational climate are likely to be more intrinsically motivated whereas children in a performance motivational climate are more likely to be extrinsically motivated (Amorose, 2007).

1   *Intrinsic motivation:* An athlete is said to be intrinsically motivated when he or she wants to perform an activity for the satisfaction gained from performing the activity (Ryan and Deci, 2007).
2   *Extrinsic motivation:* Athletes are extrinsically motivated when they perform an activity for expected rewards or outcomes, such as winning money or accolades (Vallerand, 2007).

Motivation is very important because it is related to persistence or dropout. That is, athletes who are more intrinsically motivated are more likely to continue playing sport, whereas athletes who are extrinsically motivated are more likely to drop out (Pelletier *et al.*, 2001). As such, it is crucial that coaches develop intrinsic motivation to foster long-term participation in sport. Coaches need to understand factors that influence motivation in order to generate intrinsic motivation among athletes.

Age related differences and motivation

It is important that coaches consider the age of the children they coach, because there are some age-related motivational differences among children of different ages. Nicholls (1989) argued that children aged between four and ten years of age are not able to differentiate between ability and effort. This means that children between the ages of four and ten years believe that athletes who try hard will perform well and have high ability. However, in a child's later years, he or she will begin to distinguish between effort and ability and will eventually realise that ability is not always related to effort and that sometimes athletes will perform very well even though they may not put in as much effort as other children.

As children get older, around 11–12 years of age, there is a tendency for some athletes to want to demonstrate their superior ability over other children at performing certain tasks. Not only do they want to show that they are more able, they want to do so by exerting the same or less physical effort than other children. Harwood *et al.* (2008) therefore argued that coaches should make a strong effort to create mastery motivational climates for children aged from 11–12 years so that children do not have the opportunity to demonstrate their superior ability over other children. Even though children under the age of 12 years of age are unable to discriminate between effort and ability, it could be argued that coaches should foster a mastery motivational orientation for all children. This is because the benefits of this motivational orientation include enjoyment, competence, and intrinsic motivation (Ames, 1992).

Creating a mastery-oriented motivational climate

Two studies have attempted to manipulate the motivational climate (e.g. Theeboom *et al.*, 1995; Treasure, 1993) and then assess the effects of manipulating the environment with samples of child athletes. Treasure conducted a ten-week intervention to create one of two conditions: (1) a mastery motivational climate or (2) a performance motivational climate among child soccer players. The intervention was based on the TARGET acronym that was initially proposed by Epstein (1989).

TARGET stands for *Task* (e.g. design of learning), *Authority* (e.g. location of decision making), *Recognition* (e.g. use of incentives), *Grouping* (individual vs. cooperative work), *Evaluation* (e.g. use of feedback), and *Time* (pace of instruction). Treasure (1993) found that the motivational climate could be manipulated, because the soccer players in the mastery motivation climate group perceived that they were in a motivational climate, whereas the athletes in the performance group perceived that they were in a performance-oriented climate. The study by Treasure (1993) is important, because it suggests that coaches have the potential to shape the motivational climate.

Theeboom *et al.* (1995) then conducted an intervention study that examined the effects of a motivation climate training programme (e.g. mastery vs. performance) on enjoyment, perceived competence, intrinsic motivation, and motor skill development among Wushu athletes. This study consisted of child athletes who were aged between 8 and 12 years of age, who were randomly assigned to one of two groups: (1) mastery-oriented group, or (2) the performance-oriented group. The results revealed that the children in the mastery-oriented group scored higher than the performance-oriented group in enjoyment and had better motor skills. Furthermore, Theeboom *et al.* also interviewed the athletes and found that those in the mastery-oriented group seemed to have higher levels of intrinsic motivation and perceived competence than the performance-oriented group. Collectively, these studies indicate that coaches have the potential to manipulate the motivational climate. Manipulating the motivational climate to create a mastery motivational climate has the potential to make sport more enjoyable for child athletes along with increasing perceived competence, intrinsic motivation, and improving motor performance.

Using TARGET to create a mastery motivational climate for child athletes

Task

A crucial role of the coach is to design activities that his or her athletes will participate in, such as practice drills, tactics, or even learning activities for children. It is important that the coach asks athletes to conduct tasks that are varied and diverse in nature. Research has found that tasks that have variety and diversity are more likely to interest children and develop learning (Nicholls, 1989). Additionally, coaches should devise tasks that are meaningful to the athlete. For example, if an athlete can see how a task is related to his or her sport, the task is more likely to be viewed as meaningful.

Authority

Authority refers to the degree in which the coach involves the children in decision making regarding the activities that will be carried out (Treasure, 2001). Indeed, authority is very important, because Ames (1992) suggested that decision making is related to positive motivation patterns. Therefore, the more choice children have, the more positively motivated they will be. However, when coaches give children choices, it is essential that the choices are of tasks that are similar in difficulty levels. This is because some children may opt for tasks that are very difficult, whereas other children will select tasks that are very easy tasks if they are worried that they will be compared to other athletes and they have low perceptions of ability (Ames, 1992). Furthermore, Ames stated that if choice is motivated by a child's fear, such as the fear of performing poorly compared to others, then it is unlikely to enhance personal control. Indeed, the coach should ensure that when he or she gives athletes choices, all choices are of an equal difficulty. This will ensure the child chooses the activity for reasons of personal interest as opposed to fear of performing poorly.

Recognition

Treasure (2001) stated that it is very important to reward children and give these athletes incentives to perform, however these incentives or rewards might be viewed by children as being more important than the activity itself. Furthermore, coaches have to be very careful regarding how they administer rewards or incentives, because they can have a negative influence. For example, Lepper and Hodell (1989) found that rewarding a whole group of children, with various abilities who had differing levels of interest, created less motivation. This might have occurred because the children knew they would receive an award regardless of how much effort they put into a task. Additionally, rewards can also decrease motivation if children perceive that the reward is a bribe for them to perform certain behaviours. In order to create a mastery motivational climate, coaches should reward children who improve or those who demonstrate maximum effort, as opposed to those who put in little effort. This will ensure that feelings of satisfaction and pride are a result of the improvement a child makes or the effort they put in as opposed to comparisons with other athletes.

Grouping

According to Ames (1992), how a coach:

* decides how groups are formed;
* keeps children apart from each other; and
* decides the processes in which children move from one group to another

are key factors in determining the motivational climate of a group. Indeed, if coaches select groups based on ability, such as a group of the most talented athletes, a group of athletes with average ability, and a group of athletes with the least ability, there might be a tendency for the coach to give more: (1) instructional time, (2) opportunities, (3) encouragement, and (4) attention to the most talented group of athletes (Martinek, 1989; Weinstein, 1989).

Coaches might be tempted to group individuals based on ability if they have a group of individuals with different abilities (Treasure, 2001). However, to create a mastery motivational climate, coaches should avoid creating homogeneous ability groupings. This will prevent older children making social comparisons. Rather, coaches should group individuals randomly to form heterogeneous ability groupings and regularly change groupings or move athletes from one group to another regularly to avoid social comparisons and foster a mastery motivational climate (Marshall and Weinstein, 1984).

Evaluation

How a coach evaluates the children he or she coaches is one of the most important factors that determines whether athletes perceive they are in a mastery or performance motivational climate (Treasure, 2001). Research has revealed that when children compare themselves to other children based on ability, it negatively influences motivation (Nicholls, 1989) and may result in a sense of decreased self-worth (Covington, 1984). As such, coaches should make evaluations related to the individual by commenting on progress towards the goals of an athlete, the improvement made, or the amount of effort in comparison to other training sessions or matches, thus avoiding peer comparison evaluations. Providing these types of evaluations will encourage children to focus on their own ability to improve and foster a mastery motivational climate.

Timing

Timing is related to the other five dimensions of the model (e.g. task, authority, recognition, grouping, and evaluation). That is, time is related to the task, so coaches should consider what they are asking their athletes to do and the amount of time that they are giving their athletes to complete a specific task. With regards to authority, athletes should be able to control which tasks they do first. It is imperative that the coach spends the same amount of time with each group, as opposed to a coach spending the majority of time with only one group (Keegan *et al.*, 2009). Coaches should be aware of timing, because some children may need more time than others to develop the skills that are required to play sport, but as Treasure (2001) stated 'the children who need the most practice and playing time are the ones who receive the least' (p. 93). It is important that coaches consider time when they evaluate athletes and provide feedback at the appropriate times, such as after successful attempts or when an athlete has demonstrated improvement.

Learning

Coaches who regularly coach children will probably have coached a child's first experience in a particular sport. This is because children try many sports, often prompted by their parents, to see if the child enjoys the sport or has any talent for the sport (Côté, 1999). Coaching a child that is new to a particular sport might be problematic if the child struggles to learn different skills or techniques.

Learning amongst children can be enhanced by the coach giving the child the choice about when he or she receives performance feedback, also referred to as knowledge of results (Chiviacowsky *et al.*, 2008a). However, before information will be provided on how to enhance learning among children, coaches should be aware of the differences between children and adults in their capacity to deal with information (Badan *et al.*, 2000).

As a child progresses through childhood, his or her motor behaviour (e.g. ability to perform different movements skilfully) will develop, due to: (1) hardware and (2) software changes (Connolly, 1970). Hardware refers to changes that occur due to growth such as increases in height and weight. Software changes refer to an individual's ability to use different structures. Essentially, the individual becomes more efficient at processing information. For example, Lambert and Bard (2005) found that reaction time decreases from early childhood to adolescence.

At the present time much less is known about children's information-processing abilities than with adults' abilities (Chiviacowsky *et al*., 2008a), but asking children to tell the coach when they want to receive feedback may accelerate the learning process when children are learning new tasks. For example, Chiviacowsky *et al*. found that children's performance in a bean-bag throwing exercise could be improved when the children decided when to receive feedback as opposed to when the children had no choice on when they received feedback. The children also required knowledge of results less often as they continued in the throwing task. This trend of the children requiring less feedback about their results indicates that the children learned more effectively (Wulf and Shea, 2004). Therefore coaches who ask their child athletes to tell them when they want information on the knowledge of results should expect fewer requests as a child progresses on an activity.

Furthermore, the findings from Chiviacowsky *et al*. (2008a) also indicated that children preferred feedback after successful attempts. Indeed Chiviacowsky *et al*. stated that there may be a temptation for coaches to provide feedback after unsuccessful attempts only. This is because the coach may assume that this is when the child needs the most help in order to guide the child and correct any erroneous movement patterns in a skill. However, the children in the Chiviacowsky *et al*. study only asked for feedback when they had been successful. Therefore, coaches should ask children to tell them when they want feedback or knowledge of results and refrain from providing the child with feedback when they have been unsuccessful at performing a specific task, because it is not conducive to effective learning.

Learning may also be enhanced by coaches encouraging children to ask for feedback more often when a new skill is being learned. This is because children often have a tendency to ask for feedback at less than the optimal rate according to research (Chiviacowsky *et al*., 2008b). The onus is on the coach to act in a supportive and encouraging manner so that children feel comfortable in regularly asking for feedback. Although this may be advantageous to learning among children, providing regular feedback to child athletes may only be possible when a coach is coaching an individual or a small group as opposed to a group of 20–30 children.

Another strategy that coaches could employ to facilitate learning in timing-based skills among children, especially when timing of movements is a crucial factor such as swimming, cycling, or running, is to teach children a counting strategy. This has been found to enhance learning on cycling tasks among younger children, aged between five and seven years of age, and older children aged between eight and ten years (Liu and Jensen, 2011). For example, a coach could administer the instruction 'you are at 50 right now, try and keep the same pace' to a swimmer. It is especially important that coaches encourage younger children to use strategies, because they do not automatically use strategies. Ellis (1992) stated that timing is especially important for sports, so improving a child's timing has the potential to benefit performance.

Self-awareness of coaching behaviour

It is essential that coaches consider their behaviour whether they coach children, adolescents or adult athletes. Quite often, coaches are not aware of their behaviour, with many coaches often being 'blissfully unaware of how they behaved' (Smith and Smoll, 1997: 18). A recent study found that the discrepancy between a coach's actual and reported behaviour may be as high as 40 per cent (Millar *et al.*, 2011). Sport has the potential to benefit children in a number of ways, but if the coach behaves poorly, it has a detrimental impact on the well-being of children and reduces enjoyment (Smith and Smoll, 1997).

Research has found that male coaches behave differently to female coaches, with male coaches generally offering less encouragement than female coaches (Dubois, 1990; Walters *et al.*, 2012; Wandzilak *et al.*, 1988). Indeed, in the study by Walters *et al.*, male coaches made 29 per cent more negative comments than female coaches. Negative comments by the coaches included 'Great shot' when indeed the athlete had hit a poor shot, 'you need to shoot earlier' or 'you committed yourself too early'. It is essential that coaches refrain from expressing negative comments, especially to children, because Smoll and Smith (2006) suggested that negative behaviours or comments made by coaches are likely to induce feelings of resentment among children and may even result in some children ceasing sports participation. Coaches may have used negative comments because they were frustrated that their team might have been losing. Coaches who overemphasise the importance of winning negatively influence dropout rates, self-esteem, and stress (Siegenthaler and Gonzalez, 1997). Furthermore, if a coach emphasises performance then a performance motivational climate will develop, which is not conducive to athlete development and motivation.

Another concerning finding from the Walters *et al.* (2012) study was that the coaches were more critical of male athletes than female athletes, because coaches perceived females to be less talented (Horn *et al.*, 2006). Additionally, coaches from sports of more national significance, football within the UK, rugby union in New Zealand or cricket in India for example, were also more critical of child athletes. It is essential that coaches are (a) aware of how negative behaviour may impact upon child athletes, and (b) aware of their own behaviour.

Enhancing positive experiences: fun and enjoyment

The main reasons children participate and continue participating in sport are because it is fun and enjoyable (Crocker *et al.* 2004). One of the main reasons why child cease participating in a sport is because it makes them unhappy (Cary, 2004). Indeed, Cary found that 44 per cent of parents said their child had dropped out of playing sport because it made them unhappy. For these reasons, it is essential that coaches make participating in sport a fun and enjoyable experience for all children.

Scanlan and Lewthwwaite (1986) developed a model to explain the sources of fun and enjoyment among children. Coaches should have an understanding of this model and implement the model in their coaching. Maximising the outcomes in each of the four categories has the potential to make sport more fun and enjoyable for children (MacPhail *et al.*, 2008). The model proposed by Scanlan and Lewthwaite contains four elements:

1   *Intrinsic achievement:* refers to a child's perception of his or her competence. It is related to the amount of improvement made, whether a skill has been successfully mastered or not, and perceptions of ability.
2   *Extrinsic achievement:* relates to perceptions of competence achieved through feedback from a coach or achieving recognition from a coach.
3   *Intrinsic non-achievement:* includes both competition and movement factors. For example, participating in competitions can be very exciting, and the movement sensations that a person experiences when playing sport can be very satisfying.
4   *Extrinsic non-achievement:* involves non-performance sources of fun, such as a child making friends through playing sport, spending time with their friends through playing sport, or even the feeling of being affiliated with a particular team.

A coach can maximise the enjoyment of a child by creating tasks that promote feelings of competence, provide feedback that denotes competence, and provide children with an element of competition. Finally, the coach can tell the children that they are all important members of the team or club and that their affiliation is highly appreciated and respected (see Case study 11.1).

Summary points

- Motivation is concerned with the *why* people conduct certain behaviours (Deci and Ryan, 2000).
- A motivational climate refers to the way in which coaches influence motivation through their coaching practices (e.g. providing feedback, structuring practices) and provide recognition (Ames, 1992).
- In a mastery motivational climate there is a focus on learning, making improvements, and exerting maximal effort.
- Performance motivational climates are sport settings in which the coach emphasises and rewards winning.
- Coaches can create a mastery motivational climate.
- Coaches can enhance learning among children by providing feedback when they want the feedback.
- Coaches should be aware of their behaviour and the consequences of negative comments.
- Sport should be fun and enjoyable to maintain participation rates among child athletes.

Case study 11.1 Creating a mastery motivational climate in children's soccer

This case study represents a coach's attempt to create a mastery climate in a group of children he coached. Steve has been coaching this group of 20 ten-year-olds for the last month and they play in a local league. Steve is concerned by the children being too pre-occupied with results, so made an attempt to encourage the players to focus on improvement and not the results of matches. Snippets of dialogue between Steve and some of his players are included in this case study for illustrative purposes.

Initial instructions at start of session

Steve: In today's training session I would like you to practise improving your first touch, because this is really important in soccer matches and it would be excellent if you can all improve this element of your game. I have set up four different drills and have laid out cones for each drill. In Drill 1 you receive the ball along the ground and then trap it and pass it back to your partner with your left foot, whereas in Drill 2 you receive the ball at knee height and have to try and cushion it by raising your foot and then pass it to your partner with your right foot. In Drill 3 you receive the ball at chest height and try and cushion it with your chest and pass the ball back to your partner, whereas in Drill 4 you sprint down the line at full speed and receive the ball into your feet and cushion it whilst running, get the ball under control and dribble to the line at full speed. Each person will have a go at each drill. I would like you to decide which drill to go on and start performing. I will show you how each drill works by giving a demonstration. Does anyone have any questions?

Training commences and Steve makes a number of comments

Steve : Well done Ashley, for sprinting down the line as fast as you could and then controlling the ball.

Ashley: Thanks coach

Steve: Mike, that is excellent you are really improving your technique and can cushion the ball much better now.

Mike: I don't think I am improving as I can't trap the ball as well as some of the others.

Steve: No Mike, you really are getting better. You could improve even more by making sure you keep your eye on the ball as sometimes you lift you head up more. Try that now Mike. [Steve gives demonstration.]

Mike: I see what you mean, I will try that now.

Steve: That's it Mike.

End of first round of drills

Steve: Stop everyone. Now decide which drill you want to perform next and stand by the cone ready to start. I am really pleased with the effort everyone is putting in and want you all to continue putting in maximal effort. Start now!

All drills completed

Steve: Well done everyone, you've all now had a go at each drill. I would like us all to spend the next 30-40 minutes in match practices. I would like the people who have completed Drills 1 and 4 to participate in some 2 versus 1 matches. I would like those that have just completed Drills 2 and 3 to play some 4 versus 4. For the first few minutes I want everyone to practise controlling the ball, so everyone has to take at least two touches. After each goal is scored I want each of you to swap bibs with the closest person to you on the other side.

Steve: Great effort Stevie, I can see you are all putting in maximum effort. Jonny, that was a really good first touch and it allowed you some time to look up and make a great pass. Well Done!

Final speech

Steve: Well done today, does anyone have any questions they would like to ask?

Danny: I struggled to get a good touch with my left foot, but I am good at doing it with my right foot and I can't seem to get better.

Steve: Most of us have a tendency to be better with one foot or another. I think you are making improvements with your left foot, but it is just taking a bit longer than your right. I think that if you keep on practising you will continue getting better with your left foot. Are there any other questions? I am looking forward to the game on Sunday, see you then lads.

Case study reflection

In this case study, Steve was trying to adhere to the TARGET principles and the recommendations from Scanlan and Lewthwaite (1986) regarding sources of fun among children. Steve developed a variety of tasks that were meaningful to soccer matches, he gave the players choice, he rewarded effort and improvement verbally, regularly switched the groups in the match to reduce social comparison, and carefully timed what he did.

Practice exam questions

1   Compare and contrast intrinsic and extrinsic motivation and the implications these types of motivation have among children.
2   Describe how a coach can develop a mastery motivational climate.
3   Describe how motivation may change among children based upon the framework provided by Nicholls (1989).
4   Discuss how coach behaviour affects children.
5   Discuss the influence of the coach on how a child enjoys sport.

Critical thinking questions: applying theory to practice

1   Describe how a coach can implement the TARGET principles into a coaching session.
2   How can a coach increase motivation among child athletes during training?
3   What can a coach do to enhance learning among children?
4   Consider the behaviour of a coach you have recently seen coaching. Identify positive comments that the coach made in addition to the negative comments made by the coach.
5   How can coaches make training sessions more enjoyable for children?

12 Coaching adolescents

This chapter provides information on the factors that coaches should consider when they coach adolescent athletes. In this chapter, information is provided in relation to coaching adolescent athletes and:

*   adolescence;
*   motivation;
*   coaching behaviour;
*   structuring practice activities;
*   understanding and reducing dropout;
*   enhancing self-esteem, well-being, and enjoyment.

Adolescence

In this chapter, athletes who are aged between 12 and 18 years of age are classified as being adolescents. Adolescence has the potential to be a stressful period, due to the development changes that occur in this stage of a person's life (Compas *et al.*, 2001). Athletes may experience changes in physical, physiological, emotional, social, and cognitive changes during this period (Boekaerts, 1996).

Motivation

It appears that sports participation declines throughout adolescence. Recent data from Sport Scotland (2008) revealed that 87 per cent of 8–11 year olds played sport once a week, 76 per cent of 12–15 year olds played sport once a week, and only 51 per cent of 16–24 year olds played sport once a week. Another concerning recent trend is fewer adolescents are involved in sports. For example, between 2007 and 2009 there was a 20.3 per cent reduction in the number of 16–19-year-old males playing football (Sport England, 2010). These figures are worrying, given the numerous health benefits associated with playing sport (Zaff *et al.*, 2003).

A key factor that explains why some adolescent athletes drop out is decreased motivation, which is a consequence of poor coaching (Price and Weiss, 2000). Coaches need to understand what motivates adolescent athletes and what decreases motivation, in order to ensure the athletes they coach are motivated, because there are subtle variations between adolescent athletes and either child or adult athletes in terms of motivation. Failure to recognise such differences may contribute to decreased motivation among adolescent athletes and ultimately sport withdrawal.

A review by Weiss and Williams (2004) found that adolescents have intrinsic and extrinsic motives to play sport. Intrinsic motivation has also been referred to a self-determined motivation (Ryan and Deci, 2007). An athlete exhibits self-determined motivation when he or she takes part in activities in the absence of prompts from parents or coaches, in addition to the athlete not receiving any awards. Conversely, an athlete who is motivated to play sport for the external reward or outcome is extrinsically motivated. Ryan and Deci (2007) suggested that there are four types of extrinsic motivation:

1   *Integrated regulations:* Some athletes are motivated to perform certain sports because they see that the sport fits in well with how they see themselves. Playing sport for these reasons will not provide the athlete with immediate rewards. For example, a person may play rugby union because he sees himself as being a physically tough person who likes physical confrontation.
2   *Identified regulations:* Athletes may perform a certain behaviour because they anticipate reaping the benefits at a later date. For example, a female basketball player may always spend an extra 30 minutes practising her shooting, even though she does not enjoy the extra practice, because she thinks that there might be a match in which she will have an attempt to win the game and that the extra practice may help for that anticipated moment.
3   *Introjected regulations:* Certain athletes may carry out some behaviours to: (1) experience positive emotions such as pride, happiness, and joy, or (2) avoid negative feelings such as guilt or shame. For example, a male tennis player might spend four hours practising his forehand because he would feel guilty if he did not do this.
4   *External regulations:* A number of people conduct behaviours purely for the outcome or the rewards that they will receive despite not enjoying the task. An example of this form of motivation would be the swimmer who only attends swimming training because he thinks it will help him win a university swimming scholarship.

How coaches influence motivation among adolescent athletes

Research has indicated that coaches can directly influence the intrinsic motivation levels of the athletes that they coach (Weiss *et al.*, 2009). There also appear to be differences between children and adolescent athletes with regards to the impact that a coach can have on motivation. Black and Weiss (1992) explored the relationship between motivation and coach behaviour among a sample of 312 athletes who were divided into three age groups: (1) 10–11 years of age, (2) 12–14 years of age, and (3) 15–18 years of age. Interestingly, the findings revealed that coach behaviour was not related to intrinsic motivation among the 10–11-year-old athletes, but intrinsic motivation correlated with how the coach behaved among the athletes who were aged 12–14 and 15–18 years old. There were other age-related findings, as the swimmers within the 12–14 years group who received more information after a positive performance were more intrinsically motivated. However, the swimmers that were the most intrinsically motivated among the 15–18 years of age group also felt that they had more information after a positive performance in addition to receiving praise from their coach. This study reveals the importance of coaches providing information to athletes.

In order to maximise intrinsic motivation among athletes aged between 12–14 years of age, coaches should focus their efforts on providing regular feedback after an athlete performs well. Older adolescent athletes also require regular feedback after they have performed successfully, but it is important that coaches also provides these athletes with praise regarding their accomplishments. Although the research by Black and Weiss (1992) found that coach behaviour did not influence motivation among athletes aged between 10 and 11 years of age, other research by Theeboom *et al.* (1995) revealed that coaches can increase the intrinsic motivation of their athletes by manipulating the environment that they coach in. It would therefore be incorrect for coaches who work with athletes aged between 10 and 11 years of age to dismiss how they behave, because they think it does not have an impact of intrinsic motivation. It clearly can. For information on how a coach can impact a child's intrinsic motivation please see Chapter 11 of this book.

With regards to adolescent athletes, Bengoechea and Strean (2007) found evidence to suggest that coaches influence the motivation of adolescent athletes aged between 13 and 17 years of age in a variety of different ways. Indeed, these authors identified five motivational roles that coaches may play, which included:

1   *Providers of support:* The adolescent athletes reported that they benefited from their coaches and other people acting in a supportive manner, which enhanced motivation, self-perceptions, and emotions. In particular, the results suggested that the coaches had the most impact on adolescents by adopting an approach in which the athletes felt that their coach was 'backing them'. The athletes reported that this approach allowed them to make their own decisions.

2   *Sources of pressure and control:* Coaches were also found to be a source of pressure. Athletes reported worrying about meeting the expectations of their coach. Bengoechea and Strean (2007) suggested that if coaches create a pressure to perform certain activities (e.g. compete at particular competitions) the athletes may feel they have little or no choice, which reduces intrinsic motivation. However, the results also suggested that not all controlling behaviour by a coach has a negative impact on motivation. Some of the adolescents reported that, at times, they lacked motivation to take part in the least enjoyable aspects of their sport. However, they knew they were important for their own performance or for that of the team. As

such, the athletes may need or expect some form of controlling behaviour. From a coaching perspective, if the coach has to use controlling behaviour, it is essential the coach states the perceived benefits of the athlete engaging in particular training (e.g. hill sprints). Indeed, Vallerand (2001) argued that exerting controlling behaviour may produce positive outcomes, but coaches should be cautious when adopting this approach. For instance, coaches could try and increase intrinsic motivation by trying to make tasks more enjoyable before resorting to controlling behaviours.

3   *Sources of competence-relevant information:* Athletes were motivated by coaches who increased their perception of being competent through providing feedback. Unlike children, as adolescents progress through their teenage years they tend to rely less on others to generate feelings of competence and tend to rely on judging competence based on their achievement of personal goals and skill improvement (Horn *et al.*, 1993). However, adolescents don't just exclusively use internal feedback and do also rely on feedback from coaches as a source of competence. It is therefore important that coaches provide feedback that emphasises competence in adolescent athletes such as 'you are really getting to grips with the forehand stroke and are hitting excellent strokes now'.

4   *Socialisation of achievement orientations:* Coaches play an important role in developing the environment an athlete is in, which has been referred to as being either: (1) mastery (Ames, 1992), task (Nicholls, 1989), or learning (Dweck, 1986). Athletes in this type or environment are concerned with improving and judge their accomplishments based on the improvements made or the amount of effort exerted; (2) performance (e.g. Ames; Dweck) and ego (Nicholls, 1989). In this second type of environment the athlete's main desire is to be better than other athletes. As such, the athlete would judge his or her performance based on his or her standing in relation to other athletes.

   The Bengoechea and Strean (2007) study found that the coach is pivotal in determining the environment or motivational climate among adolescent athletes, through stating how success is measured (e.g. improvements or effort vs. comparisons to other athletes or outcome such as winning). Coaches can maximise motivation by creating an environment in which athletes' success is judged on how they improve and the amount of effort exerted. Adopting this stance does not mean that coaches cannot introduce a competitive element within their coaching, because many adolescents enjoyed an element of competition. However, coaches could place less emphasis on who wins matches in training or competitive matches and focus on improvements made and what athletes can do to improve further (for a more extensive discussion of the motivational climate, see Chapter 11 on coaching children).

5   *Models to emulate:* Adolescent athletes also observe their coaches and take on board some of the behaviours of the people they are observing, which can increase motivation (Weiss, 1995). As such, if a coach demonstrates a positive attitude to improving and exerting maximal effort in training and during competitions, athletes may also adopt this approach.

Enhancing Motivation: RESISTANCE

Enhancing intrinsic motivation has the potential to benefit athletes, because intrinsically motivated athletes experience less anxiety than those who are extrinsically motivated (Weiss and Amorose, 2008). The research by Bengoechea and Strean (2007) suggested that a coach can influence and thus enhance motivation by developing a mastery or task motivation climate. An intervention study conducted by Harwood and Swain (2002) examined the effects of a season long: (a) player, (b) parent, and (c) coach intervention on goal involvement responses, self-regulation, competition cognitions, and goal orientations among four adolescent tennis players. Each participant received four 90-minute educational sessions and the set of coaches and parents received two 90-minute educational sessions. The different sessions focused on motives for playing tennis, the Competitive Performance Mentality (CPM), how the motivational climate can destroy CPM, and a series of personal tasks so the tennis players could become familiar with the aims of the intervention. (The Competitive Performance Mentality, which was developed by Harwood and Swain (2002) is a motivational approach to competition, which states that a player only ever has two challenges in a match that they participate in: (1) the self-challenge, which is the challenge to improve and maintain performance standards in all areas of performance, and (2) the game challenge, which is to use the self-challenge to overcome the test (which is the opponent) set by the game of tennis on that day.)

Furthermore, Harwood and Swain (2002) created the RESISTANCE acronym, which represented the 10 factors in tennis that could reduce an athlete's motivation. The RESISTANCE acronym stands for:

- *Rating:* Athletes were made aware that it was not their rating or ranking that produces their performance, but the effort they exerted.
- *Esteem:* Players were encouraged to separate themselves from the outcome, so if they lost they were less inclined to think of themselves in a negative fashion.
- *Seeding:* Players were encouraged to pay little attention to their seeding or their opponent's seeding, as they were told that ranking does not determine results, performance does.
- *Importance:* All matches were of the same importance and no match is more important than another match.
- *Score*: The score which a player beats another player or the score by which a player gets beaten is not important.
- *Team:* Team-mates were encouraged to play like the player who had earned and deserved his or her place on a team.
- *Audience:* The main concern of an audience is to watch players try their best and give maximal effort at all times during a match.
- *No justice:* The players were encouraged to think rationally and understand that one bad call from a referee does not determine the outcome of a match, as the performance for the rest of the match determines the outcome of matches.

- *Comparison:* Players were asked not to base what they thought they had achieved solely on making comparisons with other players (e.g. one player might have reached a semi-final, but compares himself only with the player who made the final. The player who made the semi-final could focus on the improvement he made in different areas of the game to reach the semi-final and think about what he can do to improve his technique to reach future finals).
- *Endorsements:* Players were encouraged to worry less about designer labels, and were told that fashion has never won anyone a match, performance wins matches.

Harwood and Swain (2002) successfully developed the RESISTANCE intervention to increase task involvement (e.g. desire to improve) in relation to enhancing pre-competitive task goals and reducing ego involvement (e.g. desire to show superior ability).

Coach behaviour

Desired coach behaviour and its effects

It is essential that coaches are aware of their behaviour when coaching adolescent athletes, because coach behaviour has a number of implications. In addition to it influencing intrinsic motivation, it is also related to aggression (Chow *et al.*, 2009). Indeed, Chow *et al.* (2009) found that coaches who perceived they had stronger beliefs in their abilities to coach sport and lead their team to success resulted in players who were more likely to commit violent acts of aggression than players who were coached by coaches with weaker beliefs in their ability to be successful. Chow *et al.* suggested that coaches who had strong judgements about their ability to coach may view aggressive behaviour as legitimate, given it might result in a team winning and thus achieving the coach's goal.

Additional research by Rieke *et al.* (2008) found that coaches who demonstrated a caring behaviour, involved athletes in making decisions, and wanted others to grow personally was associated with athletes who were more satisfied, mentally tough, task-oriented, and intrinsically motivated. Other research has identified the ideal coach behaviours among adolescent athletes (Martin *et al.*, 2003). The results of Martin *et al.*'s study revealed that adolescent athletes prefer a coach who can run effective instructional practices in training, can perform the sports skills that are associated with sport being coached, and provided athletes with opportunities to compete and achieve their goals. Interestingly, there were some gender differences as the female adolescent athletes preferred a coach who made practice and competitions seem more fun and exciting, than male adolescents. However, the male adolescents preferred a coach who placed an emphasis on fitness, achievements, and competition. These studies have revealed the importance of coach behaviour, but did not explore how coaches behaved during competitions. More recent research has assessed how coaches behave during competitions among adolescent athletes.

In-game behaviours of coaches

Several studies have revealed the in-game behaviour of coaches who coach adolescent athletes. Smith and Cushion (2006) examined how professional soccer coaches behaved during matches. They categorised behaviour into three themes: (1) developing performance (e.g. use of silence, use of instruction, mistake correction, decision making, and purpose of games), (2) support and encouragement (e.g. use of praise, scolding, use of names, and verbal statements to intensify the efforts of players), and (3) coaches' role and influences (e.g. the coach's job and coach's knowledge and experience). The most frequently reported in-game behaviour was the use of silence. Coaches need to be careful when adopting the strategy of silence, because some athletes might perceive that a coach is conducting ineffective coaching (Jones *et al.*, 1995). However, Smith and Cushion (2006) contended that use of silence was an appropriate behaviour because it allowed the coaches to monitor their team and performance, before reflecting on deploying an intervention. Other research has concurred with the findings of Smith and Cushion as instruction appears to be a frequent coach behaviour with samples of adolescent soccer players in the United Kingdom (Ford *et al.*, 2010) and adolescent volleyball players in Portugal (Isabel *et al.*, 2008).

Interestingly, Ford and colleagues (Ford *et al.*, 2010) examined skill and age-related differences and found that elite adolescent soccer players received more coaching behavioural responses in training activities that replicated match conditions than non-elite athletes. Furthermore, older soccer players in the under-16 category received more coaching behavioural responses than those in the under-9 and under-13 years of age category. These findings have a number of implications for players and it appears that the behaviours may result in a number of undesirable consequences. Indeed, Smith and Cushion (2006) acknowledged that the in-game behaviours of coaches were focused on developing the performance of the players to the detriment of creating a supportive and encouraging environment. Indeed, the instructional approach adopted by coaches as opposed to a more supportive and encouraging behaviour may result in decreased intrinsic motivation (Bengoechea and Strean, 2007), decreased satisfaction among athletes (Rieke *et al.*, 2008), and even mental toughness (Gucciardi *et al.*, 2008). However, other research has suggested that adolescents require coaches to demonstrate instructional practices in training (Martin *et al.*, 2003), so athletes may also require this in matches. However, research is required to assess the effects of in-game coach behaviour among athletes to assess the impact of coaches mainly providing athletes with instructional behaviours as opposed to supportive and encouraging instructions. In the meantime, coaches should become more aware of their in-game behaviour and could combine instructional behaviours with supportive behaviours to ensure that motivation levels are maintained among athletes.

Another issue with coaches providing so many instructional behaviours relates to the development of the athlete. There is evidence to suggest that coaches who provide frequent verbal instruction, feedback, or demonstrations may indeed provide too much information to athletes, which can prevent them from engaging in their own problem-solving process (Williams and Hodges, 2005). Indeed, there have been calls for coaches to provide less instruction to athletes, which is representative of the instruction they would receive in a match. Ford *et al.* (2010) stated that learners will eventually have to perform in competitions on their own without direct guidance or instruction from a coach. Therefore, Ford *et al.* (2010) stated that the challenge for coaches is 'to provide the least amount of instruction possible so as to enable athletes to solve problems independently' (p. 493). As such, coaches consider their instructions and question whether they are necessary before administering instructions, in order to foster a more problem-solving approach among athletes.

Practice activities and instruction

There appears to be a discrepancy between what coaches actually do and research regarding skill acquisition, motor learning, and expert performance among adolescent athletes (Ford *et al.*, 2010). Indeed, it has been argued that practice should reflect competition for athletes to make improvements from their training (Singer and Janelle, 1999). For example, elite wrestlers reported that mat work was the most important part of their training, whereas gymnasts have adapted their training to spend more time engaged in activities that were similar to competition (Law *et al.*, 2007). However, the results by Ford *et al.* indicate that adolescent soccer players spend 65 per cent of time in training activities that are not closely related to actual competition, whereas only 35 per cent of practice time involved activities that were similar to playing soccer. Ford and colleagues stated that this finding is very worrying, given that adolescence might be a key period in which the skills associated with playing soccer are developed (Proteau *et al.*, 1992). Others have even advocated that only activities relevant to competition should be practised (Williams and Hodges, 2005). Nevertheless, it is apparent that adolescent athletes should spend more time in activities that are relevant to competition. In addition to competition-relevant activities developing perceptual, cognitive, and motor skills, they may also enhance intrinsic motivation given that individuals are more motivated when they perceive the tasks as being relevant (Nicholls, 1989). Future research could explore the effects of playing form activities on intrinsic motivation among adolescent athletes.

Understanding and reducing dropout

Previous research has indicated that up to 35 per cent of adolescents engaged in sport might drop out or cease participation in any given year (Fraser-Thomas *et al.*, 2008). It is therefore important that coaches understand the reasons why adolescent athletes drop out so they can eliminate some of the risk factors associated with dropout. A review by Weiss and Williams (2004) identified conflict of interests, lack of fun, arguments with coaches, and a lack of playing time as the main reasons for dropping out of sport. It appears that adolescents do not make a 'snap-shot' decision to drop out. Dropping out of sport is a process. In this process the adolescent athlete would make an ongoing cost-benefit evaluation of participating in their sport, which could involve an analysis of weighing up a lack of playing time (cost) with the amount of improvement that has been made (benefit) (Fraser-Thomas *et al.*, 2008).

Fraser-Thomas *et al.* (2008) conducted a study that assessed the physical and psychosocial reasons for dropout among a sample of 25 swimmers who had dropped out and 25 swimmers who were currently engaged in swimming and were aged between 13 and 18 years of age. The results revealed that physical factors and psychosocial factors were related to dropout among these swimmers. With regards to physical factors, it was found that those who dropped out took part in few activities outside of school and spent less time participating in swimming. Additionally, those who had dropped out were more likely to have had the status of being a top swimmer in their childhood, started supplementary dry land training earlier, and went to a swimming camp earlier than those engaged in swimming. Fraser-Thomas and colleagues suggested that the swimmers who dropped out might not have been psychologically capable of handling the pressure of being a top swimmer, which indicates the need for coaches to provide athletes with the psychological skills training to ensure they are capable of coping with stress or pressure, or even the disappointment of being a child star, but mediocre in adolescence (Hill, 1988). Fraser-Thomas *et al.* (2008) identified psychosocial factors as a reason for the swimmers dropping out, such as receiving less one-on-one coaching throughout development. Another factor that was related to dropout was parents. Many of the swimmers who dropped out had parents who competed at high level. Also, those who dropped out were less likely to have best friends who were involved in swimming and the dropouts were also the youngest in their training group.

From a coaching perspective, these findings indicate that coaches need to think carefully about how they formulate training groups and that 'age' might not necessarily be the best indicator for forming groups. Creating additional activities that promote interaction and possible friendships away from swimming may help reduce dropout rates. It is clear however that coaches need to make sports training and competition more fun and enjoyable for adolescent athletes, which could mean delaying when athletes attend residential training camps (Fraser-Thomas *et al.*, 2008). Additionally, coaches could also consider what athletes do at the training camps and reduce the amount of training at training camps. This would leave more time for additional activities that athletes perceive as fun and enjoyable.

Enhancing self-esteem, well-being, and enjoyment

Self-esteem refers to an athlete's overall evaluation of his or her sense of worthiness and indicates a person's feelings regarding skills, abilities and social relationships (Coopersmith, 1967; Rosenberg, 1979). Additionally, self-esteem is a useful indicator of a person's well-being (Coatsworth and Conroy, 2006). Promoting and enhancing self-esteem is desirable, because individuals who are high in self-esteem are thought to be more psychologically healthy (Taylor and Brown, 1988). Conversely, individuals who have low self-esteem are thought to be in a distressed state (Tennen and Affleck, 1993). In general, it is accepted that self-esteem influences current and future behaviour (Harter, 1999). There is a widely held notion that adolescents who participate in sport benefit from increased levels of self-esteem (Marsh and Kleitman, 2003; Tracy and Erkut, 2002).

Although participating in sport has the potential to boost self-esteem, this is very much dependent on the coach. Research has indicated that coaching behaviours account for variances in self-esteem (Smith *et al.*, 1983) and that athletes with lower self-esteem are more sensitive and responsive to instructive and supportive behaviours from a coach (Smith and Smoll, 1990). With this in mind, a number of programmes have been developed to improve coach behaviours to enhance self-esteem among athletes. One of the most recent interventions was created by Coatsworth and Conroy (2006) who developed a two-hour coach training programme adapted from Coach Effectiveness Training (Smith and Smoll, 1996). This involved Coatsworth and Conroy emphasising the consequences of coaching behaviour, how coaches should evaluate success and failure, benefits of and techniques for team building, creating a mastery achievement goal climate, supporting coach behaviours and eliminating punitive coaching behaviours. Overall. Coatsworth and Conroy's intervention was successful in enhancing self-esteem especially among younger adolescents and females who had low self-esteem at the start of the study.

Coaches can also enhance the well-being of adolescent athletes by supporting them in the choices they make and soliciting input. For example, Adie *et al.* (2012) found that environments created by coaches that solicit an athlete's responses and opinions conveys that the coach trusts the athlete. Allowing athletes to make their own choices or decisions increases well-being. Furthermore, this type of coaching environment may even reduce symptoms of overtraining among athletes (Adie *et al.*, 2012; Raedeke and Smith, 2001).

In terms of making sport a more enjoyable experience for adolescent athletes, Fry and Gano-Overway. (2010) found that athletes who perceived that they were in a caring sporting environment were more likely to report higher enjoyment scores. A caring environment was characterised by warmth, safety, acceptance, and willingness to help. There were also a number of other interesting results with regards to athletes being in a caring environment. Athletes in a caring environment were more likely to have positive attitudes towards their team-mates, greater commitment to soccer, and engage in more caring behaviours towards their team-mates. Coaches can foster a caring environment by communicating in a positive and supportive way with their athletes. They can also encourage athletes to do the same, make their athletes feel safe by not punishing any mistakes they make, help athletes feel accepted into a group by involving them, and show willingness to help improve athletes.

Case study 12.1 Reflections on a training session

The following case study represents Kim's reflection of a practice session in the diary she keeps. Kim is an ex-international hockey player and is the coach of a regional under-18 squad that contains 18 players.

The players were a bit low after Saturday's defeat and I felt it was really important to speak to them all at the start of session, and I am really glad that I did. I tried to be very empathetic towards the players and supportive and wanted them to voice some of the reasons behind the defeat and poor performance. This worked really well as the players identified a number of factors that I had also noticed and they all seemed to take ownership of the situation and devised their own strategies regarding what we could work on. I also provided some feedback in areas that I felt we could improve on and asked for opinions from the athletes. After some positive discussion the players seemed to be uplifted, because they felt if we made improvements in the areas we had identified team performance would improve. One of the key areas the players identified was playing under pressure. As such I created some training matches that gave the players less time on the ball so they would become more used to playing with less space and time. I did this by reducing the size of the pitch by initially playing 9 versus 9 on a half pitch for 15 minutes. I then reduced the pitch even further to give the players even less space. This was a challenge for the players and I tried to be encouraging which I think really helped as more mistakes were being made, but deep down the players knew they needed to improve in this area of the game and I think most of them saw the benefits of this and quite a few asked if we could do this in future. I know that it is not going to be a quick fix, but I feel confident that the players believe that they will improve as the season progresses and that today's session helped to lift their spirits. I am looking forward to the next session with the players.

Case study summary

In this case study Kim described how she attempted to provide the players with input and decision making in a manner that was caring and supporting. She also tried to place an emphasis on the players improving and set up a training activity that was relevant to matches with the aim of helping the players become accustomed to playing under pressure with less time on the ball.

Summary points

- Adolescent athletes who are intrinsically motivated appear to experience lower levels of anxiety and are able to learn skills more efficiently than those who are extrinsically motivated (Weiss and Amorose, 2008).
- Coaches influence motivation among adolescent athletes through a variety of different ways including providing support and developing the motivational climate.
- Coach behaviour can influence aggression, decision making, and mental toughness among adolescent athletes.
- The majority of in-game behaviours by coaches appear to be of an instructional nature.
- Practice activities in training should replicate match conditions to help develop adolescent athletes, but it appears that players might only spend a third of their practice time in match-like conditions.
- There is a relationship between the age at which adolescents increase the amount of training they do (e.g. attend training camps) and drop out.
- Dropout rates could be reduced by coaches delaying specialised training camps and providing psychological support to adolescent athletes to help them combat stress.
- Coaches can enhance the self-esteem of adolescent athletes by placing less emphasis on outcome and more emphasis on rewarding improvement and view that as success, act in a supportive manner and refrain from administering punitive coaching behaviours.
- Coaches can also enhance the well-being of the adolescent athletes that they coach by supporting athletes in the choices they make and soliciting input and decision making.

Practice exam questions

1   Identify and describe the four different types of extrinsic motivation and their implications for sports performance among adolescent athletes.
2   To what extent can coaches influence motivation among adolescent athletes? Discuss.
3   What are the implications of adolescent athletes spending only 33 per cent of practice time in activities that are relevant to competition?
4   Describe the discrepancies between adolescent athletes' preferred behaviour and the in-game behaviour of coaches.
5   Discuss the role of the coach in promoting self-esteem among adolescent athletes.

Critical thinking questions: applying theory to practice

1   Describe how a coach can implement the RESISTANCE principles into a coaching session.

2 How can a coach implement the findings of Bengoechea and Strean (2007) into a training programme to enhance motivation?

3 How can coaches make training sessions more realistic of matches and what are the implications for performance?

4 Identify and discuss how coaches can devise training programmes with the goal of reducing dropout among adolescent athletes.

5 What can a coach do to develop a caring environment?

13 Coaching adults

The aim of this chapter is to provide information on the factors that coaches could consider when they coach adult athletes, who are classified as being 18 years of age and older. In this chapter, information is provided in relation to adults and:

* andragogy: learning and motivation;
* effects of coach behaviour;
* antecedents of coach behaviour.

During the period between April 2010 and April 2011 6,924,000 adults participated in sport at least three times a week for a minimum of 30 minutes each time (Sport England, 2011). Furthermore, a large number of adult athletes received tuition from professional coaches. During this time period, 345,300 adults received golf tuition, 377,100 received coaching in football, 236,000 had swimming lessons, and 161,600 had tennis lessons (Sport England, 2011). It is essential that coaches who coach adult athletes understand this population and tailor their coaching appropriately.

Andragogy: learning and motivation

Although coaches might expect to be coaching athletes with years of experience when they coach an adult athlete, this might not always be true. Adults are likely to take up new sports for a number of reasons. For example, athletes who participate in contact sports such as rugby union might take up new sports that put less strain on their bodies such as swimming or tennis. Older athletes who are not capable of performing how they want in tennis, due to their reduced speed, might take up sports such as golf or bowls. It is therefore essential that coaches understand how adult athletes learn to maximise their coaching efficiency.

In comparison with children, less is known about how adults learn. The term pedagogy is a familiar term in sport science journals and originates from the Greek words *paid* which means child and *agogus* which means leader of. Pedagogy literally means teaching children (Knowles *et al.*, 2011). The term that refers to the understanding of and supporting learning among adults is called andragogy. It is important to note that the word andragogy is not a new term of expression, as the use of this word dates back to Alexander Kapp who coined this phrase way back in 1883 (Reischmann and Jost, 2004).

Lindeman (1926) identified key principles among adult learners, which have all been supported by research in the intervening years (Knowles *et al.*, 2011), with Merriam and Brockett (1997) stating that little has changed with regards to why adults want to learn and the best ways of helping adults learn. As such Lindeman stated that:

1   Adults become motivated to learn skills when they experience needs and interests, which they feel that learning will satisfy.
2   Adults are oriented to learning that is life-centred and thus adults will want to learn when they feel that learning will benefit their wider life.
3   Adults often rely on their previous life experience when learning, so coaches should use experience as a core component of coaching adults. Within a sport setting, coaches could relate back to athletes' previous experiences of playing other sports if they are similar.
4   Adults also have a very deep need to be self-directing. The role of the coach is not to transmit his or her knowledge to the athlete; rather, the coach's role is to engage in a mutual process of enquiry with the athlete.

Based on these four points, Knowles (1995) developed eight principles that form a process to help adults learn more effectively that can be applied to coaches:

1   *Preparing learners:* It is crucial that adults are given information regarding the tasks they will be engaged in at the start of each session and why they are relevant. For example, a coach who is teaching an adult to swim could say that he or she would like the swimmer to work on his leg kicks in a session, to increase swimming speed.
2   *Developing the climate:* Coaches should teach athletes in a relaxed fashion that is supportive, collaborative, and respectful. Furthermore, coaches should also be open to the athlete's ideas. Many adult athletes will have their own ways of learning based on their previous experiences in sport and non-sport settings.
3   *Planning:* Coaches should involve the athlete in regard to the activities that the athlete will be engaged in.
4   *Diagnosis of needs:* The coach and the player should mutually assess the current state of the player's abilities and what they feel the player needs to work on to improve.
5   *Setting of objectives:* The coach and the player should work together to set realistic objectives regarding improvement and standards of attainment. For example, an adult golfer may have the objective of attaining a handicap of 5 within 12 months of starting golf, which might be unrealistic. In this instance the coach could question whether the golfer thinks that would be realistic and could give his opinion on the amount of time the golfer would have to spend practising in order to get his handicap down to 5 in such a short space of time.

6   *Designing learning plans:* Adult athletes like to understand why they could benefit from learning new skills. The coach could identify, what Knowles (1995) termed, 'problem units' that would then help determine a learning plan. Within a sporting context, a problem unit would refer to aspects of a person's ability that might prevent him or her from reaching a desired level of ability. For example, a tennis player might not be serving as he would like to because he: (1) has a poor ball toss, (2) does not have adequate power to hit the ball as hard as he wants to, (3) lacks explosive power, (4) has poor racquet position when he draws his racquet back in preparation for hitting the ball. As such, each point would be considered a problem unit. The coach could design activities that the athlete could engage in to learn new skills to eradicate each problem unit and thus serve better.

7   *Learning activities:* Adult learners will learn more effectively when the coach relates learning to an athlete's previous experience. For example, a retired tennis player may take up golf and the coach could relate aspects of golf to tennis when coaching. For example, the tennis player would be familiar with slicing the ball and hitting topspin shots, which is similar to golf when golfers hit a drawn shot or a fade. By explaining the concept of a fade as a slice and a draw as a topspin shot, the golfer can use his or her previous experiences and relate them to golf.

8   *Evaluation:* Coaches should regularly evaluate the progress made by an adult learner and involve the learner in the process. That is, the coach could ask the learner for his or her opinions on progress made. The athlete and coach could share their own ideas, which then might shape future training sessions.

Enhancing learning through control

Although the eight principles developed by Knowles were not specifically designed for sports coaches who coach adult athletes, many of the principles have been supported in the sport science literature. In summary, these eight principles indicate that the adult athlete should be given choice when learning. Within motor learning research, experimenters have attempted to explore how giving adults choices influences learning when practising. Giving an athlete choice is often referred to as self-control (Wu and Magill, 2011).

One of the first studies that explored self-control and learning among adults, was by Janelle et al. (1995). They allowed the adults to control when they received feedback during practice, for learning a ball-throwing task. Janelle and colleagues found that giving the adult learners this choice improved learning. Interestingly, Janelle and colleagues found that the participants in the self-controlled group asked for feedback after 20.8 per cent of trials in the first trial block, but only 6.7 per cent in the second trial block. From a coaching perspective, this would indicate that coaches should give athletes less feedback as they continue their learning.

Giving adults the choice regarding observations (Wrisberg and Pein, 2002), physical assistance devices (Wulf and Toole, 1999), and practice schedules (Keetch and Lee, 2007) seems to have a positive impact on learning. However, a limitation of these studies is that they did not explore the effects of self-controlled practice on learning when participants were asked to learn multiple movement patterns (Wu and Magill, 2011). Given that many sports involve multiple movement patterns, it would be interesting to explore the effects of self-controlled practice on learning multiple movement patterns. The study by Wu and Magill explored this, by giving the participants the choice of different time structures and found that individuals who chose their practice schedule performed significantly better in the 24-hour learning transfer test than individuals who did not choose their practice schedule. This provides more support for giving adults choice.

In addition to giving participants choice regarding the time structure in which they practise (Wu and Magill, 2011), other research has indicated that giving athletes a choice over the amount of practice they do may also enhance learning (Post *et al.*, 2011). With a sample of 24 participants Post and colleagues explored the effects of allowing participants to choose the amount of practice they had on a darts throwing task. The results revealed that the participants who controlled the amount of practice performed better in the retention task (performing the same task again) and a transfer task (e.g. performing a related task). From a coaching perspective, these findings indicate that allowing participants to control the amount of practice they have might reap immediate and longer-term benefits in performance.

Chiviacowsky and Wulf (2002) found that performance improvements occurred in a transfer task, but not a retention task when participants controlled the amount of practice they had. Chiviacowsky and Wulf argued that performance increments in transfer tasks are a more sensitive measure of learning than performance increases in a retention task. This is because the transfer task requires individuals to adapt a skill that they have previously attempted to learn. It also has implications for transferring skills learned in training into competitive situations. Those who control the amount of practice they do should be more able to adapt their learning to diverse situations, which is important for sports such as golf where golfers may play different courses and even team sport athletes who might have to play in different weather conditions and against opponents of different standards.

Although these results suggest that coaches should allow all athletes to decide the amount of practice they have, other researchers have found this may have a negative impact, so coaches could be cautious with all athletes. Some athletes' preferred learning conditions, such as the amount of practice one partakes in, might not result in performance increases through enhanced learning (Schmidt and Bjork, 1992). This is because learning should be most effective from maximising the number of practice attempts or sessions (Schmidt and Lee, 2005). Therefore giving an athlete complete control in the amount of practice might not be the most effective way to enhance learning in all situations, as some athletes might decide to have a small number of practice trials (Post *et al.*, 2011). Perhaps coaches and athletes could come to an agreement themselves about the amount of practice an athlete does, as learning progresses. This would give the athlete control, but also allows the coach to make an input using his or her experience.

Enhancing learning and motivation.

One method employed by coaches to help athletes learn more effectively is through providing feedback. That is, a coach may provide the athlete with knowledge of his or her results about whether a specific movement or skill execution was successful or not. The purpose of such feedback is to enable athletes to correct errors (Wulf *et al.*, 2010). Research by Chiviacowsky *et al.* (2009) explored how knowledge of results after good trials influenced learning, among a sample of 22 adults with a mean age of 65.9 years, on a bean-bag throwing experiment. It was found that knowledge of results for trials after small errors is more effective for enhancing learning than knowledge of results after trials with much larger errors. The authors provided some clues as to why only providing knowledge of results feedback might be so helpful in enhancing learning. For example, being provided with knowledge of results after a successful trial might have a reinforcing role that encourages people to perform the same movement again. Additionally, providing adults with knowledge of their results after successful trials may have a motivational impact on learning. This notion was supported by Badami *et al.* (2011) who explored whether providing a participant with feedback after good compared to bad trials influenced intrinsic motivation (e.g. performing a certain behaviour for one's own satisfaction and enjoyment). Indeed, Badami and colleagues found that individuals' motivation was higher when feedback was given after good trials, as opposed to when it was given after poorer trials. Feedback after good trials also increased perceived competence. Coaches working with adult athletes could enhance learning, intrinsic motivation, and perceived competence by only providing their athletes with knowledge of results after successful performances.

The motivational impact of feedback, as alluded to by Chiviacowsky *et al.* (2009), should not be overlooked. This is because the extent to which feedback provides a positive or negative emotional state directly influences performance among learners and psychological well-being (Hutchinson *et al.*, 2008; Lewthwaite and Wulf, 2010; Wulf *et al.*, 2010) and motivation (Badami *et al.*, 2011).

Hutchinson *et al.* found that feedback which indicated participants had performed above average in comparison to other performers, resulted in increased performance. Enjoyment of the task and increased levels of belief was also higher among athletes who were told they had performed better than average. Lewthwaite and Wulf (2010) also found that social comparison feedback can have more permanent effects on learning. Those who received positive feedback performed better in a transfer test than those who received negative feedback. Furthermore, learners who received information that they were improving at a greater rate in comparison with their peers also performed more effectively than individuals who received information that they were learning at a slower rate than their peers (Wulf *et al.*, 2010). These findings have been attributed to athletes feeling concerned about themselves when they experience negative feedback, which disrupts performance (Wulf and Lewthwaite, 2009; 2010) and feedback energising a performer when they receive positive feedback, which facilitates learning (Kühn *et al.*, 2008).

These aforementioned studies indicate the importance of coaches providing feedback that is positive in nature, because positive feedback influences motivation, which in turn is related to performance and learning. For example, if a particular athlete is improving much more than his peers the coach could mention this to the athlete to enhance his or her motivation, but should refrain from making social comparisons if the performer is below average. With regard to learners that perform below average, coaches should focus on the positive elements of an athlete's performance and provide positive feedback to maximise enjoyment and effort.

Although using feedback may increase levels of motivation (e.g. Badami *et al.*, 2011) other research has found that pep talks given by a coach has no effect on motivation (Gonzalez *et al.*, 2011). Indeed, Gonzalez *et al.* explored the influence of a video clip of a coach giving a pep talk in relation to motivation, inspiration, inspiration to perform, and emotion. The results revealed the pep talk did not have an effect on motivation, but did influence inspiration to perform. However, one should not automatically dispel the influence of coach pep talks on motivation. This is because the movie of a pep talk was given by an actor and so was not specific to the group of players nor did the players know the coach. As such, the athletes would have known that the pep talk was not directed at them. Future research could monitor the effects of pep talks with coaches that athletes are familiar with as opposed to using video clips or pep talks. Furthermore, other research has suggested that athletes need differing amounts of information and emotion according to the situation (Vargas-Tonsing and Guan, 2007). Therefore, the information and emotional content of the pep talk video clip may not have elicited motivational responses.

Enhancing learning via instructions

A goal of coaches is to teach athletes sporting techniques they can use when they play sport. There is evidence to suggest that the instructions a learner receives influences how he or she will perform under high pressure situations (Lam *et al.*, 2009; Law *et al.*, 2003; Liao and Masters, 2001). It has been suggested that when athletes learn a new task they should have as little information as possible about the mechanics of a particular movement. When an athlete learns a movement with little understanding of the mechanics or processes involved, they are said to have engaged in implicit learning. One method to help an athlete learn implicitly involves analogies (Masters, 2000). According to Masters, an analogy refers to an athlete equating a sport skill with something that is similar, yet unrelated. An analogy reduces the number of rules an athlete has about a particular movement to just one biomechanical metaphor relating to the movement.

With this in mind, Liao and Masters (2001) examined the influence of using an analogy on learning a table tennis topspin forehand shot. This involved one group of athletes thinking about a right-angled triangle when they hit a forehand compared to the other group who received 12 instructions. The analogy group had fewer rules, but the performance of the two groups was the same in learning.

However, the analogy group's performance was more resistant to the negative effects of pressure and distractions than the group that received 12 instructions. This finding is relevant for athletes, who have to play sport with many distractions such as coach communications, team-mates, and even an audience, in addition to playing in pressurised competitions. As such, analogy learning may help athletes maintain performance despite experiencing anxiety and having several distractions.

The effectiveness of analogy learning has also been found in another table tennis study using the right-angled triangle analogy of the bat travelling along the hypotenuse of a right handed triangle (Law *et al.*, 2003), and a basketball study (Lam *et al.*, 2009). In the basketball study the players used the analogy of the hand reaching for a biscuit from a biscuit jar. The results of the basketball study found that the analogy group and the group that received coaching allocated equal amounts of attention to the task throughout learning and the trials, but the analogy group had less rules or information about the mechanics of basketball shooting in addition to not having their performance influenced by pressure. Despite some literature indicating that analogy training might have a limited influence on performance during learning (Koedijker *et al.*, 2007), the majority of the evidence indicates that analogy learning helps athletes to maintain performance under pressure (Lam *et al.*, 2009; Law *et al.*, 2003; Liao and Masters 2001). A challenge for coaches when coaching beginners is to generate analogies with the players that they can understand and implement when learning, because this has the potential to help athletes circumvent the negative impact of pressure on performance.

The effects of coach behaviour

Recent research has explored how supportive a coach is in relation to giving his or her athletes choices among adult athletes and the effects of such behaviour (Sheldon and Watson, 2011; Zourbanos *et al.*, 2007; 2010). Other research has examined the factors that influence whether a coach is supportive or controlling (Stebbings *et al.*, 2011). With a sample of 264 adult athletes Sheldon and Watson examined the effects of coach behaviour with regard to varsity and recreational athletes. In particular the authors of this study explored how a supportive versus controlling behavioural approach by the coach influenced the athletes. A supportive coach involved the coach giving his or her athletes as much choice as possible regarding what they do, when they will do it, where they will do it, and with whom (Deci and Ryan, 2000). Conversely, a controlling behaviour involves the coach assigning tasks and activities to athletes without allowing the athletes any input and with little interest in the views of the athlete. Sheldon and Watson found that supportive coaching was associated with increased intrinsic motivation and positive evaluations of team experiences.

Interestingly, there were some key differences between varsity and recreational athletes. The coach behaviour affected the varsity athletes more than it did the recreational athletes, in terms of intrinsic motivation and overall evaluations of the sport team experience. The authors suggested that this is because varsity athletes spend more time with their coach than recreational athletes. Varsity coaches also make decisions that influence a student's scholarship and therefore future life. Furthermore, Sheldon and Watson (2011) also found that the behaviour of the coach predicted objective performance. Athletes from supportive teams had better performance records. This study has implications for the behaviour of coaches, especially those working at higher levels of the game. Coaches should attempt to provide a supportive environment for their athletes and avoid controlling behaviours. As Sheldon and Watson acknowledged, this does not mean coaches have to adopt a softly, softly approach to coaching athletes, rather the challenge is to provide structure and intensity to athletes' training, while at the same time maintaining the connection each athlete has with the practice activities they engage in. The framework provided by Knowles (1995) and his eight principles seem as though they could be very useful in helping coaches achieve a supportive and also productive relationship with their athletes. The research by Sheldon and Watson (2011) is useful in illustrating the effects of a supportive versus controlling behaviour by coaches on athletes.

In addition to coach behaviour being associated with motivation and positive evaluations of team experiences (Sheldon and Watson, 2011), how supportive a coach is also influences self-talk (Zourbanos *et al.*, 2007; 2010). Zourbanos *et al.* (2007) explored the relationship between coach behaviour and statements, and athletes' self-talk. Self-talk refers to the inner dialogue that individuals have regarding thoughts, which influences behaviours and emotions, and may even distract athletes from performing at their best (Meichenbaum, 1977). Zourbanos *et al.* (2007) found that how supportive a coach was predicted whether the coach would give positive statements to athletes, which in turn predicted positive self-talk among the athletes. Interestingly, the relationship between the coach and positive self-talk explained 32 per cent of the variance of athletes' self-talk indicating the key role that coaches play in shaping the self-talk content of athletes. The research of Zourbanos *et al.* (2007) was cross-sectional, so causality cannot be inferred from that study. That is, it is unclear whether positive coach behaviour caused positive self-talk among the athletes, or whether positive self-talk among the athletes caused positive coach behaviour.

Zourbanos *et al.* (2011) published a three-study paper that in part addressed this limitation, with Study 3 of the paper being an experiment to assess the relationship between coach behaviour and self-talk. The experiment study found that positive coaching behaviour directly reduced the amount of negative self-talk, whereas the cross-sectional questionnaire-based studies (Study 2 and Study 3) provided support for the notion that positive coach behaviour is related to positive self-talk whereas negative coach behaviour is related to negative self-talk among athletes. As such, Zourbanos *et al.* (2007) stated that coaches should adopt a supportive stance to the athletes they coach by encouraging athletes, use positive language, give constructive comments, but avoid negative verbalisations such as criticism and irrational comments.

Antecedents of coaching behaviour

Understanding why certain coaches provide a supportive versus controlling type of behaviour may be the key to reducing controlling behaviours among coaches and thus has the potential to improve motivation, positive team experiences, and self-talk (Sheldon and Watson, 2011; Zourbanos *et al.*, 2007; 2011). To this end, Stebbings *et al.* (2011) examined the antecedents of such behaviours among a sample of 443 coaches. It was reported that coaches' psychological well-being predicted coaching behaviour, with the coaches who had higher levels of psychological well-being providing more supportive behaviours and less controlling behaviours. An important implication from this research is that coaches should seek help when they suffer from poor psychological well-being. Providing support to coaches might indirectly improve the supportive behaviours of coaches (Stebbings *et al.*, 2011).

Case study 13.1 Coaching an experienced golfer how to draw the ball using an analogy

Peter is an experienced golf coach who played on the European Tour for 12 years and then took up coaching and has coached winners on the European Tour. He has been coaching Robert for three months, who is 31 years old and has a handicap of five. Peter believes that Robert should learn to shape the ball, such as right to left (known as draw for right-handed players) and left to right (known as a fade for left-handed players) in order to make improvements to his game. Peter discussed his thoughts with Robert, who was very keen to learn this new skill so he can improve his handicap even further. Robert was a former county tennis champion, so Peter used Robert's previous learning experiences by suggesting that a draw is similar to a topspin forehand in tennis, whereas a fade feels like a sliced backhand. This really helped Robert understand the difference between the two. As such, Peter instructed Robert to address the ball with a slightly closed stance, but then once he was in position all he had to do was swing normally and 'roll your wrists' on impact. This analogy of 'roll your wrists' helped Robert not to get too bogged down in trying to manufacture a right to left ball flight and allowed him just to focus on that simple instruction.

Case study reflection

This case study illustrates how a golf coach used an analogy to illustrate how a new skill, drawing the ball, could be taught. In this example, the instructions that the golfer had were very limited other than ensuring his stance was correct and then focusing on the movement in his hands.

Summary points

- Andragogy refers to the understanding of and supporting learning among adults.
- Adults become motivated to learn skills when they experience needs and interests, which they feel that learning will satisfy.
- Adults may learn more effectively if coaches adhere to the eight principles proposed by Knowles (1995).
- Coaches should provide feedback after successful performances of a skill and positive feedback enhances intrinsic motivation.
- Coaches could provide the smallest amount of instruction as possible when coaching adult athletes a new skill.
- Coach behaviour influences motivation and self-talk among adult athletes.

Practice exam questions

1 Discuss how control may influence learning among adults.
2 Describe how the feedback a coach provides influences learning.
3 Discuss how the instructions a coach provides influences learning.
4 How does the behaviour of a coach influence athletes and what factors influence this behaviour? Discuss.
5 What are the key principles of adult learning and how might these differ from child athletes?

Critical thinking questions: applying theory to practice

1 How could a coach incorporate the eight principles proposed by Knowles (1995) within a training session?
2 Describe how a coach could enhance learning feedback within a coaching session.
3 How can a coach enhance the motivation of the adult athletes he or she coaches?
4 How should a coach instruct his or her athletes to maximise learning?
5 Describe how coaches should behave when coaching adult athletes.

14 Coaching athletes with learning disabilities

The purpose of this chapter is to provide coaches with information on the different types of learning disabilities and how this could influence their coaching practice. In particular, this chapter contains information about the following learning disabilities:

- attention-deficit hyperactivity disorder (ADHD);
- language processing disabilities;
- visual-perception disabilities;
- fine motor disabilities.

Additionally, this chapter will also contain information on:

- attitudes of coaches towards athletes with learning disabilities;
- typical behaviour of individuals with learning disabilities;
- managing challenging behaviour whilst coaching;
- increasing compliance;
- coaching principles when coaching athletes with learning disabilities to facilitate learning;
- communicating and instructing athletes;
- facilitating learning.

It should be noted from the outset that a purpose of this chapter is not to provide coaches with information so that they can diagnose the athletes they coach. Indeed, it is imperative that coaches do not use the information they acquire to diagnose any athlete that they coach, because diagnosing learning disabilities can be a long process that requires individuals to sit a variety of tests before a diagnosis can be made. The information presented in this chapter is to help coaches understand different learning disabilities should they work with athletes diagnosed with learning disabilities.

A learning disability refers to a person's neurological handicap that affects his or her ability to understand what he or she is told or reads. Athletes with learning disabilities will also have difficulties remembering what they have been taught (Smith and Strick, 2010). It is thought that learning disabilities may affect up to five per cent of general populations, but Smith and Strick argued that this number may be an underestimation, because many instances of learning disabilities will remain undiagnosed. Some people that are just thought of as being lazy or unmotivated, might be suffering from a learning disability. Within the United States, it has been estimated that 10 per cent of school children have some form of learning disability (U.S. Department of Education, 2007). Beyer *et al.* (2009) stated that although individuals with learning disabilities receive special care in educational settings, there is little information regarding how coaches can help these individuals in sport settings. Indeed, when a person with a learning difficulty is outside of an educational setting such as playing sport or going shopping, he or she may not appear any different from their peers (Friend and Bursuck, 2009), which is why learning disabilities are often referred to as 'invisible' disabilities (Beyer *et al.*, 2008; 2009).

Typical behaviour of individuals with learning disabilities

Coaching athletes with a learning disability may be challenging due to the behaviour they may display. According to Smith and Strick (2010), individuals with a learning difficulty may have:

- *A short attention span:* Athletes with short attention spans are easily distracted from what they are doing, lose interest in what they are doing very quickly, move around from activity to activity very quickly even without completing a task or activity, and cannot pay attention for more than a minute at a time.
- *Difficulty following directions:* An athlete with a learning disability often finds it difficult to follow the instructions and understand instructions from the coach. A consequence of this is that an athlete might continually ask the coach questions, such as: 'What am I meant to do on this drill?', 'Where do I have to pass the ball to?', 'How long are we doing this for?'.
- *Social immaturity:* Athletes with learning disabilities may act younger than their age, which is especially prevalent among children and younger adolescents. Furthermore, athletes with learning disabilities are sometimes unable to process non-verbal information such as facial expressions or body language.
- *Problems with conversation:* Another behaviour common among individuals with learning disabilities is rambling at a rate which others cannot understand. This is often caused by people with learning disabilities struggling to find the right words to express themselves, which often results in the athlete being frustrated.
- *Inflexibility:* Some athletes with a learning disability may act in a stubborn fashion and ignore suggestions or help from a coach, regarding the different ways he or she may complete a task more successfully.
- *Poor planning and organisational skills:* Athletes with a learning disability may have no sense of time and can often be late to training sessions. If a coach gives the athlete a task that has many parts or instructions, the athlete

may struggle to know where to begin due to an inability to break down the task into manageable segments of movements.

- *Absentmindedness:* The athlete with a learning disability often forgets equipment that might be needed for a session or forgets to do additional tasks that a coach might set between sessions, such as additional practice of a certain skill.
- *Clumsiness:* Athletes with learning disabilities may often appear awkward or un-coordinated when they play sport, such as bumping into other athletes, losing control of the ball if they are dribbling in soccer, or struggling to perform certain movements such as catching a ball.
- *Impulsiveness:* Athletes with a learning disability may also interrupt the coach when he or she is talking, have difficulty waiting for their turn on an activity, and voice a variety of observations that may be completely unrelated to the sport they are playing or practising.

Types of learning disabilities

There are four main types of learning disabilities. Before providing information on each learning disability, it should be noted that athletes with learning disabilities may have more than one type of disability (Smith and Strick, 2010).

Attention deficit hyperactivity disorder (ADHD)

ADHD stands for attention deficit hyperactivity disorder and it represents an umbrella term for three forms of ADHD (Rief, 2008), which include:

1   *ADHD-I:* Athletes with ADHD-I have problems with their attention-span, but they are not hyperactive or impulsive. As such, this form of ADHD is often referred to as the pre-dominantly inattentive type.
2   *ADHD-HI:* Individuals with this type of ADHD are hyperactive and can also be very impulsive, so this form of ADHD is labelled the pre-dominantly hyperactive and impulsive type.
3   *ADH*D-C: Most people that are diagnosed with ADHD have the combined type of ADHD, referred to as the combined type. These athletes display significant symptoms of inattention, impulsivity, and hyperactivity.

   For the remainder of this chapter, the term ADHD will be used, rather than distinguishing between ADHD-I, ADHD-HI, and ADHD-C. As such this is inclusive of all three forms of ADHD and is common practice among medical professionals (Rief, 2008).
   According to the American Psychiatric Association (1994; 2000), ADHD is characterised by the following behaviours:

1   The athlete has difficulty sustaining attention, does not listen to instructions, and has problems completing tasks. Indeed, athletes with ADHD tend not to

follow through on instructions and may fail to finish activities such as sprint drills, training matches, or even competitive matches. Athletes afflicted with ADHD may also avoid tasks that require a sustained mental effort.

2 The second main symptom of ADHD is hyperactivity, which includes behaviours such as excessive fidgeting and an inability to remain still in which remaining still would be expected (e.g. sitting in a classroom). Other symptoms include excessive talking, and running about in situations that are inappropriate such as a busy shopping centre or a classroom. Of relevance to sport, individuals with ADHD may find it difficult to listen to instructions and play sport quietly.

3 The third symptom associated with ADHD is impulsivity, with ADHD sufferers having a tendency to interrupt others by butting in to conversations, blurting out answers to questions before the questions have been completed, and difficulties waiting for their turn during sporting activities.

It may be challenging coaching children with ADHD, especially in larger groups due to the behaviour associated with ADHD not being conducive to group work. However, it is important that athletes with learning disabilities such as ADHD have positive experiences of playing sport and thus continue sport participation. This is because previous research has found that children with ADHD who play sport experience more psychological well-being compared to those who do not play sport. Indeed, Kiluk *et al.* (2009) explored the relationship between sport participation and mood among 65 children diagnosed with ADHD. They found that children with ADHD who participated in sport were significantly less likely to report anxiety or depression symptoms. One factor that may determine whether an individual with learning disabilities, such as ADHD, participates in sport is the attitude of the coach towards athletes with learning disabilities (Beyer *et al.*, 2008; Rizzo *et al.*, 1997).

Visual-perception disabilities

Visual perception refers to the ability of the eyes to gather information, interpret that information, and then translate it into visual attributes such as luminance, colour, motion, and depth (Spaniol *et al.*, 2011). A variety of brain structures are involved in making their own contribution to the images that people see (Morozova *et al.*, 2008).Visual perception such as motion and depth are important in sporting contexts in which athletes have to make decisions about the direction in which a ball is moving, the speed at which it is moving, and whether a ball is accelerating or decelerating, in addition to other competitors or team-mates moving. Athletes who have visual-perception disabilities have problems making sense out of what they see. They do not have problems with their eyesight as such, rather the way in which the brain processes visual images (Smith and Strick, 2010).

According to Smith and Strick (2010) there are a number of symptoms that are common among individuals with visual-perception disabilities, relating to writing (e.g. disliking writing and avoiding writing, slow and sloppy writing, and a difficulty in remembering shapes or numbers), reading (e.g. confusing similar looking letters such as 'b' and 'd', frequently losing his or her place when reading, and struggling to comprehend the main ideas and themes), and mathematics (e.g. difficulty memorising mathematic facts and interpreting charts). Due to the nature of sports coaching, which typically does not involve athletes writing or reading, coaches are unlikely to see the people they coach experiencing these difficulties. However, Smith and Strick (2010) reported that there are a number of behaviours associated with visual-perception disabilities that might be apparent when an athlete is playing sport such as:

- confusing left and right;
- poor spatial judgement, so athletes might run into spaces that are simply not big enough for them to run into;
- poor sense of direction;
- difficulty judging speed and distance;
- poor visual imagery, so an athlete might struggle to see what they should do in a training task such as dribbling round cones;
- struggling to understand different strategies that a coach might ask his or her team to perform;
- slow to react to visual information;
- appearing clumsy.

Language-processing disabilities

Language processing refers to an athlete's ability to read, write, and spell (Taylor and Walter, 2003). It has been estimated that language-processing disabilities related to reading, writing, and spelling affect between 5–10 per cent of all children within the United Kingdom (Stein *et al.*, 2000). The common term for such language-processing disabilities is dyslexia. Reid (2009) suggested that defining dyslexia is a very difficult process and even questioned the need for defining this learning disability, because capturing the feelings and experiences of those who have dyslexia in a single statement might be very difficult, if not impossible. There are a variety of definitions regarding dyslexia, but Reid suggests that four main themes emerge from many definitions on dyslexia:

1   Dyslexia is developmental in that individuals who have dyslexia find it very difficult to develop literacy (e.g. writing) and language (e.g. punctuation) related skills. As such, athletes with dyslexia may be poor at understanding the instructions that a coach gives them due to under-developed language capabilities.
2   The central theme of dyslexia is related to literacy, which includes word recognition, spelling, decoding abilities, and writing. Within a sport setting, athletes may struggle to decode a series of instructions, such as the tactics, given by a coach for a soccer match.

3   Different teaching and learning approaches for athletes with dyslexia are required. As such, if a coach knows that an athlete he or she coaches has dyslexia, the coach might want to adjust his or her style (information on coaching styles and facilitating learning with dyslexic athletes and athletes with other learning disabilities is provided in this chapter).

4   There may also be a number of additional secondary factors associated with dyslexia which include problems organising, sequencing events, and motor skill problems. That is, athletes who have dyslexia might be very unorganised in aspects such as turning up to training sessions with the correct kit, have problems comprehending team tactics, or co-ordination problems.

Fine motor skill disabilities

Motor ability refers to a person's ability to perform a specific movement with precision (Haibach *et al.*, 2011). Indeed, Haibach and colleagues distinguished between gross motor skills that involve movement created by large muscle groups such as quadriceps, hamstrings, and biceps and fine motor skills, which are created by much smaller muscle groups. Gross motor skills are generally less precise than fine motor skills.

A person with a fine motor skill disability has problems controlling small muscle groups, such as the muscles in their hand, so although this disability has no impact on the individual's intellectual performance, it interferes with their classroom performance due to problems with writing (Smith and Strick, 2010). This disability also has the potential to impact an athlete's sport performance, especially those sports that involve fine motor skills and hand movements. Indeed, athletes with fine motor skill disabilities may struggle in certain elements of sports such as basketball shooting, putting in golf, and volleying in tennis due to the movements required in these skills.

Attitudes of coaches towards athletes with learning disabilities

Rizzo *et al.* (1997) explored 82 coaches' attitudes towards coaching athletes with mild learning disabilities in youth soccer. They found that the coach's attitude is a critical factor in whether individuals with learning disabilities play sport. However, Rizzo *et al.* also found some particularly concerning results as the coaches seemed to disagree with coaching athletes with learning disabilities, although the attitudes and intentions of the coaches show agreement in coaching athletes with learning disabilities.

The authors tried to explain their findings by suggesting that the coaches did not have the opportunity to state that they were undecided in their beliefs about coaching athletes with learning disabilities, but nevertheless, this is a worrying and concerning finding. Rizzo and colleagues also found that as the perceived competence of the coach increased, the coaches were more willing to coach a team that included athletes with learning disabilities in it. The authors cited experience as a reason why coaches did not feel competent to coach athletes with learning disabilities, because only 38 per cent of the sample had previously coached athletes with learning difficulties and 75% per cent did not have a family member with a learning disability, so they may have had little contact with individuals who have a learning disability.

The notion that coach experience might influence a coach's attitudes towards athletes with learning disabilities was supported by Beyer *et al.* (2008), who: (1) compared the attitudes of coaches with previous experience of coaching athletes with learning disabilities (ADHD) with those coaches who had no experience, and (2) collected information on coaches' experiences of coaching athletes with ADHD with a sample of 221 sport coaches. It was found that coaches who had experiences of coaching athletes with ADHD had a more positive attitude to athletes with this learning disability than those who had no experience at all. These positive attitudes were related to their experiences of coaching athletes with ADHD.

Only 26 per cent of the coaches in the Beyer *et al.* (2008) sample had experience of coaching athletes with ADHD, which is less than previous research by Rizzo *et al.* (1997). Indeed, Beyer *et al.* argued that because the prevalence of children with ADHD is relatively high, up to 10 per cent of all children (U.S. Department of Education, 2007), it is more than likely that most of these coaches will have coached an athlete with a learning disability, but not known about it. As experience appears to be a crucial factor in shaping a coach's attitude towards coaching athletes with learning disabilities, a way to improve coaches' attitudes and then behaviour may be to give coaches hands-on experience of coaching athletes with learning disabilities, such as ADHD or dyslexia (Rizzo *et al.*, 1997). At the very least, there is a need to improve coach education regarding coaching athletes with learning disabilities, which could involve information on understanding the behaviour and recognising the signs of children with learning difficulties and how coaches should behave (Beyer *et al.*, 2008; DePauw and Gavron, 1991).

Coaching principles when coaching athletes with learning disabilities

Stowe (2000) and Reid (2009) have outlined a number of principles that coaches can take on board when they are coaching athletes with disabilities to improve the effectiveness of their coaching. These include:

1 *Involving the athlete:* All athletes, but especially those with learning disabilities, need to be involved in the planning sessions so they take ownership. Generally, athletes with learning disabilities will learn more effectively when they are presented with small amounts of information at a time. It may also important to:
   • Tell the athlete what the coach would like him or her to achieve at the start of each coaching session in addition to asking the athlete what he or she would like to achieve. Some athletes may have problems articulating their goals and when this happens, coaches should reassure athletes that this often happens, but that it is important to have goals.

- When coaching athletes with learning disabilities it is important that coaches tell the athletes how they will be coached and explain the rationale for the activities that will be carried out in each session. Some athletes might want to discuss certain activities or have a preference for some tasks, but not others.
- Coaches should regularly ask athletes how they feel they are progressing with certain skills, which parts of the coaching session are the easiest and which are the most difficult, and the tasks that generate the most learning.

2   *Multisensory coaching:* Athletes with learning disabilities, especially dyslexia, require more interactive learning. Coaches could describe feelings and sights when they perform different tasks and encourage athletes to also describe their own feelings when performing different tasks.

3   *Promote logic and not memory:* Athletes with learning disabilities may have problems with their short- and long-term memory, so coaches should teach strategies that encourage athletes to focus on the logical processes of different movements as opposed to encouraging athletes to use their memory. As such, coaches could encourage athletes to learn movement patterns. For example, if a coach is teaching an athlete how to kick a soccer ball, he or she could emphasise two movements: (1) the back lift and (2) the forward leg motion when teaching this skill.

4   *Present material sequentially:* When coaches are teaching different concepts, especially new skills, they should start from the very beginning and build very slowly. It is important that the coach emphasises the importance of the athlete understanding each principle associated with certain tasks (e.g. transfer of weight in tennis serve, hitting the ball at highest point, following through etc).

5   *Present material in small units:* For athletes with learning disabilities 'less' is usually better, so coaches should present much less information at a time than they would to athletes without learning disabilities. If a lot of material is presented at any one time, it is highly likely that the athlete will forget all of the information that has been presented. The coach can monitor whether he or she is presenting enough or too much information at a time by speaking directly to the athlete to check the pacing of the coaching.

6   *Review:* Training sessions could start with a review of the previous session, in which the coach describes what he or she did and can ask the athlete for his or her thoughts on that session. The coach can then provide information regarding how the current session is related to the previous session, because one of the most important aspects of learning is making connections between different tasks. Athletes with learning disabilities may struggle to comprehend how different tasks or training sessions are related to each other.

7   *Provide more opportunities for practice:* Athletes with learning disabilities may need more opportunities for reinforcement than other athletes, so coaches should provide athletes with lots of opportunities to practise what they have learned.

8   *Individualise instruction:* Athletes with learning disabilities often have very different needs. Coaches should bear this in mind and could, for

example, encourage athletes to work at their own pace and incorporate this individualised coaching within their coaching plans. Furthermore, it is imperative that coaches only ask athletes to perform tasks that they know they are capable of achieving to avoid embarrassing athletes who are not successful.

Increasing compliance

Athletes with learning disorders such as ADHD are often non-compliant to the instructions they receive (Gudjonsson and Sigurdsson, 2010; Singh *et al.*, 2010). This might mean that coaching athletes with learning disorders such as ADHD is problematic for coaches, especially when coaching larger groups. One method that coaches can employ to increase compliance is to make prolonged eye contact with the athlete (Kapalka, 2004). Indeed, if coaches maintain eye contact for a period of around 20 seconds after giving an athlete some instructions, this gives the athlete more time to process what has been asked of them and whether they want to comply or non-comply.

In addition to maintaining eye contact when providing instructions, Beyer *et al.* (2009) stated that coaches should stand a little closer than normal prior to giving the instruction. The coach can also ask the athlete to clarify that he or she has understood the instructions that they have been given.

Managing disruptive behaviour

Research from non-sport domains has found that athletes diagnosed with learning disorders, including ADHD, perform and behave at their best when they receive immediate and frequent feedback (Fiore *et al.*, 1993). Praise and token reinforcements can also improve behaviour (O'Leary and O'Leary, 1977). Based on these research findings, Anhalt *et al.* (1998) developed a behavioural management programme that can be adapted for coaches in sport settings. The programme includes consequences for appropriate and inappropriate behaviour and peer-mediated interventions.

Consequences for appropriate behaviour

1   *Labelled praises:* A labelled praise refers to positive feedback in response to a specific behaviour, as opposed to praises that are unlabelled and do not specify which behaviour is being praised (Hembree-Kigin and McNeil, 1995). Within a sporting context, the comment 'Excellent pass Shawn, the pace of the pass and the direction were brilliant' is an example of a labelled praise, whereas 'Good pass, Shawn' is an example of an unlabelled praise. Coaches are encouraged to provide as many labelled praises as possible and refrain from giving unlabelled praises. This is because praise has been shown to increase the amount of effort individuals put on a task and improve behaviour among disruptive individuals (Kirby and Shields, 1972).

2 *Happy face or point rewards:* When coaching children with learning disorders, coaches can reward behaviours such as adhering to a task and working well with other athletes. The coach would award the happy faces or points at the end of each training session and award happy faces for each compliant behaviour observed. It is crucial that the coach explains why he or she has awarded each happy face. Although some research has indicated that labelled praises are effective in improving disruptive behaviour (e.g. Kirby and Shields, 1972), other research has suggested that behaviour and performance can be further enhanced by including positive consequences in addition to labelled praise, such as happy faces (Pfiffner and Barkley, 1990).

3 *Reward activity:* Coaches could reward athletes who have accumulated the most points or happy faces with the choice of taking part in a reward activity. The reward activity should be a different activity to the tasks within the training session and should be fun. For example, within swimming, a coach might have the reward of allowing swimmers with more happy faces than sad faces to play with inflatable toys or balls in the swimming pool. In an hour's training session coaches could have three to four reward breaks, as frequent breaks appear to enhance behaviour (Sulzer-Azaroff and Mayer, 1991). After each break each athlete starts from zero with regard to happy faces or points so each athlete has a renewed opportunity to experience the reward activity.

Consequences for inappropriate behaviour

1 *Sad face warning signal:* A coach can give a sad face warning signal if the children behave in a manner that disrupts the coaching sessions. When the coach issues the warning he or she would call out the athlete's name and hold up two fingers, which represent the choices the athlete has. The coach would say something along the lines of 'You have two choices. You can either improve your behaviour and you will not receive a sad face, or you can receive a sad face. It is your choice'. Prior to each session, the athletes are told about the two choice statements a coach will make and the reasons for these statements. It is imperative that when coaches give the warning, they do so causing minimal attention and are as quiet as possible. Negative attention often reinforces an athlete's poor behaviour (Zentall and Zentall, 1983).

2 *Awarding of sad faces:* Athletes who continue to behave poorly following the warning signal will be given a sad face or have points taken off their score if that system is being used. It is imperative that the voice of the coach remains calm and constant when the sad face is given to minimise the attention given to children for negative behaviour. It has been found that mild punishment behaviours along with rewards tend to improve on-task behaviours and decreases in disruptive behaviours of children (Abramowitz and O'Leary, 1991).

3 *Losing the privilege of the reward activity:* Athletes who behave in an inappropriate manner are not allowed to take part in the reward activity. DuPaul and Stoner (1994) found that removing privileges can be very

effective in increasing target behaviours. The coach sets a clean slate of happy and sad faces after each reward activity, so each athlete knows he or she has a chance of doing the reward activity if they behave well in the next phase of the session.

Peer-mediated interventions

Anhalt *et al.* (1998) suggested that individuals can be put into groups, with these groups receiving awards for working together. This may be advantageous in sport settings, in which a coach might be coaching a number of athletes or because the coach wants to practise teamwork skills for team sports such as soccer or rugby. In addition to grouping athletes being more suitable in coaching sessions, having athletes work together in what was termed a 'cooperative learning environment' has been found to enhance self-esteem, interpersonal co-operation, tolerance of others, and social acceptance (Furman and Gavin, 1989). As such, the coach would separate athletes into different groups and would administer the consequences for appropriate and inappropriate behaviour at the group level.

In addition to providing rewards, coaches could identify a different leader every coaching session. The coach would inform the leader that it is his or her responsibility to motivate the group to follow the rules and behave appropriately. The leader also has the privilege of using the warning signal, but only the coach can award unhappy faces.

Summary points

- Athletes with learning difficulties may have a short attention span, have difficulty following instructions, be socially immature, have problems conversing with others, and might be poor at planning.
- There are four main types of learning disabilities, which are ADHD, visual-perception, language-processing (also known as dyslexia) and fine motor disabilities.
- Coaches who have limited experiences or no experience of coaching athletes with learning disabilities may have a negative attitude towards coaching athletes with learning disabilities.
- Coaches who are more competent are more likely to have a positive attitude towards coaching athletes with learning disabilities.
- Providing coaches with guidance on how to coach athletes with learning disabilities and behaviour management techniques may enhance an coaches's attitude towards coaching athletes with learning disabilities.
- Coaches should adapt their coaching when working with athletes with learning disabilities to maximise learning.
- There are a variety of techniques to increase compliance and manage disruptive behaviour that coaches can use.

Case study 14.1 Experiences of managing challenging behaviour

The following case study represents the dialogue between Jon, a 24-year-old rugby union coach and a very talented rugby union player called Chris. Jon is a volunteer coach and has coached Chris for nearly one season. Chris is eight years old, and has been playing rugby since he was four years of age. Within the last six months Chris was diagnosed with ADHD and although he is very keen to play rugby and learn, he can be quite disruptive, rude, and violent to other players. The dialogue in this case study starts after Chris has been very disruptive in a training session when Jon had been giving out instructions. He spoke to Chris in a calm manner so the other players could not hear what he had said:

Jon: Chris, I know you know what you have to do in these drills, but other players don't know what to do. If you talk to other players when I am speaking they won't understand. You have two choices, you can either listen and not receive some minus penalty points, or you can choose not to listen and receive minus penalty points [Jon made a conscious effort to hold a prolonged eye contact with Chris].

Chris: Shane was the person who started talking to me and I wasn't doing anything coach.

Jon: Chris, you have two choices: you can either listen to me and not receive minus penalty points or not listen and you will receive some penalty points.

Chris: OK I will listen.

However, within two minutes of the warning Chris continued to be disruptive and would not listen and the following dialogue ensued.

Jon: Chris, two minutes ago I gave you two choices and you have continued not listening. I am therefore giving you a minus point. Your score for the session is –1.

Within the next 10 minutes Chris showed some exemplary behaviour by helping a team-mate out who was struggling after he missed a tackle by encouraging him and saying what he did wrong to which Jon said:

Jon: Chris, that was excellent that you encouraged your team-mate after he made a mistake and then gave him some advice. I am awarding you one point for each of those things, so you are now on plus one.

Case study reflection

Coaching athletes with learning disabilities might be very challenging, and a coach may spend more time monitoring and managing the behaviour of these athletes than other athletes.

Practice exam questions

1   Compare and contrast the four main types of learning disabilities.
2   Describe the different types of ADHD and the behaviours associated with each type.
3   Describe how a coach's attitude might be influenced by whether an athlete has a learning disability or not.
4   Describe the principles that coaches could adhere to when coaching athletes with learning disabilities.
5   Describe the behaviours that athletes with learning disabilities might display.

Critical thinking questions: applying theory to practice

1   Describe how coaching training programmes could improve the attitudes of coaches towards athletes with learning difficulties.
2   Compare and contrast coaching instructions among athletes with learning disabilities and athletes who do not have learning disabilities.
3   What are the advantages and disadvantages of awarding happy and unhappy faces in coaching sessions?
4   David has ADHD and is very disruptive. Describe how a coach could manage David's challenging behaviours.
5   Describe how a peer-mediated intervention could be incorporated into a training session with athletes with learning disabilities.

Part V
Relationships and support

15 The coach–athlete relationship

The purpose of this chapter is to provide coaches with information on the complexities of the relationships with their athletes and factors that influence this relationship. In particular this chapter will provide information on:

- the definition of the coach–athlete relationship;
- the importance of the coach–athlete relationship;
- the different types of coach–athlete relationships;
- conceptualising the coach–athlete relationship;
- factors that influence the coach–athlete relationship;
- how coaches can improve the coach–athlete relationship;
- how a coach can manage conflict in the coach–athlete relationship.

Definition of the coach–athlete relationship

Jowett and colleagues (Jowett and Cockerill, 2002, 2003; Jowett and Poczwardowski, 2007) defined the coach–athlete relationship as any situation in which a coach's and athlete's thoughts, feelings and behaviours are interrelated. According to Jowett and colleagues this relationship is a dynamic process, which would imply that both the coach and the athlete can influence the quality of this relationship. Additionally, the coach–athlete relationship is thought to change over time and can thus be viewed as a process (Jowett and Poczwardowski, 2007).

How athletes and coaches behave, think, and feel shape the coach–athlete relationship. This is because thoughts and feelings influence behaviours between athletes and coaches. As such, how a coach or athlete behaves to one another influences how the other will respond in return (Jowett and Poczwardowski, 2007). For example, if a coach believes strongly in the ability of his or her player, he or she will have positive thoughts and feelings about the coaching sessions that take place. This is likely to influence the coach's behaviours as he or she will be enthusiastic about training and helping the player reach his or her full potential. In response to this positive behaviour from the coach, the athlete will trust his or her coach and behave in a manner that is conducive to improving and maximising performance. This is an example of a positive coach–athlete relationship, but if the coach did not believe in the player and had negative opinions about the player, he or she may behave negatively towards the player and the player might respond in a negative fashion by not trusting his or her coach and putting in less effort (Jowett and Poczwardowski, 2007).

The importance of the coach–athlete relationship

Jowett (2005) suggested that the coach–athlete relationship is important because it:

1   Facilitates athletic excellence. In an optimal coach–athlete relationship the athlete will reach his or her full potential by working with his or her coach.
2   Facilitates personal growth among both the athlete and the coach, as both the coach and the athlete can grow as people due to this relationship.

Describing the coach–athlete relationship

Although it has been implied in this chapter that coach–athlete relationships are either positive or negative, this classification is perhaps too simplistic. Jowett (2005) explored different types of coach–athlete relationships and suggested that every coach–athlete relationship contains two key elements: (1) successfulness and (2) effectiveness.

1   *Successfulness*: The successfulness element of the coach–athlete relationship refers to the degree in which the athlete is successful. This is relative, as success for one athlete might be winning a gold medal, whereas success for another athlete might be making his or her school team, but the key ingredient is that the coach and the athlete perceive that there is an element of success.
2   *Effectiveness:* The effectiveness of the coach–athlete relationship refers to the degree in which the athlete and the coach get on with each other. For example, an effective relationship would include trust, empathy, respect, and closeness between the coach and the athlete. Conversely, an ineffective relationship would be used to describe a relationship between the coach and the athlete in which there is no respect, no trust, and in which the coach and the athlete do not get on.

Based on the notion of success and effectiveness in the coach–athlete relationship, Jowett (2005) argued that there are four types of coach–athlete relationships: effective and successful, effective and unsuccessful, ineffective and successful, and ineffective and unsuccessful:

•   *Effective and successful:* Effective and successful coach–athlete relationships occur when the coach and the athlete get on very well and trust each other implicitly. They also have lots of success in terms of the results achieved by the athlete, whether that is winning events or selection into national teams. An example of an effective and successful relationship would be a coach who spends lots of time working with a tennis player and develops trust and a great friendship with the player over a number of years. The player performs well and even wins on professional tour. The relationship is effective because the coach and the athlete get on well together, which enhances well-being and it is successful in that the tennis player has achieved one of his or her main goals, such as playing and winning on tour.

- *Effective and unsuccessful:* A relationship in which the coach and the athlete get on very well and trust each other, but have limited sporting success is described as an effective and unsuccessful relationship. An example of this type of relationship would be a coach who gets on really well with a badminton player, but the badminton player does not fulfil his or her potential at badminton competitions.
- *Ineffective and successful:* A relationship in which the player and coach do not get on or trust each other, but have an element of success in terms of what the player achieves, is described as an ineffective and successful coach–athlete relationship. Even though there is performance success in this relationship in terms of competition results and improvements made, there might be arguments between the player and coach. This can result in the coach and athlete disliking each other. An example would be a coach and player who do not get on at all in terms of disagreeing on how they feel performance can be maximised, with the player taking part in training sessions that he or she does not value. However, the player performs well in competition despite not valuing his or her training sessions.
- *Ineffective and unsuccessful:* If a coach has a very poor relationship with his or her athlete that yields poor results, it can be classified as an ineffective and unsuccessful coach–athlete relationship. An example would be a coach and a player who don't get on well together, find it difficult to open up, and have poor competitive results.

Conceptualising the coach–athlete relationship

Several researchers have conceptualised the coach–athlete relationship, such as Jowett (Jowett, 2005; Jowett *et al.*, 2005). She suggested that the coach–athlete relationship consists of 3+1 Cs: closeness, commitment, complementarity, and co-orientation. LaVoi (2004) suggested that the coach–athlete relationship has four main components: authenticity, engagement, empowerment, and ability, whereas Poczwardowski (Poczwardowski, 1997; Poczwardowski *et al.*, 2002) conceptualised the coach–athlete relationship as a recurring pattern of mutual care between the athlete and the coach.

3+1 Cs conceptualisation of the coach–athlete relationship

- *Closeness:* Closeness refers to the relationship between the athlete and the coach. If an athlete has a close relationship with his or her coach, it would be characterised by the athlete and coach valuing one another, supporting each other, in addition to caring for the well-being of each other (Hellstedt, 1987). On the other hand, coach–athlete relationships that lack the quality of closeness, involve the athlete and coach not caring, valuing, or supporting each other.

- *Commitment:* Jowett and Poczwardowski (2007) defined commitment as the coach's and athlete's intent to maintain the relationship. As such the athlete will want to continue working with his or her coach. There will be intent from both parties to maximise successful outcomes, such as winning competitions and achieving selection onto different teams.
- *Complementarity:* Complementarity refers to how the behaviours between the coach and the athlete correspond to each other. For example, a coach–athlete relationship would be high in complementarity if the coach acts in a caring and encouraging manner, which is reciprocated by the athlete who also acts in a caring manner and is enthusiastic about training sessions with the coach.
- *Co-orientation:* Co-orientation between the athlete and the coach occurs when the athlete and the coach have established a common ground on the views that they both hold, such as how they think it might be best for the athlete to progress. This common ground is achieved via the coach and athlete discussing their views regarding future accomplishment goals (Clark and Reiss, 1988; Jowett and Meek, 2000).

LaVoi's conceptual model

LaVoi's (2007) conceptual model of the coach–athlete relationship centres on the need for human beings to belong and have close relationships with other individuals. It was also argued that athletes will achieve more growth and satisfaction when they have a close relationship with their coach (Jowett and Poczwardowski, 2007). There are four component parts in this conceptualisation:

- *Authenticity:* This refers to how genuinely the athlete and coach expresses himself or herself in the coach–athlete relationship. The more authentic the expression, the closer the relationship will be.
- *Engagement:* Engagement in the coach–athlete relationship is measured by how committed the coach and the athlete are towards their working relationship and how responsive they are to one another. *Empowerment:* A coach–athlete relationship would be high in empowerment if both the coach and the athlete encourage and inspire each other to be active. The coach and the athlete will also have equal input within the relationship. *Ability:* Ability, in LaVoi's (2007) conceptualisation, refers to the coach and the athlete's capacity to deal with any conflict that might occur.

Poczwardowski's conceptual model

Poczwardowski and colleagues (Poczwardowski, 1997; Poczwardowski *et al.*, 2002) suggested that the coach–athlete relationship relates to the constantly re-occurring pattern of mutual behaviour between a coach and an athlete. The relationship involves technical conversations and affective conversations about each others' needs. As such, Poczwardowski (1997) stated that the coach–athlete relationship involves both sport and non-sporting interactions between the coach and the athlete.

Summary of conceptual models

The conceptual model of the coach–athlete relationship that dominates peer-reviewed activity within the sport psychology literature is that of the 3+1 Cs, proposed by Jowett (Jowett, 2005; Jowett *et al.*, 2005).

Factors that influence the coach–athlete relationship

Researchers have identified a number of factors that appear to influence the coach–athlete relationship (Jackson *et al.*, 2011; Lafrenière *et al.*, 2011; Lorimer and Jowett, 2009). For example, Jackson and colleagues explored how personality influenced the commitment and trust among 91 athletes and their coaches. Interestingly, the more dissimilar the athlete and coach were in terms of extraversion (e.g. outgoing) and openness (e.g. inventiveness) the less committed and close they were.

Lafrenière *et al.* (2011) explored how coaches' passion for coaching influenced the athlete's perception of the coach–athlete relationship. They found that harmonious passion (e.g. a strong desire to take part in activity that one loves) predicted whether a coach would support his or her athletes to make their own choices, leading to a high quality coach–athlete relationship, and the athlete being happier. Conversely, obsessive passion predicted controlling behaviours from the coach, which resulted in a low-quality relationship.

Lorimer and Jowett (2009) explored empathetic accuracy (e.g. the degree to which the coach and the athlete could accurately perceive the psychological condition of one another) and meta-perspective (e.g. how the coach thinks the athlete views the relationship or how the athlete thinks the coach views the relationship), among 121 athletes and coaches. Athletes and coaches who had a positive meta-perspective, such as thinking the other partner is trusting, were more able to accurately predict the psychological condition of the other. In turn, the relationships in which the coach and the athlete could accurately predict the psychological condition of the other were rated as being more satisfying.

How coaches can improve the coach–athlete relationship

Sport psychology researchers such as Mageau and Vallerand (2003) and Rhind and Jowett (2010) have provided suggestions regarding how a coach can improve or maintain the relationship with his or her athlete. Mageau and Vallerand outlined the following strategies:

- *Give your player or players some choice – within reason*: Coaches could give their players choices, although it is important to impose rules and limits within the choices.
- *Provide a rationale*: It is important that the coach explains why he or she would like a player to work on certain aspects (e.g. conditioning or technical skills).
- *Acknowledge feelings*: A coach can empathise with a player by demonstrating that he or she knows how a player is feeling, by acknowledging the player's feelings.
- *Give players the chance to show their initiative*: Coaches could also allow players to use their own initiative by asking them what they would like to work on and then how they would go about doing it, or what tactics they would like to play.
- *Provide feedback that is informative and non-controlling*: Feedback from the coach should allow the athlete to improve and thus be constructive, but non-controlling. Controlling feedback is when the coach uses his or her comments to control the athlete's behaviour. For example 'Your passing was excellent today, if you carry on passing like that in the future I will pick you in every match' is an example of controlling feedback, whereas 'The direction and the weight of your passes was spot on' places more emphasis on information and is not controlling.
- *Avoid ego-oriented behaviour*: It is important that coaches do not compare their players with other players, because this could lead to frustration on the part of the player.

Alternatively, Rhind and Jowett (2010) proposed the COMPASS model of maintenance strategies within the coach–athlete relationship. The acronym COMPASS stands for:

- *Conflict management:* Conflict management includes proactive strategies such as the coach taking steps to avoid conflict in the future, by clarifying his or her expression. Also included in conflict management are re-active strategies, such as the coach cooperating with the athlete during discussions about any disagreements, to repair conflict that has already ensued.
- *Openness:* This strategy refers to the coach being open about his or her feelings and also encouraging the athlete to do the same. As such, the coach could encourage the athlete to talk about how he or she is feeling.
- *Motivation:* The coach can show the athlete that he or she is motivated to continue working with the athlete and helping the athlete develop. The coach can also demonstrate that he or she has the knowledge, skills, and also the coaching ability to help the athlete achieve his or her goals.
- *Positivity:* The coach can demonstrate a positive attitude to the player by adapting his or her behaviour to suit the needs of the player and also show fairness with the player.
- *Advice:* Coaches can maintain the coach–athlete relationship by giving the athlete advice on problems the player may be encountering. This advice may

be sport-based advice on technical skills and advice on non-sporting matters such as relationships.

- *Support:* A coach can demonstrate support to the athlete by letting the athlete know of this support and being available for the athlete to discuss both sport and non-sporting matters.
- *Social networks:* The relationship between the coach and the athlete can be improved or maintained by the athlete and coach spending time with each other away from the sporting environment.

Both Mageau and Vallerand (2003) and Rhind and Jowett (2010) have outlined some excellent strategies that coaches can adhere to in order to maintain or improve their relationships with athletes.

Conflict in the coach–athlete relationship and what to do when it happens

Even though a coach might adhere to the strategies proposed by Mageau and Vallerand (2003) and Rhind and Jowett (2010), conflict may still occur. LaVoi (2004) suggested that attitude, work rate, commitment, rule breaking, and undermining team cohesion are factors that irritate coaches and might be the source of conflict among a coach and a player. If conflict does occur between the coach and the player, Rahim (2002) suggested a number of strategies that the coach can engage in to manage the conflict. These strategies include:

- *Integrating*: The coach and the player have an open and honest exchange regarding their views. It is hoped that this process will allow the coach and the athlete to identify alternative solutions to the issues that are causing conflicts (e.g. training schedules or technical aspects of performance).
- *Compromising*: The coach and the athlete can make a compromise by agreeing that they are wrong and listen to the desires of each other. For example, a tennis coach might want a player to spend more time working on her serve, but the tennis player does not want to. In this instance the compromise could be the player and coach agreeing that the player will work on her serve, but only spend half the amount of time doing this that the coach had wanted.
- *Obliging*: The coach could attempt to minimise different points of view between himself or herself and the athlete through discussion.
- *Dominating*: A coach can dominate, by telling the player what he or she has to do.
- *Avoiding*: In certain circumstances, the coach might avoid confronting the player about the issues that cause conflict, and let the conflict persist.

These examples of conflict management provided by Rahim (2002) are very different in nature. Ideally, coaches would want to avoid either dominating or avoiding approaches to conflict management, because these have the potential to be the most disruptive.

Case study 15.1 Managing conflict in the coach–athlete relationship

Mickey is a 29-year-old golf coach who had an all-time high world ranking of 155. He coaches a variety of high-level players, but has been having some problems with Lucy, a player Mickey has coached since she was 14 years old. She is now 16 years old and plays for England. Over the last six months Mickey and Lucy's relationship has become very strained, yet her performances in the last six months are better than they have ever been and she won a national age group championship during this time. They disagree on how Lucy can take her game forward, what training activities they do, and even who Lucy trains with. Mickey felt as though every idea he suggested could result in argument and believed the problems started when Lucy started receiving coaching with the England setup. As such, Mickey feels the only way forward is to resolve the conflict or face the possibility of terminating their relationship. Mickey knows that he is a strong character and can sometimes be difficult to deal with. He attempted to resolve the conflict by arranging a meeting with Lucy, so they could discuss their views. In this meeting, Mickey encouraged Lucy to be honest at all times and wanted to hear her views regarding what aspects of training she felt were beneficial, what aspects she did not like, how she saw their relationship moving on, and what he could do differently. Following this, Mickey gave his viewpoints. As it turned out, Lucy and Mickey had too many differing views that could not be resolved. For example, Lucy wanted to spend more time working on the take-back phase of the golf swing based on the advice she had received from England coaches, whereas Mickey said she needed to work on her impact position to make more improvements. In the end Mickey and Lucy decided to terminate their relationship, because they had differing opinions on what to work on next.

Case study reflection

Coaches may be very frustrated and upset if a player no longer believes in the advice that is given to him or her and ultimately decides to visit another coach. This is something that happens across all sports. Coaches have to accept that it will happen, especially in sports where the athlete has power over who he or she is coached by.

Summary points

- The coach–athlete relationship is any situation in which a coach's and athlete's thoughts, feelings, and behaviours are interrelated.
- Athletic excellence and personal growth can be facilitated by the coach–athlete relationship.

- There are two key elements to the coach–athlete relationship: (1) successfulness and (2) effectiveness.
- Closeness, commitment, complementarity, and co-orientation are key components of the coach–athlete relationship.
- Coaches can improve the coach–athlete relationship by giving their athletes choices and rationale, acknowledging feelings of athletes, and providing athletes with non-controlling feedback.
- The COMPASS model can be implemented by coaches to maintain a coach–athlete relationship.
- Conflict in the coach–athlete relationship will arise from time to time. There are a number of steps that coaches can take to manage any conflict.

Practice exam questions

1   What is the coach–athlete relationship, and why is it important that coaches understand more about this relationship?
2   Describe the different types of coach–athlete relationship, with regard to effectiveness and successfulness and the implications.
3   Compare and contrast Jowett's (2005), LaVoi's (2007) and Poczwardowski's (1997) conceptualisations of the coach–athlete relationship.
4   Compare and contrast Mageau and Vallerand's (2003) and Rhind and Jowett's (2010) models regarding improving the coach–athlete relationship.
5   Discuss the factors that influence the coach–athlete relationship.

Critical thinking questions: applying theory to practice

1   Describe how a coach can provide an athlete with more choice and what this would entail in training sessions.
2   Describe and provide examples of controlling and non-controlling feedback and comment upon the implications of providing different types of feedback.
3   How can coaches show athletes that they are motivated to working with an athlete?
4   Describe how a coach could integrate with his or her player to manage conflict.
5   What are the implications of a coach and athlete avoiding conflict management?

16 Understanding and building team cohesion

This chapter provides information on the factors that coaches could consider when they coach team sports such as soccer, rugby, and hockey. Coaches who coach individual sports, but in team settings such as golf or tennis teams may also find this chapter useful. As such, information is provided on:

- defining team cohesion;
- conceptual model of team cohesion;
- characteristics of team cohesion;
- the importance of cohesion;
- the effects of coach behaviour and leadership on team cohesion;
- team-building strategies;
- factors to consider when planning team building interventions.

Defining team cohesion

A widely used definition indicates that team cohesion is 'a dynamic process which is reflected in the tendency for a group to stick together and remain united in the pursuit of its instrumental objectives and/or for the satisfaction of member affective needs' (Carron *et al.*, 1998: 213).

Conceptual model of team cohesion

The definition of team cohesion provided by Carron *et al.* (1998) is related to the proposed four-dimensional conceptual model of team cohesion, provided by Carron *et al.* (1985). As such, Carron *et al.* (1985) suggested that each athlete, who is a member of a team, holds two specific perceptions about the team he or she plays in. These are referred to as individual attractions to the group and group integration:

- *Individual attractions to the group (ATG):* This part of the model holds that individuals have perceptions regarding why others (e.g. a coach or captain) might be motivated to keep them in their team, in addition to the athlete's own personal feelings about the team he or she plays for.

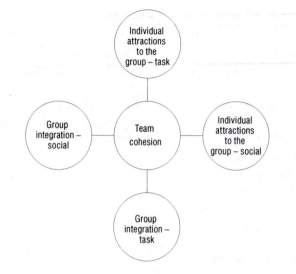

Figure 16.1 The four-dimensional model of group cohesion

- *Group integration (GI):* Group integration refers to the athlete's perceptions regarding the bonding, closeness, and similarity within a particular team.

The model proposed by Carron *et al.* (1985) is four-dimensional because both ATG and GI also have a component of either social cohesion (S) or task cohesion (T), based on the perceptions of each athlete in a team. Task cohesion refers to the extent to which team-mates work in unison together to achieve their team's overall goal. Some athletes might not be motivated to achieve team objectives (e.g. winning league, reducing number of suspensions in a season, or avoiding relegation). Social cohesion refers to an athlete's perceptions regarding how well he or she gets on with and likes his or her team-mates. As such, group cohesiveness can be represented as four different manifestations (see Figure 16.1), which would be (Carron *et al.*, 2007):

1   *Individual attractions to the group – task (ATG-T):* A team that has athletes that score highly in ATG-T would feel strongly about playing for their team and are highly motivated to work hard in order to achieve team goals.
2   *Individual attractions to the group – social (AGT-S):* Teams that have athletes who score highly on AGT-S would be characterised by athletes who feel a strong bond within the team with many members being friends.
3   *Group integration – task (GI-T):* Athletes within teams who score highly on GI-T would feel close to their team-mates and motivated to achieve common team goals, which would be reflected in their behaviour.
4   *Group integration – social (GI-S):* Teams with athletes that score highly on GI-S would have athletes that feel a close bond and friendships, who are keen to maintain the level of friendship and closeness that they have.

Table 16.1 Factors that influence task and social cohesion

Factors that influenced task cohesion	Factors that influenced social cohesion
Athletes working together	Athletes knowing one another
Effective communication among team-mates	Being friends and getting along with other athletes
Bonding between team-mates	Feeling well supported
Team members understanding their team-mates' abilities	Engaging in non-sport activities with each other
Athletes being unselfish	Not having any conflict or cliques
Athletes having experiences of attempting to achieve goals	
Being led well by other team-mates	
Being in a team full of committed athletes	
Having parity in terms of status with other team-mates	
Having a good coach–team relationship	

Characteristics of team cohesion

Carron *et al.* (1998) suggested that team cohesion is multi-dimensional, instrumental, and affective. First, Carron and colleagues stated that team cohesion is multi-dimensional as it has four dimensions (e.g. ATG-T, AGT-S, GI-T, GI-S). Second, team cohesion was referred to as being dynamic, because each dimension can influence the other and it can change on a regular basis. Third, athletes in teams do not stay close or form bonds for the sake of staying close or have tighter bonds amongst one another, all teams need a specific purpose to stay together. Fourth, team cohesion has an affective element, because being in a team can be very pleasing and satisfying to individual athletes among a team. From a coaching perspective, coaches should understand the multidimensionality of teams, accept that cohesion is a dynamic process, give athletes a reason to stick together, and ensure the athletes experience positive emotions from being part of a team by making being in a team enjoyable and fun.

Research by Eys *et al.* (2009), extended the findings of Carron *et al.* (1998) by exploring the perceptions of cohesion among a sample of 56 youth team sport athletes. The authors identified 10 categories that influenced task cohesion and seven categories that reflected social cohesion (see Table 16.1).

The importance of team cohesion

It is imperative that coaches have an understanding of why this construct is important when coaching teams. Team cohesion has been associated with a variety of desirable outcomes such as:

1   *Enhanced team performance:* A meta-analysis containing 46 studies, by Carron *et al.* (2002), revealed that there was an effect size of .66 for the relationship between team cohesiveness and team performance. This finding indicates that team cohesion has moderate to large effect on sporting performance. Interestingly, Carron and colleagues also explored the relationship between social cohesion and performance in addition to the task cohesion and performance. Social cohesion had an effect size of .70, whereas task cohesion had an effect size of .61 indicating that both are strongly related to the sporting performance of teams.

2   *Reduced anxiety for team members:* Prapavessis and Carron (1996) reported that athletes who reported higher levels of team cohesion experienced less cognitive anxiety (e.g. worry) than athletes with lower levels of team cohesion. Furthermore, Eys *et al.* (2003) also explored whether team cohesion was related to perceptions of anxiety and found that athletes who perceived their anxiety as facilitative reported higher levels of ATG-T and GI-T. Although whether anxiety can ever be facilitative is questionable (Burton, 1998; Burton and Naylor, 1997).

3   *Enhanced mood among team members:* Terry *et al.* (1996) explored the relationship between team cohesion and mood among a sample of rugby players, rowers, and netballers. The results of this study revealed that athletes who played in teams that were more cohesive reported lower levels of depression, anger, and tension, but higher levels of vigour compared to athletes who perceived they were in less cohesive teams.

4   *Increased peer efficacy:* Marcos *et al.* (2010) explored the relationship between team cohesion and perceived peer efficacy among athletes and coaches participating in semi-professional soccer and basketball. Peer efficacy was conceptualised as each athlete's belief about their team-mates' abilities to be successful in completing a task (Lent and Lopez, 2002). Athletes who reported higher levels of cohesion also reported higher levels of peer efficacy.

5   *Decreased jealousy:* Research has suggested that team cohesion is negatively associated with jealousy, which refers to an athlete wanting to be another person or wanting what another athlete has (Kamphoff *et al.*, 2005).

6   *Increased effort:* Bray and Whaley (2001) explored the amount of effort exerted by basketball players along with team cohesion. They found that athletes in more cohesive teams exerted more effort than those who felt their teams lacked cohesiveness.

There are a number of benefits from higher levels of cohesion, relating to increased team performance, reduced anxiety among team members, and even increased effort among basketball players. However, coaches should be aware of some of the pitfalls associated with highly cohesive teams. For example, in Hardy *et al.*'s (2005) sample, 56 per cent of athletes reported there were disadvantages of being in a highly cohesive team such as problematic communication with other athletes and the potential for social isolation for athletes who are not in the main group. Furthermore, 31 per cent of athletes reported disadvantages of high task cohesion such as communication problems, increased pressure, and reduced personal enjoyment.

However, the benefits of highly cohesive teams outweigh the negatives (Carron *et al.*, 2007). Coaches should be aware of the negative consequences of coaching highly cohesive teams and take steps to ensure that athletes do not feel isolated, more pressure, or enjoy playing sport less.

The effects of coach behaviour and leadership on team cohesion

Researchers have explored the relationship between coach behaviours and team cohesion. Westre and Weiss (1991) explored whether team cohesion was related to coach leadership style and coach behaviour, among a sample of 163 athletes. They found a significant relationship between coach behaviour and cohesion. In particular, higher frequencies of instruction by the coach, social support from the coach, a democratic style of leadership in which athletes had their say over decisions, and positive feedback were associated with more task cohesion among athletes. Based on these findings, Westre and Weiss (1991) advocated a number of strategies that coaches can apply to their coaching to enhance the cohesiveness of their teams. For instance, the coach can facilitate feelings of cohesion by providing regular instruction about skills, strategies, and tactics. Coaches should also provide positive feedback and demonstrate that they support their athletes (information on how coaches can provide social support is presented in Chapter 17).

Callow *et al.* (2009) explored the effects of coach leadership behaviours on cohesion among 309 frisbee players, who competed at different levels. The authors found that when the coach fostered acceptance of group goals (e.g. the team working together to achieve the same goal), promoted teamwork (e.g. promoting team members working together to achieve a set goal), had high performance expectations (e.g. expecting athletes to achieve high standards), and gave individual consideration to athletes (e.g. recognising that athletes have different needs), there was a positive association with task cohesion. Furthermore, when the coach encouraged athletes to accept group goals and promoted teamwork there was a positive association with social cohesion.

Interestingly, these results were influenced by the level at which the participants played, which has important ramifications for coaches who want to apply these findings to their coaching. Within the high-performance group of frisbee players, there was no significant relationship between the coach fostering acceptance of group goals and promoting teamwork with task cohesion. With the athletes from the lower group there was a positive association between cohesion and both fostering acceptance of group goals and a coach who promotes teamwork. Individual consideration by the coach predicted cohesion with the higher level athletes, but not the lower level athletes.

These findings indicate that coaches should consider the performance level of their group when deciding how to behave. Promoting team goals and teamwork, such as developing a strong team attitude and team spirit among athletes may be important for lower level performers (Callow *et al.*, 2009; Holt and Sparkes,

2001). Providing higher level athletes with more individualised coaching behaviours such as treating athletes as individuals, considering the different strengths of individuals, and helping them develop their individual strengths may build cohesion among this group of athletes (Callow *et al.*, 2009). Regardless of the performance level, coaches could show their athletes that they have a high performance expectation, by insisting athletes perform at their best, not settling for second-best, and always expecting athletes to do their best, because this is associated with team cohesion regardless of performance level.

More recent research has also found a relationship between coach behaviour and task and social cohesion. De Backer *et al.* (2011) found that perceived justice by the coach (e.g. coach rewarding athlete with appropriate match time based on his or her contribution to the team) and support (e.g. a coach allowing and supporting athletes in making their own choices regarding training) was positively related to task and social cohesion. As such, coaches should be very concerned about their athletes' perceptions of justice (De Backer *et al.*, 2011) and improve their players' sense of perceived justice by providing information on the decisions they have made. Coaches should also allow athletes to have their say, and then provide justification (Cropanzano and Greenberg, 1997).

Reinboth *et al.* (2004) found that socially supportive behaviours by the coach enhanced cohesion. Reinboth *et al.* suggested that coaches can give their athletes options regarding what activities they do, consider the needs of athletes as individual people, and evaluate athletes based only on whether they have improved or not. Coaches should not evaluate athletes based on how they compare to other members of their team.

Although the aforementioned studies indicate that coach behaviour is related to both task and social cohesion in sports teams (Callow *et al.*, 2009; De Backer *et al.*, 2011; Westre and Weiss, 1991), other research indicates that athletes' perceptions of their relationship with the coach is a more important predictor of group cohesion than coach behaviours alone. Indeed, Jowett and Chaundry (2004) found that behaviours such as supporting athletes, providing feedback, and allowing athletes to have their say accounted for 26 per cent of task cohesion. When the relationship between the coach and the athlete was considered along with coaching behaviour these two factors accounted for 34 per cent of task cohesion. Similarly, considering only coach behaviours accounted for 12 per cent of social cohesion, which rose to 15 per cent when the authors also considered the perceived relationship the athlete had with his or her coach. The results from this study and other studies suggest that coach behaviours are important in influencing cohesion; but that coaches can also enhance cohesion by considering their relationship with the athletes they coach (information regarding how coaches can improve the coach–athlete relationship is presented in Chapter 15).

Team-building strategies

Team building refers to the process in which a team is enhanced or improved. This may result in enhanced team performance (Carron and Hausenblas, 1998).

Bloom *et al.* (2003) examined expert coaches' perceptions of team building and revealed that coaches planned team-building strategies before the season began, and knew when different team-building activities would take place during the season, such as different training sessions and social activities (team dinners and social gatherings). Another interesting finding was that the coaches wanted control over all team-building activities, but they did not want to be seen as the person who dictated to the players what activities would be undertaken. Coaches gave their ideas to team captains, with the hope that these captains would accept the role of being responsible for such activities.

Team goal setting

Information on goal setting, and in particular, team goal setting is presented in Chapter 9 of this book; see this chapter for more information. A team goal involves athletes having a shared perception regarding what they want to achieve (Mills, 1984). It is important that coaches set team goals as well as individual goals, when working with team sport athletes, because team goals are strongly linked to overall team success (Prapavessis and Carron, 1996) and team motivation (Munroe *et al.*, 2002). Martin *et al.* (2009), in their meta-analysis, found that goal setting was a very effective intervention strategy.

Team performance profiling

Information on how coaches can implement performance profiling techniques is presented in Chapter 10 of this book. Researchers such as Carron and Hausenblas (1998) suggested that team performance profiling is a technique that allows coaches to gather the opinion of his or her team members before creating a team-building intervention.

Athlete Integration

To ensure that athletes feel integrated in their team, coaches can develop activities that encourage athletes to learn information about each other, ask athletes to accept that there will be personality differences among group members, and break up cliques. Conducting these integration strategies should allow individual team members to feel a sense of personal belonging to the team (Ryska *et al.*, 1999).

Role development or role clarity

Ryska *et al.* (1999) also found evidence to suggest that it is important for coaches to develop strategies, which help athletes understand and accept their roles within the team. These roles should develop over time. In particular, Ryska and colleagues stated that coaches could try and develop unique roles for athletes within their team and promote open and continuous dialogue or communication among team-mates.

Factors to consider when planning team-building interventions

There are several factors that coaches could consider when designing a team-building intervention, which include:

- *Duration:* The meta-analysis by Martin *et al.* (2009) revealed that as the length of the intervention increases, so does the effectiveness. Interventions that lasted more than 20 weeks were more effective than team-building interventions that lasted only two weeks. Indeed, Brawley and Paskevich (1997) stated that team-building interventions should be at least a season long. From a coaching perspective, it appears that interventions take time to be introduced to athletes, for athletes to trust an intervention, and for their behaviour to change (Martin *et al.*). Coaches should understand that team-building interventions are not quick fixes and they will not produce immediate improvements in cohesion or team performance.
- *Less might be more!:* The review by Martin *et al.* (2009a) also revealed team-building interventions with less component parts (e.g. just goal setting vs. goal setting, role development training, performance profiling, and athlete integration) might be more effective. Martin *et al.* contended that if athletes have fewer activities to focus on, their attention can be directed towards one activity. However, if coaches just use goal setting techniques they will exclude other activities that could benefit their team. Martin *et al.* concluded that these findings may be influenced by the team-building interventions being too short in duration. As such, coaches should conduct team interventions over a longer time frame (e.g. one season) and introduce different team-building strategies gradually, and once the coach feels that his or her team members have become familiar with each strategy.
- *Direct versus indirect approaches:* With regard to how a coach can implement team-building strategies, they can be implemented via a direct approach or an indirect approach (Carron *et al.*, 2007). The direct approach involves the coach or the sport psychologist giving the team-building training. The indirect approach is when an individual who has the team-building knowledge passes his information onto to an individual such as a coach who runs the team-building sessions. A recent meta-analysis on team-building interventions by Martin *et al.* (2009) revealed that direct and indirect approaches are equally as effective.
- *Team building for individual sport athletes playing in a team:* Carron *et al.* (2002) and Martin *et al.* (2009a) found that team-building interventions may have a greater effect among individual sport athletes who come together to form a team (e.g. tennis players, golfers, or badminton players). However, Martin *et al.* stated that team sport athletes do benefit from team-building interventions; it is just that the improvements among these athletes might be less. This is because athletes in a team sport setting will probably have a higher level of cohesion. Although, team-building interventions may be especially useful for newly formed teams. From a coaching perspective,

coaches should not get frustrated if they feel their team-building interventions are having little effect among team sport athletes, especially in established teams.

Case study 16.1 A plan to improve team performance in an academy rugby team

Stuart, is a 29-year-old academy manager in a professional rugby league club. He felt that the previous season's academy team was not a cohesive unit and did not perform as a team. Therefore, Stuart implemented a season-long team-building intervention, which he ran himself. Stuart was aware of the need for players to bond outside of rugby and planned several social functions during the first half of the season in which players would be able to get together and have some fun. These included paintballing and going out for drinks when they toured Scotland, a pre-season barbeque, go-karting in November, club Christmas dinner in December, and a night out in December.

With regards to team-building strategies, Stuart planned individual and team goal setting, individual and team performance profiling, athlete integration, and role development sessions. Stuart started off with team goal-setting sessions which involved getting the players together to discuss team goals for the season, followed by individual goal-setting sessions. Stuart did not put a specific time period on how long he worked on goal setting with the players for, and only started performance profiling once he felt the players had fully grasped the goal-setting techniques and their behaviours had changed. Furthermore, Stuart planned not to forget about goal setting and performance profiling when he introduced role development training sessions and regularly conducted goal setting and performance profiling across the season. This sent a clear message to players that all aspects of team building were processes that need constant attention and work. Stuart also acknowledged his own behaviour as a factor that may have contributed to his team's poor cohesion in the previous season. After reading books and journal articles, Stuart changed his behaviour. He felt he did not acknowledge the individuals in the group, so he spent more time taking individuals aside to listen to their views and opinions and listen to any individual needs they have. This included asking players which areas of their game they feel they need to work on. One behaviour that Stuart did not change was his desire for players to always give their best, whether that be in training or matches.

Summary points

- Team cohesion is multi-dimensional, dynamic, instrumental, and dynamic.
- Task cohesion refers to the extent to which team-mates work in unison together to achieve their team's overall goal.
- Social cohesion refers to an athlete's perceptions regarding how well he or she gets on with and likes his or her team-mates.
- Team cohesion is associated with enhanced performance, positive mood, peer efficacy, and effort, but reduced anxiety and jealousy among team-mates.
- Coaches' behaviour influences team cohesion, as does a coach's relationship with his or her athletes.
- Team-building interventions should include goal setting, performance profiling, athlete integration, and role development.
- Team-building interventions should be at least a season long.

Practice exam questions

1. Compare and contrast task cohesion and social cohesion.
2. Critically evaluate Carron *et al.*'s (1998) conceptual model of team cohesion.
3. Discuss the importance of team cohesion.
4. Coach behaviour influences team cohesion. Discuss.
5. What factors should coaches consider when designing team-building interventions?

Critical thinking questions: applying theory to practice

1. How can a coach promote task cohesion among the team he or she coaches?
2. What can a coach do to ensure that his or her team has high levels of social cohesion?
3. What behaviours should a coach use when coaching beginners compared to higher level athletes?
4. How can a coach ensure that his or her players have high levels of perceived justice?
5. Design your own team-building intervention and justify your plan with supporting evidence.

17 Providing social support

The purpose of this chapter is to provide coaches with information on the importance of socially supporting athletes and how they can provide social support. This chapter provides information on:

- defining social support;
- benefits of social support;
- the multi-dimensional nature of social support;
- the different types of social support;
- social support preferences;
- creating a social support network.

Defining social support

A definition of social support that has been widely used in the sport literature is 'an exchange of resources between at least two individuals perceived by the provider or the recipient to be intended to enhance the well-being of the recipient' (Shumaker and Brownell, 1984:13). Rees (2007), however, suggested that there is little consensus regarding how social support is defined. This is because it is very difficult to encapsulate fully the reasons why a person may support another person. In the definition provided by Shumaker and Brownell, it is implied that the provider of social support does this to improve the recipient's well-being. Within sport however, there are a number of reasons why a coach may give an athlete social support, such as to improve a technical fault in an athlete's technique, to help cope with stress, or to help him or her feel part of the team. Although helping an athlete improve technical faults, cope with stress, and making him or her feel part of the team may enhance the well-being of an athlete, the coach does not specifically intend to enhance well-being through providing his or her athlete with social support, this is just a by-product. For the remainder of this chapter, social support from a coach will refer to the processes in which coaches attempt to help their athletes. The key aspect is that the coach attempts to help his or her athlete, but the intentions regarding why a coach wants to help the athlete or the reasons why the coach is supporting his or her athlete is not specifically considered, because this makes defining social support unnecessarily complicated.

Benefits of social support

A variety of studies have found that the social support provided by a coach has a variety of desirable consequences for the athlete:

1   *Fun:* Smoll *et al.* (1993) developed a coaching effectiveness training programme to increase both supportiveness and instructional behaviours of coaches, who worked in male youth sport settings. As such, coaches were encouraged to immediately reinforce effort and give encouragement to athletes after they made a mistake. The results indicated that athletes who had been coached by individuals who had received coach effectiveness training reported having more fun and were more attracted to playing in their team, compared to athletes who received coaching from untrained coaches.

2   *Enjoyment:* Researchers with a sample of 1,342 athletes from sports such as American football, soccer, and volleyball found that athletes who felt they received positive coach support were more likely to enjoy sport (Scanlan *et al.*, 1993). Positive support included coaches saying things to make the athletes feel good.

3   *Sporting performance:* Sport psychology scholars have explored the relationship between social support and sporting performance (Rees and Freeman, 2009, 2010; Rees *et al.*, 2007), and have found evidence to suggest that social support may account for up to 24 per cent of the variance in performance. For example, Rees *et al.* (2007) explored the relationship between social support, stressors, and performance among a sample of 117 high-level golfers, who completed questionnaires within two days of a competitive round and reported their performance after the round. Overall, social support aided the performance of the golfers.

4   *Overcoming adversity:* Morgan and Giacobbi (2006) explored the experiences of eight highly talented collegiate athletes, the parents of these athletes, and their coaches. Social support from the coaches included helping the athletes with emotional difficulties such as low self-esteem. It also involved providing information to athletes, which enabled them to achieve their goals and develop. Indeed, Morgan and Giacobbi stated the social support received by these players from coaches and parents was indispensable. From a coaching perspective, coaches should also encourage the parents of their athletes to provide social support, especially to child and adolescent athletes.

5   *Self-talk:* Social support from coaches also influences self-talk (e.g. verbalisations that an athlete addresses to himself or herself; Hardy *et al.*, 2005). Self-talk can involve positive statements or negative statements. Zourbanos *et al.* (2011) explored the relationship between social support and self-talk among 888 athletes and found that social support was positively related to positive self-talk and negatively related to negative self-talk.

The multi-dimensional nature of social support

It is commonly accepted that social support is a multi-dimensional construct (Rees, 2007; Rosenfeld and Richman, 1997; Rosenfeld *et al.*, 1989). Indeed, Rosenfeld and Richman suggested that support can be classified in one of three broad dimensions:

1   *Tangible:* Tangible social support refers to support that involves a coach assisting his or her athlete complete a task (e.g. gymnastic coach helping gymnast perform a hand stand by holding the legs of the athlete).
2   *Informational:* A coach's communication with an athlete that involves the coach telling the athlete that he or she is part of a network of communication in which the athlete is free to speak to people in the network is an example of informational social support. That is, the coach provides the athlete with information on the support structures in place.
3   *Emotional:* A coach who comforts and encourages an athlete would be considered as using emotional social support.

The different types of social support

Although social support can be broadly classified with three broad dimensions (Rees, 2007; Rosenfeld and Richman, 1997; Rosenfeld *et al.*, 1989), researchers have identified eight specific types of social support, which coaches could deploy when coaching. As such, Rosenfeld and Richman suggested the following social support strategies, which coaches can use:

1   *Listening support:* A coach can provide listening support by simply listening to the athlete without giving the athlete any advice or judging what the athlete tells the coach. This may be difficult for some coaches, especially if they hear information that they are not happy with. It is important that the coach keeps quiet and lets the athlete say what he or she wants to say.
2   *Emotional support:* Coaches can provide emotional support showing an understanding of the problems an athlete may be encountering. The coach should also demonstrate that he cares about the problems encountered by the athlete and comfort the athlete.
3   *Emotional challenge:* Sometimes it may be beneficial for the coach to challenge the athlete, so he or she may evaluate their own attitudes, values, and feelings towards another team-mate or coach. This may be beneficial when athletes think that certain players or coaches do not like them. Challenging their views may create positive attitudes if players accept that there is no reason to think they are disliked by particular coaches or players.
4   *Reality confirmation support:* In order for athletes to confirm that their views are real or reflective of other team-mates, coaches can ask players to discuss pertinent factors that athletes might be having problems with together as a group (e.g. managing stress or balancing a busy schedule). This will allow

players to listen to other players who have the same problems and shared ideas may generate new ideas for managing problems.

5   *Task appreciation support:* Coaches should recognise the amount of effort athletes put in to certain tasks (e.g. a training session) and express an appreciation for the work that athletes do, whether that is a midfielder in soccer who continually tracks back or a golfer who spends hours practising his or her putting. The coach should always show an appreciation for hard work.

6   *Task challenge support:* A coach can challenge an athlete's way of thinking about a training session activity in order to motivate and stretch an athlete. This may result in more creativity, excitement, and involvement for a particular training activity. For example, a coach could ask athletes to comment upon why a certain training activity is important and the benefits athletes acquire from participating in certain training activities. Coaches could also ask athletes how they would like to adapt different training sessions or drills to make them more relevant to competitions.

Social support preferences

The strategies outlined by Rosenfeld and Richman (1997) provide coaches with a number of strategies that they can use to enhance the social support they give to athletes. However, emerging research indicates that there are a number of factors that coaches should consider, which may influence how they provide social support.

Horn *et al.* (2011) explored the relationship between preferred coach behaviour and different psychological characteristics such as motivation and anxiety among a sample of 195 collegiate athletes. Athletes who were intrinsically motivated (e.g. played sport for the enjoyment of playing) required frequent social support, as did the athletes who were highly anxious. From a coaching perspective, coaches should recognise athletes who are intrinsically motivated and anxious, and tailor their coaching to the individual needs of the athlete, by providing more frequent social support. The guidelines by Rosenfeld and Richman (1997) state how coaches can provide social support, whereas the research by Horn *et al.* (2011) indicates the factors that influence how often coaches should provide social support.

Coaches could also consider the age and the experience of the athlete when deciding how much social support an athlete requires. Høigaard *et al.* (2008) examined preferred coach behaviours in successful (e.g. team winning first 10 of season) and unsuccessful (e.g. team losing first 10 games of the season) soccer scenarios among a sample of 88 soccer players of different ages, experience, and skill level. They found that the younger and less experienced soccer players required more social support from their coach than the older and more experienced players. The authors provided a very interesting explanation regarding why the younger players need more social support from their coach. They suggested that playing in the Norwegian Premier League or First Division is both challenging and stressful, so those who were inexperienced needed frequent social support from their coach. Høigaard and colleagues suggested that the younger players may rely more on their coach for social support, because they had not established a support network in the team or their private life. Indeed, older players are more likely to be married than younger players and can rely on their wives as a source of social support. It is important that coaches consider the age and personal circumstances of the athlete when deciding how frequently to give their athletes social support.

Coaches could also consider the team circumstances when providing social support. Høigaard *et al.* (2008) found evidence to suggest that athletes require more social support in the unsuccessful performance scenario. Indeed, Høigaard and colleagues suggested that preferring more social support during times of adversity is a natural consequence of athletes having to deal with difficult and stressful situations. From a coaching perspective, it seems imperative that coaches should consider team success when deciding how much support they provide. For example, when a team loses several matches, the coach could increase the amount of social support he or she provides.

Creating a social support network

In addition to coaches providing social support to athletes using the strategies outlined in this chapter, coaches can also set up a social support network which encourages team-mates, friends, and parents of the athletes to provide social support. Indeed, Rosenfeld *et al.* (1989) found that athletes who receive social support from their coaches, team-mates, friends, and parents, so developing a formal network, may be beneficial. Furthermore, the nature of the social support that an athlete receives appears to differ depending on the person providing the social support. Coaches and team-mates tended to provide sport related social support, whereas parents and friends provided non-sport social support.

Coaches could also foster a supporting network within their teams by encouraging athletes to be supportive of one another. One example of ways in which coaches could create a supportive network during training would be to have players lead coaching sessions. This would result in players helping other players when they take on the role of the coach. The coach could praise this type of behaviour and positive communication among athletes.

Although a coach can influence how much support they give athletes and how supportive other players are of each other, they may have less influence regarding how much support parents and friends provide their athletes. Coaches could speak to the parents of athletes at the start of the season and illustrate the importance of social support and provide information regarding how parents, wives, siblings, or friends can provide social support and encourage these people to be supportive.

Summary points

- Coaches may provide social support to athletes for a number of reasons.
- Social support is associated with athletes having more fun and enjoyment, performing better, dealing with adversity, and positive self-talk.

Case study 17.1 Providing social support in difficult circumstances

Christine is a 25-year-old badminton coach who has recently started coaching a new player, called Louise, two weeks ago. Louise is a 12-year-old aspiring badminton player who left her previous coach because Louise's dad (Eric) felt that the other coach was not good enough. From the outset of their relationship Christine could see that Louise was quite nervous and lacked confidence in her game. Alternatively, Eric was a robust character with many strong opinions about his daughter. After several phone calls with Eric during the first two weeks of coaching and assessing Louise's levels of anxiety and confidence using a questionnaire, Christine felt that Louise needed more social support from her and from her father. She felt more confident about providing Louise with additional social support than she did about asking Eric to change how he supported his daughter. She knew this was going to be a very delicate matter, but thought the benefits would really help Louise.

In the subsequent training sessions that Christine had with Louise, she really emphasised how supportive of Louise she was and would listen to what she had to say in a non-judgmental way. She demonstrated that she cared about Louise, and really praised her when she put in lots of effort during training. Incidentally, Christine felt that Eric was more concerned with Louise's results. The sessions went well and Louise responded well to Christine's caring behaviour. At the end of a session, Christine asked if she could have a quick word alone with Eric and spoke about how she felt Louise's enjoyment and performance at badminton could be enhanced by creating a supportive network that places little emphasis on the outcomes of competitions and more on caring for and supporting Louise regardless of the results that she obtained. This was met with resistance from Eric who asked Christine what she thought he had been doing all of these years. Christine agreed that he had been very supportive of Louise and then mentioned some additional strategies and provided a rationale for each strategy such as listening and emotional support. When Christine described the listening support strategy, Eric admitted that listening was not his strong point, but agreed that this was something he was going to work on.

Case study reflection

As a coach, providing social support to an athlete may only be half of the solution to really helping an athlete, because the social support an athlete receives away from sports training or competition is also very important. However, it can be a delicate process speaking to parents about how they could socially support their own child and thus diplomacy is required.

- Social support is multi-dimensional and includes tangible, informational, and emotional support.
- Coaches can socially support their athletes by engaging in a variety of different strategies.
- Coaches should consider the age, experience level, motivation, and how anxious an athlete is when deciding how to socially support the athlete.
- Creating a social support network has the potential to enhance social support in teams.

Practice exam questions

1   What is social support and who provides social support to athletes?
2   What are the potential benefits of providing social support to athletes?
3   Social support is a multi-dimensional construct. Discuss.
4   What factors influence how a coach can socially support his or her athletes? Discuss.
5   Discuss the importance of creating a social support network in team sports.

Critical thinking questions: applying theory to practice

1   What are the telltale signs that an athlete might be receiving enough support and how may this manifest itself?
2   Describe how a coach can ensure that the support he or she provides is tangible, informational, and emotional.
3   How could a coach's behaviour change after his or her team is on a run of four defeats?
4   Compare and contrast the social support a coach provides to an eight-year-old golfer with a 35-year-old golfer.
5   How can a coach create a social support network in his or her team?

Part VI
Concluding thoughts

18 Ethics, referrals and the Health Professions Council

The aim of this final chapter is to provide some concluding thoughts that coaches might want to consider when they provide psychological support to athletes. More specifically, information is presented on:

- ethical issues associated with providing sport psychology to athletes: some dos and don'ts;
- the regulation of sport psychologists and protected terms;
- referrals;
- practical implications of coaches providing sport psychology.

Ethical issues associated with providing sport psychology to athletes: some don'ts and dos

When a coach provides psychological help to his or her athlete, the coach is entering into what Ebert (1997) termed a dual-role relationship. Brewer (2000) suggested that dual-role relationships have the potential to be problematic from an ethical perspective. Some scholars have even suggested that coaches should not provide psychological help to athletes (e.g. Ellickson and Brown, 1990), because there might be problems establishing a boundary between the coach and the athlete and problems regarding confidentiality, given that coaches often provide public statements to media organisations about their athletes. Additionally, coaches who provide psychological help may not be able to do so without seeing a reduction in their competency as a coach due to time pressures (Buceta, 1993). Perhaps the most important ethical issue relating to coaches providing psychological guidance to athletes relates to whether they are competent to do so, without causing harm to the athlete (Koocher and Keith-Spiegel, 1998).

However, others such as Smith (1992) and Brewer (2000) have stated that a coach providing psychological help to an athlete is compatible with coaching roles, as long as the coach provides psychology geared towards performance and not clinical concerns. There are several dos and don'ts that coaches could consider when they provide psychological help to athletes:

Don'ts

- Provide psychological help for non-performance issues (e.g. depression, drug abuse, alcohol addiction, gambling, eating disorders, or relationships). In instances that these cases are presented to the coach, the athlete should be referred to either a general practitioner or clinical psychologist immediately (Andersen and Van Raalte, 2005).
- Put pressure on an athlete to receive psychological help.
- Let the psychological help provided to an athlete reduce the quality of coaching provided.

Dos

- Consult a registered sport and exercise psychologist or clinical psychologist if there are any doubts regarding the aspects of the psychological help.
- Provide athletes with information on the different psychological skills that can be taught by a coach and the commitment the athlete will have to make before starting any psychology training interventions.

The regulation of sport psychologists and protected terms

Even though a coach may acquire very extensive information on sport psychology and be very effective at creating psychological training programmes, coaches cannot call themselves sport psychologists or advertise for work in this capacity within the United Kingdom, United States, Canada, or Australia if they are not registered within the United Kingdom or licensed in the United States, Canada, or Australia.

Since 13 May 2009 the Health Professions Council (HPC) regulates individuals who practise as psychologists under statutory regulation. As such, the terms 'registered psychologist', 'practitioner psychologist' and 'sport and exercise psychologist' are protected terms, and only individuals who are registered with the HPC can use this title. There are still examples of the title being misused in the sport psychology literature such as: 'initial contact was made with the first author, a British Association of Sport and Exercise Sciences (BASES) accredited sport psychologist' (Hays *et al.*, 2010b: 398). Individuals who are accredited by BASES in the sport psychology pathway are breaking the law if they refer to themselves as BASES accredited sport psychologists, given that it is a protected term exclusive to the HPC and not BASES.

Should a coach wish to become a HPC-registered sport and exercise psychologist, there is a specific pathway, which involves the completion of:

- an undergraduate degree that is accredited by the British Psychological Society (BPS);
- a masters' degree, which is accredited by the BPS, in sport and exercise psychology;
- two years of supervision by a HPC-registered sport and exercise psychologist.

Within the United States, Canada, and Australia individuals are required to obtain a licence in order to practise as a psychologist. The formal training involves:

- achieving an undergraduate degree that is accredited by the relevant country's psychological society (e.g. American Psychological Association, Canadian Psychological Association, or Australian Psychological Society);
- a professional doctorate in psychology.

For clarification, coaches are legally allowed to provide training in the psychological skills outlined in this book, but they cannot call themselves sport and exercise psychologists.

Referrals

A referral is when a coach contacts another professional to help the athlete he or she is working with, because the coach lacks sufficient expertise to manage the problem. Referrals might also be made when a coach might not think it is appropriate to work with a specific athlete (Brewer, 2000). A coach should contact a clinical psychologist or ask his athlete to contact his or her general practitioner if the athlete has problems relating to:

- depression
- drug abuse
- alcohol addiction
- gambling
- eating disorders
- relationships.

Under no circumstances should coaches attempt to provide psychological support to athletes for these problems.

In circumstances that are performance-related and when a coach feels the needs of an athlete are beyond his or her capabilities, the coach should refer the athlete to a registered sport and exercise psychologist.

Telling an athlete that he or she should be referred to another professional such as a clinical psychologist or a sport and exercise psychologist has the potential to be awkward for a coach. The coach should explain to the player why a referral has been made, provide information about the professional who the referral has been made to, and answer any questions the athlete has.

Practical implications of coaches providing sport psychology

Although many athletes would potentially benefit from receiving training in sport psychology by their coach, some coaches will simply not have the time to learn about different psychological techniques and then implement the techniques with athletes. Before asking an athlete whether he or she would like to engage in some psychological training, the coach should make sure that he or she has enough time to coach the athlete and provide psychological help too.

When coaches have the time and an interest in using sport psychology within their coaching, they have the potential to improve the performance, enjoyment, and well-being of the athletes that they coach. As with all new skills, coaching psychological skills will be difficult at times and improvements in an athlete's performance may take a long time, but by providing psychological skills training, coaches are providing a more complete service.

References

Abramowitz, A. J., and O'Leary, S. G. (1991) 'Behavioural interventions for the classroom: Implications for students with ADHD', *School Psychology Review*, 20, 220–234.

Adie, J. W., Duda, J. L., and Ntoumanis, N. (2012) 'Perceived coach-autonomy support, basic need satisfaction and the well- and ill-being of elite youth soccer players: A longitudinal investigation', *Psychology of Sport and Exercise*, 13, 51–59.

Ahsen, A. (1984) 'The triple code model for imagery and psycho-physiology', *Journal of Mental Imagery*, 8, 15–42.

Aldwin, C. M. (2007) *Stress, coping and development: An integrative perspective*, (2nd edn), New York: Guilford Press.

American Psychiatric Association (1994) *Diagnostic and statistical manual of mental disorders*, Washington, DC: American Psychiatric Association.

American Psychiatric Association (2000) *Diagnostic and statistical manual of mental disorders- IV-TR*, (4th edn), Washington, DC: American Psychiatric Association.

Ames, C. (1992) 'Achievement goals, motivational climate, and motivational processes', in G. C. Roberts (ed.), *Advances in motivation in sport and exercise*, Champaign, IL: Human Kinetics, pp. 161–176.

Amorose, A. J. (2007) 'Coaching effectiveness,' in M. S. Hagger amd N. L. D. Chatzisarantis (eds), *Intrinsic motivation and self-determination in exercise and sport*, Champaign, IL: Human Kinetics, pp. 209–228.

Andersen, M. B. (2000) 'Beginnings: Intakes and the initiation of relationships', in M. B. Andersen (ed.), *Doing sport psychology*, Champaign, IL: Human Kinetics, pp. 3–16.

Andersen, M. B. (2011) 'Who's mental, who's tough and who's both? Mutton constructs dressed up as lamb', in D. Gucciardi and S. Gordon (eds), *Mental toughness in sport: Developments in research and theory*, London: Routledge, pp. 69–88.

Andersen, M. B., and Van Raalte, J. L. (2005) 'Over one's head: Referral processes', in M. B. Andersen (ed.), *Sport psychology in practice*, Champaign, IL: Human Kinetics, pp. 159–170.

Anhalt, K., McNeil, C. B., and Bahl, A. B. (1998) 'The ADHD classroom kit: A whole-classroom approach for managing disruptive behaviour', *Psychology in the Schools*, 35, 67–79.

Anshel, M. H. (2001) 'Qualitative validation of a model for coping with acute stress in sport', *Journal of Sport Behaviour*, 24, 223–246.

Anshel, M. H., Gregory, W. L., and Kaczmarek, M. (1990) 'The effectiveness of a stress training program in coping with criticism in sport: A test of the COPE model', *Journal of Sport Behaviour*, 13, 194–217.

Badami, R., Vaez Mousavi, M., Wulf, G., and Namazizadeh, M. (2011) 'Feedback after good versus poor trials after intrinsic motivation', *Research Quarterly for Exercise and Sport,* 82, 360–364.

Badan, M., Hauert, C. A., and Moumoud, P. (2000) 'Sequential pointing in children and adults', *Journal of Experimental Child Psychology,* 75, 43–69.

Bandura, A. (1977) 'Self-efficacy: Toward a unifying theory of behavioural change', *Psychological Review,* 84, 191–215.

Bandura, A. (1997) *Self-efficacy: The exercise of control,* New York: Freeman.

Baumeister, R. F. (1984) 'Choking under pressure: Self-consciousness and paradoxical effects of incentives on skilful performance', *Journal of Personality and Social Psychology,* 46, 610–620.

Beauchamp, P. H., Halliwell, W. R., Fournier, J. F., and Koestner, R. (1996) 'Effects of cognitive-behavioural psychological skills training on motivation, preparation, and putting performance of novice golfers', *The Sport Psychologist,* 10, 157–170.

Beilock, S. L., and Carr, T. H. (2001) 'On the fragility of skilled performance: What governs choking under pressure?', *Journal of Experimental Psychology: General,* 130, 701–725.

Beilock, S. L., and Gray, R. (2007) 'Why do athletes choke under pressure?', in G. Tenenbaum, and R.C. Eklund (eds), *Handbook of sport psychology* (3rd edn) Hoboken, NJ: John Wiley and Sons, pp. 425–444.

Beilock, S. L., Kulp, C. A., Holt, L. E., and Carr, T. H. (2004) 'More on the fragility of performance: Choking under pressure in mathematical problem solving', *Journal of Experimental Psychology: General,* 133, 584–600.

Bengoechea, E. G., and Strean, W. B. (2007) 'On the interpersonal context of adolescents' sport motivation', *Psychology of Sport and Exercise,* 8, 195–217.

Bernstein, D. A., and Nietzel, M. T. (1980) *Introduction to clinical psychology,* New York: McGraw-Hill.

Beyer, R., Flores, M. M., Vargas-Tonsing, T. M. (2008) 'Coaches' attitudes towards youth sport participants with attention deficit hyperactivity disorder', *International Journal of Sport Science & Coaching,* 3, 555–563.

Beyer, R., Flores, M. M., Vargas-Tonsing, T. M. (2009) 'Strategies and methods for coaching athletes with invisible disabilities in youth sport activities', *The Journal of Youth Sports,* 4, 10–15.

Bianco, T. (2001) 'Social support and recovery from sport injury: Elite skiers share their experiences', *Research Quarterly for Exercise and Sport,* 72, 376–388.

Black, S. J., and Weiss, M. R. (1992) 'The relationship among perceived coaching behaviours, perceptions of ability, and motivation in competitive age-group swimmers, *Journal of Sport and Exercise Psychology,* 14, 309–325.

Blakeslee, T. R. (1980) *The right brain,* New York: Anchor Press.

Bloom. G., Stevens, D. E., and Wickwire, T. L. (2003) 'Expert coaches perceptions of team building', *Journal of Applied Sport Psychology,* 15, 129–143.

Boekaerts, M. (1996) 'Coping with stress in childhood and adolescence', in M. Zeidner and N.S. Endler (eds), *Handbook of coping: Theory research and applications,* New York: Wiley, pp. 452–484.

Brawley, L.R., and Paskevich, D.M. (1997) 'Conducting team building research in context of sport and exercise', *Journal of Applied Sport Psychology,* 9, 11–40.

Bray, C.D., and Whaley, D. E. (2001) 'Team cohesion, effort and objective individual performance of high school basketball players', *The Sport Psychologist,* 15, 260–275.

Brewer, B. W. (2000) 'Doing sport psychology in the coaching role', in M. B. Andersen (ed.), *Doing sport psychology*, Champaign, IL: Human Kinetics, pp. 237–248.

Buceta, J. M. (1993) 'The sport psychologist/athletic dual role: Advantages, difficulties, and ethical considerations', *Journal of Applied Sport Psychology*, 5, 64–77.

Bull, S. J., Shambrook, C. J., James, W., and Brooks, J. E. (2005) 'Towards an understanding of mental toughness in elite English cricketers', *Journal of Applied Sport Psychology*, 17, 209–27.

Burton, D. (1989) 'Winning isn't everything: Examining the impact of performance goals on collegiate swimmers' cognitions and performance', *The Sport Psychologist*, 3, 105–132.

Burton, D. (1998) 'Measuring competitive state anxiety', in J. Duda (ed.), *Advances in sport and exercise psychology*, Morgantown, WV: Fitness Informational Technology, pp. 129–148.

Burton, D., and Naylor, S. (1997) 'Is anxiety really facilitative? Reaction to the myth that cognitive anxiety always impairs sport performance', *Journal of Applied Sport Psychology*, 9, 295–302.

Burton, D., and Naylor, S. (2002) 'The Jekyll/Hyde nature of goals: Revisiting and updating goal setting in sport', in T. Horn (ed.), *Advances in sport psychology*, Champaign, IL: Human Kinetics, pp. 459–499.

Burton, D., Naylor, S., and Holliday, B. (2001) 'Goal setting in sport: Investigating the goal effectiveness paradigm', in R. Singer, H. Hausenblas, and C. Janelle (eds), *Handbook of sport psychology*, New York: Wiley, pp. 497–528.

Butler, R. J. (1989) *The performance profile: Developing elite performance*, London: British Olympic Association.

Butler, R. J. (1996a) *Performance profiling*, Leeds: National Coaching Foundation.

Butler, R. J. (1996b) 'Performance profiling' in R. J. Butler (ed.), *Sports psychology in action*, London: Hodder Arnold, pp. 9–19.

Butler, R. J., and Hardy, L. (1992) 'The performance profile: Theory and application', *The Sport Psychologist*, 6, 253–264.

Butler, R. J., Smith, M., and Irwin, I. (1993) 'The performance profile in practice', *Journal of Applied Sport Psychology*, 5, 48–63.

Callow, N., and Hardy, L. (2001) 'Types of imagery associated with sport confidence in netball players of varying skill levels', *Journal of Applied Sport Psychology*, 13, 1–17.

Callow, N., and Walters, A. (2005) 'The effect of kinaesthetic imagery on the sport confidence of flat-race horse jockeys', *Psychology of Sport and Exercise*, 6, 443–459.

Callow, N., Smith, M. J., Hardy, L., Arthur, C. A., and Hardy, J. (2009) 'Measurement of transformational leadership and its relationship with team cohesion and performance level', *Journal of Applied Sport Psychology*, 21, 395–412.

Calmels, C., Berthoumieux, C., and d'Arrie-Longueville, F. (2004) 'Effects of an imagery training programme on selective attention of national softball players', *The Sport Psychologist*, 18, 272–296.

Cannon, W. B. (1915) *Bodily changes in pain, hunger, fear, and rage: An account of recent researches into the functions of emotional excitement*, New York: Appleton.

Carpenter, (1894) *Principles of mental physiology*, New York: Appleton.

Carron, A. V., and Hausenblas, H. A. (1998) *Group dynamics in sport*, Morgantown, WV: Fitness Information Technology.

Carron, A. V., Brawley, L. R., and Widmeyer, W. N. (1998) 'The measurement of cohesiveness in sport groups', in Duda, J. (ed.), *Advances in sport and exercise psychology measurement*, Morgantown, WV: Fitness Information Technology, pp. 213–226.

Carron, A. V., Colman, M. M., Wheeler, J., and Stevens, D. (2002) 'Cohesion and performance in sport: A meta-analysis', *Journal of Sport & Exercise Psychology*, 24, 168–188.

Carron, A. V., Eys, M. A., and Burke, S. M. (2007) 'Team cohesion: Nature, correlates, and development', in S. Jowett and D. Lavallee (eds), *Social Psychology in sport*, Champaign, IL: Human Kinetics, pp. 91–101.

Carron, A. V., Widmeyer, W. N., and Brawley, L. R. (1985) 'The development of an instrument to assess cohesion in sport teams: The group environment questionnaire', *Journal of Sport Psychology*, 7, 244–266.

Carson, F., and Polman, R. C. J. (2010) 'The facilitative nature of avoidance coping within sports injury rehabilitation', *Scandinavian Journal of Medicine and Science in Sports*, 20, 235–240.

Cary, P. (2004) 'Fixing kids' sport', *U.S. News and World Report*, 136, 44–53.

Chesney, M. A., Folkman, S., and Chambers, D. B. (1996) 'Coping effectiveness training for men living with HIV: preliminary findings', *International Journal of STD & AIDS*, 7, 75–82.

Chesney, M. A., Chambers, D. B., Taylor, J. M., Johnson, L. M., and Folkman, S. (2003) 'Coping effectiveness training for men living with HIV: Results from a randomized clinical trial testing a group-based intervention', *Psychosomatic Medicine*, 65, 1038–1046.

Chesney, M.A., Neilands, T. B., Chambers, D. B., Taylor, J. M., and Folkman, S. (2006) 'A validity and reliability study of the coping self-efficacy scale', *British Journal of Health Psychology*, 11, 421–437.

Chiviacowsky, S., and Wulf, G. (2002) 'Self-controlled feedback: Does it enhance learning because performers get feedback when they need it? *Research Quarterly for Exercise and Sport*, 73, 408–415.

Chiviacowsky, S., Wulf, G., Laroque de Medeiros, F., Kaefer, A., and Tani, G. (2008a) 'Learning benefits of self-controlled knowledge of results in 10-year-old children', *Research Quarterly for Exercise and Sport*, 79, 405–410.

Chiviacowsky, S., Wulf, G., Laroque de Medeiros, F., and Kaefer, A. (2008b) 'Self-controlled feedback in 10-year-old children: Higher feedback frequencies enhance learning', *Research Quarterly for Exercise and Sport*, 79,122–127.

Chiviacowsky, S., Wulf, G., Wally, R., and Borges, T. (2009) 'Knowledge of results after good trials enhances learning in older adults', *Research Quarterly for Exercise and Sport*, 80, 663–668.

Chow, G. M., Murray, K. E., and Feltz, D. L. (2009) 'Individual, team, and coach predictors of players' likelihood to aggress in youth soccer', *Journal of Sport & Exercise Psychology*, 31, 425–443.

Clark, M. S., and Reiss, H. T. (1988) 'Interpersonal processes in close relationships', *Annual Review of Psychology*, 39, 609–672.

Clough, P., Earle, K., and Sewell, D. (2002) 'Mental toughness: The concept and its measurement', in I. Cockerill (ed.), *Solutions in Sport Psychology*, London: Thomson, pp. 32–45.

Coatsworth, J. D., and Conroy, D. E. (2006) 'Enhancing the self-esteem of youth swimmers through coach training: Gender and age effects', *Psychology of Sport and Exercise*, 7, 173–192.

Compas, B.E., Connor-Smith, J.K., Saltzman, H., Harding Thomsen, A., and Wadsworth, M.E. (2001) 'Coping with stress during childhood and adolescence: Problems, progress, and potential in theory and research', *Psychological Bulletin*, 12, 87–127.

Connaughton, D., Hanton, S., and Jones, G. (2010) 'The development and maintenance of mental toughness in the world's best performers', *The Sport Psychologist*, 24, 168–193.

Connaughton, D., Thelwell, R., and Hanton, S. (2011) 'Mental toughness development: Issues, practical implications, and future directions, in D. F. Gucciardi & S. Gordon (eds), *Mental toughness in sport: Developments in theory and research*, London: Routledge, pp. 135–162.

Connaughton, D., Hanton, S., Jones, G., and Wadey, R. (2008a) 'Mental toughness research: Key issues in this area', *International Journal of Sport Psychology*, 39, 192–204.

Connaughton, D., Wadey, R., Hanton, S., and Jones, G. (2008b) 'The development and maintenance of mental toughness: Perceptions of elite performers', *Journal of Sports Sciences*, 26, 83–95.

Connolly, K. (1970) *Mechanisms of motor skill development*, London: Academic Press.

Conroy, D. E., Elliot, A. J., and Coatsworth, J. D. (2007) 'Competence motivation in sport and exercise', in M. S. Hagger amd N. L. D. Chatzisarantis (eds), *Intrinsic motivation and self-determination in exercise and sport*, Champaign, IL: Human Kinetics, pp. 181–192.

Coopersmith, S. (1967) *The antecedents of self-esteem*, San Francisco, CA: Freeman.

Côté, J. (1999) 'The influence of the family in the development of talent in sport', *The Sport Psychologist*, 13, 395–417.

Côté, J., and Gilbert, W. D. (2009) 'An integrative definition of coaching effectiveness and expertise', *International Journal of Sports Science & Coaching*, 4, 307–323.

Côté, J., Bruner, M., Erickson, K., Strachan, L., and Fraser-Thomas, J. (2010) 'Athlete development and coaching', in J. Lyle and C. Cushion (eds), *Sports coaching: Professionalisation and practice*, Edinburgh: Churchill Livingston, pp. 63–84.

Cotterill, S., Sanders, R., and Collins, D. (2010) 'Developing effective pre-performance routines in golf: Why don't we ask the golfer?', *Journal of Applied Sport Psychology*, 22, 51–64.

Coulter, T. J., Mallet, C., and Gucciardi, D. F. (2010) 'Understanding mental toughness in Australian soccer: Perceptions of players, parents, and coaches', *Journal of Sports Sciences*, 28, 699–716.

Covington, M. V. (1984) 'The motive for self worth', in R. Ames and C. Ames (eds), *Research on motivation in education: Student motivation*, New York: Academic Press, pp. 77–113.

Craft, L. L., Magyar, M., Becker, B. J., and Feltz, D. L. (2003) 'The relationship between the Competitive State Anxiety Inventory-2 and sport performance: A meta-analysis', *Journal of Sport & Exercise Psychology*, 25, 44–65.

Crocker, P. R. E., and Graham, T. R. (1995) 'Coping with competitive athletes with performance stress: Gender differences and relationships with affect', *The Sport Psychologist*, 9, 325–338.

Crocker, P. R. E., Alderman, R. B., and Smith, F. M. (1988) 'Cognitive-affective stress management training with high performance youth volleyball players: Effects on affect, cognition, and performance', *Journal of Sport & Exercise Psychology*, 10, 448–460.

Crocker, P. R. E., Hoar, S., McDonough, M., Kowalski, K., and Niefer, C. (2004) 'Emotional experience in youth sport', in M. Weiss (ed.), *Development sport and exercise psychology: A lifespan perspective*, Morgantown, WV: Fitness Information Technology, pp. 197–222.

Cropanzano, R., and Greenberg, J. (1997) 'Progress in organizational justice: tunnelling through the maze', in C. L. Cooper, and I. T. Robertson (eds), *International review of industrial and organizational psychology*, New York: Wiley, pp. 317–372.

Crossman, J. (1997) 'Psychological rehabilitation from sports injuries', *Sports Medicine*, 23, 333–339.

Crust, L. (2008) 'A review and conceptual re-examination of mental toughness: Implications for future researchers', *Personality and Individual Differences*, 45, 576–83.

Cushion, C. J. (2007a) 'Modelling the complexity of the coaching process', *International Journal of Sports Science & Coaching*, 2, 395–401.

Cushion, C. J. (2007b) 'Modelling the complexity of the coaching process: A response to commentaries', *International Journal of Sports Science & Coaching*, 2, 427–433.

Dale, G. A., and Wrisberg, C. A. (1996) 'The use of a performance profiling technique in a team setting: Getting the athletes and the coach on the "same page"', *The Sport Psychologist*, 10, 261–277.

Deci, E. L., and Ryan, R. M. (1987) 'The support of autonomy and the control of behaviour', *Journal of Personality and Social Psychology*, 53, 1024–1037.

Deci, E. L., and Ryan, R. M. (2000) 'The "what" and "why" of goal pursuits: Human needs and the self-determination of behaviour', *Psychological Inquiry*, 11, 227–268.

De Backer, M., Boen, F., Ceux, T., De Cuyper, B., Høigaard, R., Callens, F., Fransen, K., and Vande Broek, G. (2011) 'Do perceived justice and need support of the coach predict team identification and cohesion? Testing their relative importance among top volleyball and handball players in Belgium and Norway', *Psychology of Sport and Exercise*, 12, 192–201.

DePauw, K. P., and Gavron, S.J. (1991) 'Coaches of athletes with disabilities', *Physical Educator*, 48, 33–40.

Driskell, J. E., Cooper, C., and Moran, A. (1994) 'Does mental practice enhance performance?', *Journal of Applied Psychology*, 79, 481–492.

Dubois, P. (1990). 'The youth sport coach as an agent of socialisation: An exploratory study' *Journal of Sport Behavior*, 4, 95–107.

DuPaul, G. J., and Stoner, G. (1994) *ADHD in the schools: Assessment and intervention strategies*, New York: Guilford Press.

Durso-Cupal, D. D. (1996) 'The efficacy of guided imagery for recovery from anterior cruciate ligament (ACL) replacement', *Journal of Applied Sport Psychology*, 8(Suppl.), S56.

D'Urso, V., Petrosso, A., and Robazza, C. (2002) 'Emotions, perceived qualities, and performance of rugby players', *The Sport Psychologist*, 16, 173–199.

Dweck, C. S. (1986) 'Motivational process affecting learning', *American Psychologist*, 41, 1040–1048.

Ebert, B. W. (1997) 'Dual-relationship prohibitions: A concept whose time never should have come', *Applied and Preventive Psychology*, 6, 137–156.

Ellickson, K. A., and Brown, D. R. (1990) 'Ethical considerations in dual relationships: The sport psychologist-coach', *Journal of Applied Sport Psychology*, 2, 186–190.

Ellis, M. C. (1992) 'Tempo perception and performance of elementary students, grades 3–6', *Journal of Research in Music and Education*, 40, 329–341.

Epstein, J. (1989) 'Family structures and student motivation: A development perspective', in C. Ames and R. Ames (eds), *Research and motivation in edcation*, New York: Academic Press, pp. 259–295.

Eys, M. A., Hardy, J., Carron, A. V., and Beauchamp, M. R. (2003) 'The relationship between task cohesion and competitive state anxiety', *Journal of Sport and Exercise Psychology*, 25, 66–76.

Eys, M. A., Loughead, T. M., Bray, S. R., and Carron, A. V. (2009) 'Perceptions of cohesion by youth sport participants', *The Sport Psychologist*, 23, 330–345.

Feltz, D. L. (1980) 'Teaching a high-avoidance motor task to a retarded child through participant modelling', *Education and Training of the Mentally Retarded*, 15, 152–155.

Feltz, D. L. (1994) 'Self-confidence and performance', in D. Druckman and R. A. Bjork (eds), *Learning, remembering, believing: Enhancing human performance*, Washington, DC: National Academy Press, pp. 173–206.

Feltz, D. L., Short, S. E., and Sullivan, P. J. (2008) *Self-efficacy in sport: Research and strategies for working with athletes, teams, and coaches*, Champaign, IL: Human Kinetics.

Fiore, T. A., Becker, E. A., and Nero, R. C. (1993) 'Educational interventions for students with attention deficit disorder', *Exceptional Children*, 60, 163–173.

Folkman, S. (1984) 'Personal control and stress and coping processes: A theoretical analysis', *Journal of Personality and Social Psychology*, 46, 839–852.

Ford, P. R., Yates, I., and Williams, A. M. (2010) 'An analysis of practice activities and instructional behaviours used by youth soccer coaches during practice: Exploring the link between science and application', *Journal of Sports Sciences*, 28, 483–495.

Fraser-Thomas, J., Côté , J., and Deakin, J. (2008) 'Examining adolescent sport dropout and prolonged engagement from a developmental perspective', *Journal of Applied Sport Psychology*, 20, 318–333.

Friend, M., and Bursuck, W. D. (2009) *Including students with special needs: A practical guide for classroom teachers*, Boston, MA: Allyn and Bacon.

Fry, M. D., and Gano-Overway, L. A. (2010) 'Exploring the contribution of the caring climate to the youth sport experience, *Journal of Applied Sport Psychology*, 22, 294–304.

Furman, W., and Gavin, L. A. (1989) 'Peers' influence on adjustment and development: A view from the intervention literature', in T. J. Berndt and G. W. Ladd (eds), *Peer relationships in child development*, New York: Wiley, pp. 319–340.

Gaudreau, P., and Blondin, J.-P. (2002) 'Development of a questionnaire for the assessment of coping strategies employed by athletes in competitive sport settings', *Psychology of Sport and Exercise*, 3, 1–34.

Giges, B. (2000) 'Removing psychological barriers: Clearing the way', in M. B. Andersen (ed.), *Doing sport psychology*, Champaign, IL: Human Kinetics, pp. 17–32.

Gonzalez, S. P., Metzler, J. N., and Newton, M. (2011) 'The influence of a simulated "pep talk" on athlete inspiration, situational motivation, and emotion', *International Journal of Sports Science & Coaching*, 3, 445–459.

Gould, D., Eklund, R.C., and Jackson, S. A. (1993) 'Coping strategies used by US Olympic wrestlers', *Research Quarterly for Exercise and Sport*, 64, 83–93.

Gould, D., Hodge, K., Peterson, K., and Petlichkoff, L. (1987) 'Psychological foundations of coaching: similarities and differences among intercollegiate wrestling coaches', *The Sport Psychologist*, 1, 293–308.

Gould, D., Udry, E., Bridges, D., and Beck, L. (1997) 'Coping with season-ending injuries', *The Sport Psychologist*, 11, 379–399.

Gucciardi, D. F., Gordon, S., and Dimmock, J. A. (2008) 'Towards an understanding of mental toughness in Australian football', *Journal of Applied Sport Psychology*, 20, 261–81.

Gucciardi, D. F., Gordon, S., and Dimmock, J. A. (2009a) 'Advancing mental toughness research and theory using personal construct psychology', *International Review of Sport and Exercise Psychology*, 2, 54–72.

Gucciardi, D. F., Gordon, S., and Dimmock, J. A. (2009c) 'Evaluation of a mental toughness training program for youth aged Australian footballers: I. A quantitative analysis', *Journal of Applied Sport Psychology*, 21, 307–23.

Gucciardi, D. F., Gordon, S., Dimmock, J. A., and Mallett, C. J. (2009b) 'Understanding the coach's role in the development of mental toughness: Perspective of elite Australian football coaches', *Journal of Sports Sciences*, 27, 1483–1496.

Gucciardi, D. F., Mallett, C. J., Hanrahan, S. J., and Gordon, S. (2011) 'Measuring mental toughness in sport: Current status and future directions', in D. F. Gucciardi and S. Gordon (eds), *Mental toughness in sport: Developments in theory and research*, London: Routledge, pp. 108–132.

Gudjonsson, G. H., and Sigurdsson, J. F. (2010) 'The relationship of compliance with inattention and hyperactivity/impulsivity', *Personality and Individual Differences*, 49, 651–654.

Haibach, P. S., Reid, G., and Collier, D. H. (2011) *Motor learning and development*, Champaign, IL: Human Kinetics.

Hall, C. R., and Martin, K. A. (1997) 'Measuring movement imagery abilities: A revision of the Movement Imagery Questionnaire', *Journal of Mental Imagery*, 21, 143–154.

Haney, C. J., and Long, B. C. (1995) 'Coping effectiveness: A path analysis of self-efficacy, control, coping and performance in sport competitions', *Journal of Applied Social Psychology*, 25, 1726–46.

Hanin, Y.L. (2004) 'Emotions in sport: an individualized approach', in C. D. Spielberger (ed.), *Encyclopaedia of Applied Psychology* (Vol. 1) Oxford: Elsevier Academic Press, pp. 739–750.

Hanin Y. (2007) 'Emotions in sport: Current issues and perspectives', in G. Tenenbaum and R.C. Eklund (eds), *Handbook of Sport Psychology* (3rd edn), Hoboken, NJ: John Wiley & Sons, pp. 31–58.

Hanin, Y. L. (2010) 'Coping with anxiety in sport', in A. R Nicholls (ed.), *Coping in sport: Theory, methods, and related constructs*, New York: Nova Science Inc., pp. 159–176.

Hardy, J., Hall, C. R., and Hardy, L. (2005) 'Quantifying athlete self-talk', *Journal of Sports Sciences*, 23, 905–917.

Hardy, L., Mullen, R., and Jones, G. (1996) 'Knowledge and conscious control of motor actions under stress', *British Journal of Psychology*, 87, 621–636.

Hardy, L., Mullen, R., and Martin, N. (2001) 'Effect of task-relevant cues and state anxiety on motor performance', *Perceptual and Motor Skills*, 92, 942–946.

Harwood, C., and Swain, A. (2002) 'The development and activation of achievement goals within tennis: II. A player, parent, and coach intervention', *The Sport Psychologist*, 16, 111–137.

Harwood, C., Spray, C. M., and Keegan, R. (2008) 'Achievement goal theories in sport', in T. S. Horn (ed.), *Advances in sport psychology*, (3rd edn), Champaign, IL: Human Kinetics, pp. 157–185.

Harter, S. (1999) '*The construction of the self: A developmental perspective*' New York: Guilford Press.

Hays, K., Maynard, I., Thomas, O., and Bawden, M. (2007) 'Sources and types of confidence identified by world class sport performers', *Journal of Applied Sport Psychology*, 19, 434–456.

Hays, K., Thomas, O., Maynard, I., and Bawden, M. (2009) 'The role of confidence in world class sport performance', *Journal of Sports Sciences*, 27, 1185–1199.

Hays, K., Thomas, O., Maynard, I., and Butt, J. (2010a) 'The development of confidence profiling for sport', *The Sport Psychologist*, 18, 373–392.

Hays, K., Thomas, O., Maynard, I., and Butt, J. (2010b) 'The role of confidence profiling in cognitive-behavioural interventions in sport', *The Sport Psychologist*, 18, 393–414.

Heil, J. (1993) *Psychology of sport injury*, Champaign, IL: Human Kinetics.

Hellstedt, J. C. (1987) 'The coach/parent/athlete relationship' *The Sport Psychologist*, 1, 151–160.

Hembree-Kigin, T. L., and McNeil, C. B. (1995) *Parent–child interaction therapy*, New York: Plenum.

Hill, G. M. (1988) 'Celebrate diversity (not specialisation) in school sports', *The Executive Educator*, *10*, 24.

Høigaard, R., Jones, G. W., and Peters, D. M. (2008) 'Preferred coach leadership behaviour in elite soccer in relation to success and failure', *International Journal of Sport Sciences & Coaching*, 2, 241–250.

Holmes, P., and Collins, D. (2001) 'The PETTLEP approach to motor imagery: A functional equivalence model for sport psychologists', *Journal of Applied Sport Psychology*, 13, 60–83.

Holt, N. L., and Hogg, J. M. (2002) 'Perceptions of stress and coping during preparations for the 1999 women's soccer world cup finals', *The Sport Psychologist*, 16, 251–71.

Holt, N. L., and Mandigo, J. L. (2004) 'Coping with performance worries among male youth cricket players', *Journal of Sport Behaviour*, 27, 39–57.

Holt, N. L., and Sparkes, A. C. (2001) 'An ethnographic study of cohesiveness in a college soccer team over a season', *The Sport Psychologist*, 15, 237–259.

Horn, T. S., Glenn, S. D., and Wentzell, A. B. (1993) 'Sources of information underlying personal ability judgements in high school athletes', *Paediatric Exercise Science*, 5, 263–274.

Horn, T. S., Lox, C. L., and Labrador, F. (2006) 'The self-fulfilling prophecy theory: When coaches' expectations become reality', in J. Williams (ed.), *Applied sport psychology: Personal growth to peak performance*, (5th edn), Boston, MA: McGraw Hill, pp. 82–108.

Horn, T. S., Bloom, P., Berglund, K. M., and Packard, S. (2011) 'Relationship between collegiate athletes' psychological characteristics and their preferences for different types of coaching behaviour', *The Sport Psychologist*, 25, 190–211.

Hurst, J. R., Thompson, A., Visek, A. J., Fisher, B., and Gaudreau, P. (2011) 'Towards a dispositional version of the Coping Inventory for Competitive Sport', *Journal of Sport and Exercise Psychology*, 42, 167–185.

Hutchinson, J. C., Sherman, T., Martinovic, N., and Tenenbaum, G. (2008) 'The effect of manipulated self-efficacy on perceived and sustained effort' *Journal of Applied Sport Psychology*, 20, 457–472.

Isabel, M., António, S., António, R., Felismina, P., and Michef, M. (2008) 'A systematic observation of youth amateur volleyball coaches behaviours', *International Journal of Applied Sports Sciences*, 2, 37–58.

Ievleva, L., and Orlick, T. (1991) 'Mental links to enhanced healing', *The Sport Psychologist*, 5, 25–40.

Jackson, B., Dimmock, J. A., Gucciardi, D. F., and Grove, J. R. (2011) 'Personality traits and relationship perceptions in coach–athlete dyads: Do opposites really attract?', *Psychology of Sport and Exercise*, 12, 222–230.

Janelle, C. M., Kim, J., and Singer, R. N. (1995) 'Subject-controlled performance feedback and learning of a closed motor skill', *Perceptual and Motor Skills*, 81, 627–634.

Johnson, D. W., and Johnson, F. P. (1987) *'Joining together: Group therapy and group skills:* Englewood Cliffs, NJ: Prentice Hall.

Johnston, L. H., and Carroll, D. (1998) 'The provision of social support to injured athletes: A qualitative analysis', *Journal of Sport Rehabilitation*, 7, 267–284.

Jones, D. F., Housner, L. D., and Kornspan, A. S. (1995) 'A comparative analysis of expert and novice basketball coaches' practice planning', *Applied Research in Coaching and Athletics Annual*, 10, 201–226.

Jones, G. (1993) 'The role of performance profiling in cognitive behavioral interventions in sport', *The Sport Psychologist*, 7, 160–172.

Jones, G., and Swain, A. (1995) 'Predisposition to experience debilitative and facilitative anxiety in elite and non-elite performers', *The Sport Psychologist*, 9, 201–211.

Jones, G., Hanton, S., and Connaughton, D. (2002) 'What is this thing called mental toughness? An investigation of elite performers', *Journal of Applied Sport Psychology*, 14, 205–18.

Jones, G., Hanton, S., and Connaughton, D. (2007) 'A framework of mental toughness in the world's best performers', *The Sport Psychologist*, 21, 243–64.

Jordet, G. (2010) 'Choking under pressure as self-destructive behavior', in A. R. Nicholls (ed.), *Coping in sport: theory, methods, and related constructs*, New York: Nova Science Inc., pp. 239–259.

Jourden, F. J., Bandura, A., and Banfield, J. T. (1991) 'The impact of conceptions of ability on self-regulatory factors and motor skill acquisition', *Journal of Sport and Exercise Psychology*, 8, 213–226.

Jowett, S. (2005) 'On enhancing and repairing the coach–athlete relationship', in S. Jowett and M. Jones (eds), *The psychology of coaching*, Leicester: British Psychological Society, pp. 14–26.

Jowett, S., and Chaundry, V. (2004) 'An investigation into the impact of the coach leadership and coach–athlete relationship on group cohesion', *Group Dynamics: Theory, Research, and Practice*, 8, 302–311.

Jowett, S., and Cockerill, I. M. (2002) 'Incompatibility in the coach–athlete relationship', in I. M. Cockerill (ed.) *Solutions in sport psychology*, London: Thompson Learning, pp. 16–31.

Jowett, S., and Cockerill, I. M. (2003) 'Olympic Medallists' perspective of the athlete-coach relationship', *Psychology of Sport and Exercise*, 4, 313–331.

Jowett, S., and Meek, G.A. (2000) 'Coach–athlete relationships in married couples: An exploratory content analysis', *The Sport Psychologist*, 14, 157–175.

Jowett, S., and Poczwardowski, A. (2007) 'Understanding the coach-athlete relationship', in S. Jowett and D. Lavallee (eds), *Social Psychology in sport*, Champaign, IL: Human Kinetics, pp. 3–14.

Jowett, S., Paull, G., and Pensgaard, A. M. (2005) 'Coach–athlete relationship', in J. Taylor and G. S. Wilson (eds), *Applying sport psychology: Four perspectives*, Champaign, IL: Human Kinetics, pp. 153–170.

Kamphoff, C. S., Gill, D. L., and Huddleston, S. (2005) 'Jealousy in sport: Exploring jealousy's relationship to cohesion', *Journal of Applied Sport Psychology*, 17, 290–305.

Kapalka, G. M. (2004) 'Longer eye contact improves ADHD children's compliance with parents' commands', *Journal of Attention Disorders*, 8, 17–23.

Keegan, R. J., Harwood, C. G., Spray, C. M., and Lavallee, D. E. (2009) 'A qualitative investigation exploring the motivational climate in early career sports participants: Coach, parent and peer influences on sport motivation', *Psychology of Sport and Exercise*, 10, 361–372.

Keetch, K.M., and Lee, T. D. (2007) 'The effect of self-regulated and experimenter-imposed practice schedules on motor learning for tasks of varying difficulty', *Research Quarterly for Exercise and Sport*, 78, 476–486.

Kelly, G.A. (1991) *The psychology of personal constructs: A theory of personality,* Vol 1, London: Routledge (Original work published 1955).

Kerr, H. A., Curtis, C., Micheli, L. J., Kocher, M. S., Zurakowski, D., Kemp, S. P. T., and Brooks, J. H. M. (2008) 'Collegiate rugby union injury patterns in New England: A prospective cohort study', *British Journal of Sports Medicine,* 42, 595–603.

Kiluk, B. D., Weden, S., and Culotta, V. P. (2009) 'Sport participant and anxiety in children with ADHD', *Journal of Attention Disorders,* 12, 499–506.

Kindermann, W. (1988) 'Metabolic and hormonal reactions in overtraining', *Seminars in Orthopaedics,* 3, 207–216.

Kingston, K. M., and Hardy, L. (1997) 'Effects of different types of goals on processes that support performance', *The Sport Psychologist,* 11, 277–293.

Kirby, F. D., and Shields, F. (1972) 'Modification of arithmetic response rate and attending behaviour in a seventh-grade student', *Journal of Applied Behaviour Analysis,* 5, 79–84.

Koedijker, J. M., Oudejans, R. R. D., and Beck, P. J. (2007) 'Explicit rules and directions of attention in learning and performing the table tennis forehand', *International Journal of Sport Psychology,* 38, 227–244.

Knowles, M. S. (1995) *Designs for adult learning,* Alexandria, VA: American Society for Training and Development.

Knowles, M. S., Holton, E. F., and Swanson, R. A. (2011) *The adult learner: The definitive classic in adult education and human resource development,* Oxford: Butterworth-Heinemann.

Kobasa, S. C. (1979) 'Stressful life events, personality, and health: An inquiry into hardiness', *Journal of Personality and Social Psychology,* 37, 1–11.

Koocher, G. P., and Keith-Spiegel, P. (1998) *Ethics in psychology: Professional standards and cases* (2nd edn), New York: Oxford University Press.

Kowalski, K. C., and Crocker, P. R. (2001) 'Development and validation of the Coping Function Questionnaire for adolescents in sport', *Journal of Sport and Exercise Psychology,* 23, 136–55.

Krohne, H. W. (1993) 'Vigilance and cognitive avoidance as concepts in coping research', in H.W. Krohne (ed.), *Attention and avoidance: strategies in coping with adversiveness,* Seattle, WA: Hogrefe & Huber, pp. 19–50.

Kühn, A. A., Brücke, C., Hübl, J., Schneider, G. H., Kupsch, A., Eusebio, A., and Brown, P. (2008) 'Motivation modulates motor-related feedback activity in the human basal ganglia', *Current Biology,* 18, R648–R650.

Kvist, J., Ek, A., Sporrstedt, K., and Good, L. (2005) 'Fear of re-injury: a hindrance for returning to sports after anterior cruciate ligament reconstruction', *Knee Surgery, Sports Traumatology, Arthroscopy,* 13, 393–397.

Lafrenière, M-A. K., Jowett, S., Vallerand, R. J., and Carbonneau, N. (2011) 'Passion for coaching and the quality of the coach–athlete relationship: The mediating role of coaching behaviours', *Psychology of Sport and Exercise,* 12, 144–152.

Lam, W. K., Maxwell, J. P., and Masters, R. (2009) 'Analogy learning and the performance of motor skills under pressure', *Journal of Sport & Exercise Psychology,* 31, 337–357.

Lambert, J., and Bard, C. (2005) 'Acquisition of visuo-manual skills and improvement of information processing capacities in 6- to 10-year-old children performing a 2D pointing task', *Neuroscience Letters,* 377, 1–6.

Lang, P. J. (1977) 'Imagery in therapy: An information-processing analysis of fear', *Behaviour Therapy,* 8, 862–886.

LaVoi, N. M. (2004) 'Dimensions of closeness and conflict in the coach–athlete relationship', Paper presented at the meeting of the Association for the Advancement of Applied Sport Psychology, Minneapolis, MN, 29th September to 3rd October.

LaVoi, N. M. (2007) 'Expanding the interpersonal dimension: Closeness in the coach–athlete relationship', *International Journal of Sport Science and Coaching,* 4, 497–512.

Law, J., Masters, R., Bray, S. R., Eves, F., and Bardswell, I. (2003) 'Motor performances as a function of audience affability and metaknowledge', *Journal of Sport & Exercise Psychology,* 25, 484–500.

Law, M., Côté, J., and Ericsson, K. A. (2007) 'Characteristics of expert development in rhythmic gymnastics: A retrospective study', *International Journal of Sport and Exercise Psychology,* 5, 82–103.

Lazarus, R.S. (1991) *'Emotion and adaptation,* New York: Oxford University Press.

Lazarus, R. S. (1999) *Stress and emotion: A new synthesis,* New York: Springer.

Lazarus, R. S. (2000a) 'How emotions influence performance in competitive sports', *The Sport Psychologist,* 14, 229–252.

Lazarus, R. S. (2000b) 'Cognitive-motivational-relational theory of emotion', in Y.L. Hanin (ed.), *Emotions in sport,* Champaign, IL: Human Kinetics, pp. 39–63.

Lazarus, R. S., and Folkman, S. (1984) *Stress, appraisal and coping,* New York: Springer.

Leary, M. R. (2004) *'The curse of the self: Self-awareness, egotism, and the quality of human life.',* New York: Oxford University Press.

Lent, R.W., and Lopez, F.G. (2002) 'Cognitive ties that bind: a tripartite view of efficacy beliefs in growth-promoting relationships', *Journal of Social and Clinical Psychology,* 21, 256–286.

Lepper, M. R., and Hodell, M. (1989) 'Intrinsic motivation in the classroom', in C. Ames and R. Ames (eds), *Research on motivation in education,* New York: Academic Press, 73–105.

Lewthwaite, R., and Wulf, G. (2010) 'Social-comparative feedback affects motor skill learning', *Quarterly Journal of Experimental Psychology,* 63, 738–749.

Liao, C. M., and Masters, R. S. W. (2001) 'Analogy learning: A means to implicit motor learning', *Journal of Sports Sciences,* 19, 307–319.

Lindeman, E. C. (1926) 'Andragogik: The method of teaching adults', *Workers' Education,* 4, 38–45.

Liu, T., and Jensen, J. L. (2011) 'Effects of strategy use on children's motor performance in continuous timing task', *Research Quarterly for Exercise and Sport,* 82, 198–209.

Locke, E. A., and Latham, G. P. (1990) *A theory of goal setting and task performance.* Englewood Cliffs, NJ: Prentice Hall.

Locke, E.A., and Latham, G.P. (2002) 'Building a practically useful theory of goal setting and task motivation: A 35-year odyssey', *American Psychologist,* 57, 705–717.

Loko, J., Aule, R., Sikkut, T., Ereline, J., and Viru, A. (2000) 'Motor performance status in 10- to 17-year-old Estonian girls', *Scandinavian Journal of Medicine and Science in Sports,* 10, 109–113.

Lonsdale, C., and Tam, J. T. M. (2008) 'On the temporal and behavioural consistency of pre-performance routines: An intra-individual analysis of elite basketball players' free throw shooting accuracy', *Journal of Sports Sciences,* 26, 259–266.

Lorimer, R., and Jowett, S. (2009) 'Empathic accuracy, meta perspective, and satisfaction in the coach–athlete relationship, *Journal of Applied Sport Psycholgy,* 21, 201–212.

Lyle, J. (2007) 'Modelling the complexity of the coaching process: A commentary', *International Journal of Sports Science & Coaching,* 2, 407–409.

Lyle, J. (2011) 'What is a coach and what is coaching?', in I. Stanford (ed.), *Coaching children in sport,* London: Routledge, pp. 5–16.

MacPhail, A., Gorley, T., Kirk, D., and Kinchin, G. (2008) 'Children's experiences of fun and enjoyment during a season of sport education', *Research Quarterly for Exercise and Sport,* 79, 344–355.

Marcos, F. M. L., Miguel, P. A. S., Olivia, D. S., and Calvo, T. G. (2010) 'Interactive effects of team cohesion on perceived efficacy in semi-professional sport', *Journal of Sport Science and Medicine,* 9, 320–325.

Marsh, H. W., and Kleitman, S. (2003) 'School athletic participation: Mostly gain with little pain', *Journal of Sport & Exercise Psychology*, 25, 205–228.

Marshall, H. H., and Weinstein, R. S. (1984) 'Classroom factors affecting students' self evaluations: An interactional model', *Review of Educational Research,* 54, 301–325.

Martin, K. A., Moritz, S. E., and Hall, C. R. (1999) 'Imagery use in sport: A literature review and applied model', *The Sport Psychologist,* 13, 245–268.

Martin, L. J., Carron, A. V., and Burke, S. M. (2009) 'Team building interventions in sport: A meta-analysis', *Sport and Exercise Psychology Review,* 5, 3–18.

Martin, S. B., Dale, G. A., and Jackson, A. W. (2003) 'Youth coaching preferences of adolescent athletes and their parents', *Journal of Sport Behavior,* 24, 197–212.

Martinek, T. (1989) 'The psycho-social dynamics of the Pygmalion phenomenon in physical education and sport', in T. Templin and P. Schemp (eds), *Socialisation into physical education: Learning to teach,* Indianapolis, IN: Benchmark Press, pp. 199–217,

Masters, R.S.W. (1992) 'Knowledge, nerves and know-how', *British Journal of Psychology*, 83, 343–58.

Masters, R. S. W. (2000) 'Theoretical aspects of implicit learning in sport', *International Journal of Sport Psychology,* 31, 530–541.

Matteri, R. L., Carroll, J. A., and Dyer, C. J. (2000) 'Neuroendocrine responses to stress' in G. P. Moberg and J. A. Mench (eds) *The Biology of Animal Stress: Basic principles and implications for animal welfare,* Oxford: CABI Publishing, pp. 43–75.

McArdle, S., and Duda, J. K. (2002) 'Implications of the motivational climate in youth sports, in F. L. Smoll and R. E. Smith (eds), *Children and youth in sport,* Dubuque, IA: Kendall/Hunt.

Mageau, G.A., and Vallerand, R.J. (2003) 'The coach–athlete relationship: A motivational model', *Journal of Sports Sciences,* 21, 883–904.

Meichenbaum, D. (1977) *Cognitive-behaviour modification: An intergrative approach,* New York: Plenum Press.

Merriam, S., and Brockett, R. G. (1997) *The profession and practice of adult education: An introduction,* San Francisco, CA: Jossey-Bass.

Mesagno, C., and Mullane-Grant, T. (2010) 'A comparison of different pre-performance routines as possible choking interventions', *Journal of Applied Sport Psychology,* 22, 343–360.

Mesagno, C., Marchant, D., and Morris, T. (2008) 'Using a pre-performance routine to alleviate choking under pressure in "choking-susceptible" athletes', *The Sport Psychologist,* 22, 439–457.

Millar, S.-K., Oldham, A. R. H., and Donovan, M. (2011) 'Coaches' self-awareness of timing, nature and intent of verbal instructions to athletes', *International Journal of Sports Science and Coaching,* 6, 503–513.

Miller, A., and Donohue, B. (2003) 'The development and controlled evaluation of athletic mental preparation strategies in high school distance runners', *Journal of Applied Sport Psychology,* 15, 321–334.

Miller, S., and Weinberg, R. (1991) 'Perceptions of psychological momentum and their relationship to performance', *The Sport Psychologist*, 211–222.

Mills, T. M. (1984) *The sociology of small groups*, Englewood Cliffs, NJ: Prentice Hall.

Moran, A. P. (1996) *The psychology of concentration in sport performers: A cognitive analysis*, London: Taylor & Francis.

Morgan, T. K., and Giacobbi, P. R. (2006) 'Toward two grounded theories of the talent development and social support process of highly successful collegiate athletes, *The Sport Psychologist*, 20, 295–313.

Morozova, L. V., Zvyagina, N. V., and Terebova, N. N. (2008) 'Characteristics of visual perception in seven-year-old children differing in functional maturity of brain structures', *Human Physiology*, 34, 14–21.

Mullen, R., Hardy, L., and Tattersall, A. (2005) 'The effects of anxiety on motor performance: A test of the conscious processing hypothesis', *Journal of Sport & Exercise Psychology*, 27, 212–225.

Munroe, K., Giacobbi, P., Hall, C., and Weinberg, R. (2000) 'The 4W's of imagery use: Where, when, why, and what', *The Sport Psychologist*, 14, 119–137.

Munroe, K., Terry, P. C., and Carron, A. (2002) 'Cohesion and teamwork', in B. Hale and D. Collins (eds), *Rugby tough*, Champaign, IL: Human Kinetics, pp. 137–154.

Murphy, S. (1996) *'The achievement zone'*, New York: Putnam's.

Murphy, S. M., Fleck, S. J., and Callister, R. (1990) 'Psychological and performance concomitants of increased volume training in athletics', *Journal of Applied Sport Psychology*, 2, 34–50.

Murphy, S., Nordin, S., and Cumming, J. (2008) 'Imagery in sport, exercise, and dance', in T. S. Horn (ed.), *Advances in sport psychology*, Champaign, IL: Human Kinetics, pp. 297–324.

Nicholls, A. R. (2007a) 'A longitudinal phenomenological analysis of coping effectiveness among Scottish international adolescent golfers', *European Journal of Sport Science*, 7, 169–178.

Nicholls, A. R. (2007b) 'Can an athlete be taught to cope more effectively? The experiences of an international level adolescent golfer during a training program for coping', *Perceptual and Motor Skills*, 104, 494–500.

Nicholls, A. R. (2010) 'Effective versus ineffective coping', in A. R. Nicholls (ed.), *Coping in sport: theory, methods, and related constructs*, New York: Nova Science Inc., pp. 263–276.

Nicholls, A. R. (2011) 'Mental toughness and coping in sport', in D. Gucciardi and S. Gordon (eds), *Mental toughness in sport: Developments in research and theory*, London: Routledge, pp. 30–46.

Nicholls, A. R., and Callard, J. (2012) *Focused for rugby*, Champaign, IL: Human Kinetics.

Nicholls, A. R., and Thelwell, R. (2010) 'Coping conceptualized and unravelled', in A. R. Nicholls (ed.), *Coping in sport: theory, methods, and related constructs*, New York: Nova Science Inc., pp. 3–14.

Nicholls, A. R., Hemmings, B., and Clough, P. J. (2010) 'Stressors, coping, and emotion among international adolescent golfers', *Scandinavian Journal of Medicine & Science in Sports*, 20, 346–355.

Nicholls, A. R., Holt, N. L., and Polman, R. C. J. (2005b) 'A phenomenological analysis of coping effectiveness in golf', *The Sport Psychologist*, 19, 111–30.

Nicholls, A. R., Levy, A. R., and Polman, R. C. J. (2012) 'A path analysis of stress appraisals, emotions, coping, and performance satisfaction among athletes', *Psychology of Sport and Exercise*, 13, 263–270.

Nicholls, A. R., Holt, N. L., Polman, R. C. J., and James, D. W. G. (2005a) 'Stress and coping among international adolescent golfers', *Journal of Applied Sport Psychology*, 17, 333–40.

Nicholls, A.R., Jones, C. R., Polman, R. C. J., and Borkoles, E. (2009) 'Stressors, coping, and emotion among professional rugby union players during training and matches', *Scandinavian Journal of Medicine and Science in Sports*, 19, 113–20.

Nicholls, A. R., Levy, A. R., Jones, L., Rengamani, M., and Polman, R. C. J. (2011) 'An exploration of the two-factor schematization of relational meaning and emotions among professional rugby union players', *International Journal of Sport and Exercise Psychology*, 9, 78–91.

Nicholls, A. R., Polman, R. C. J., Levy, A. R., and Backhouse, S. H. (2008) 'Mental toughness, optimism, pessimism, and coping among athletes', *Personality and Individual Differences*, 44, 1182–92.

Nicholls, A. R., Polman, R.C. J., Levy, A. R., Taylor, J. A., and Cobley, S. P. (2007) 'Stressors, coping, and coping effectiveness: Gender, sport type, and skill differences', *Journal of Sports Sciences*, 25, 1521–1530.

Nicholls, A. R., and Polman, R. C. J. (2007) 'Coping in sport: A systematic review', *Journal of Sport Sciences*, 25, 11–31.

Nicholls, J. G. (1989) *The competitive ethos and democratic education*, Cambridge, MA: Harvard University Press.

Nideffer, R. M. (1992) *Psyched to win*, Champaign, IL: Leisure Press.

Nippert, A. H., and Smith, A. M. (2008) 'Psychological stress related to injury and impact on sport performance', *Physical Medicine and Rehabilitation Clinics of North America*, 19, 399–418.

Nordin, S., and Cumming, J. (2005) 'More than meets the eye: Investigating imagery type, direction, and outcome', *The Sport Psychologist*, 19, 1–17.

O'Leary, K. D., and O'Leary, S. G. (1977) *Classroom management: The successful use of behaviour modification*, (2nd edn), New York: Pergamon Press.

Oudejans, R. R. D., and Pijpers, J. R. (2010). 'Training with mild anxiety may prevent choking under high levels of anxiety', *Psychology of Sport & Exercise*, 11, 44–50.

Pain, M. A., Harwood, C., and Anderson, R. (2011) 'Pre-competition imagery and music: The impact on flow and performance in competitive soccer', *The Sport Psychologist*, 25, 212–232.

Pelletier, I. G., Fortier, M. S., Vallerand, R. J., and Brière, N. M. (2001) 'Associations among perceived autonomy support, forms of self-regulation, and persistence: A prospective study', *Motivation and Emotion*, 25, 279–306.

Petitpas, A. J. (2000) 'Managing stress on and off the field: The littlefoot approach to learned resourcefulness', in M. B. Andersen (ed.), *Doing sport psychology*, Champaign, IL: Human Kinetics, pp. 33–44.

Pfiffner, L. J., and Barkley, R. A. (1990) 'Educational placement and classroom management', in R. A. Barkley (ed.), *Attention-deficit hyperactivity disorder: A handbook for diagnosis and treatment*, New York: Guilford Press, pp. 498–539.

Poczwardowski, A. (1997) 'Athletes and coaches: An exploration of their relationship and its meaning', Unpublished doctoral dissertation, University of Utah, Salt Lake City.

Poczwardowski, A., and Conroy, D. E. (2002) 'Coping responses to failure and success among elite athletes and performing artists', *Journal of Applied Sport Psychology*, 14, 313–329.

Poczwardowski, A., Henschen, K. P., and Barott, J. E. (2002) 'The athlete and the coach: Their relationship and its meaning. Results of an interpretive study', *International Journal of Sport Psychology*, 33, 114–140.

Podlog, L., and Dionigi, R. (2010) 'Coach strategies for addressing psychosocial challenges during the return to sport from injury', *Journal of Sports Sciences*, 28, 1197–1208.

Post, P. G., Fairbrother, J. T., and Barros, J. A. C. (2011) 'Self-controlled amount of practice benefits learning of a motor skill', *Research Quarterly for Exercise and Sport*, 82, 474–481.

Prapavessis, H., and Carron, A. V. (1996) 'The effect of group cohesion on competitive state anxiety', *Journal of Sport & Exercise Psychology*, 18, 64–74.

Price, M. S., and Weiss, M. R. (2000) 'Relationships among coach burnout, coach behaviours, and athletes' psychological responses', *The Sport Psychologist*, 14, 391–409.

Proteau, L., Marteniuk, R. G., and Lévesque, L. (1992) 'A sensorimotor basis for motor learning: Evidence indicating specificity of practice', *Quarterly Journal of Experimental Psychology*, 44A, 557–575.

Raedeke, T. D., and Smith, A. L. (2001) 'Development and preliminary validation of an athlete burnout questionnaire', *Journal of Sport & Exercise Psychology*, 23, 281–306.

Rahim, M. (2002) 'Toward a theory of managing organizational conflict' *International Journal of Conflict Management*, 13, 206–235.

Rees, T. (2007) 'Influence of social support on athletes', in S. Jowett and D. Lavallee (eds), *Social psychology in sport*, Champaign, IL: Human Kinetics, pp. 223–232.

Rees, T., and Freeman, P. (2009) 'Social support moderates the relationship between stressors and task performance through self-efficacy', *Journal of Social and Clinical Psychology*, 28, 245–264.

Rees, T., and Freeman, P. (2010) 'Social support and performance in a golf-putting experiment', *The Sport Psychologist*, 18, 333–348.

Rees, T., Hardy, L., and Freeman, P. (2007) 'Stressors, social support and effects upon performance in golf', *Journal of Sports Sciences*, 25, 33–42.

Reeves, C. W., Nicholls, A. R., and McKenna, J. (2009) 'Stress and coping among academy footballers: Age-related differences', *Journal of Applied Sport Psychology*, 21, 31–48.

Reeves, C. W., Nicholls, A. R., and McKenna, J. (2011) 'The effects of a coping intervention on coping self-efficacy, coping effectiveness, and subjective performance among adolescent soccer players', *International Journal of Sport and Exercise Psychology*, 9, 126–142

Reid, G. (2009) *Dyslexia: A practitioner's handbook*, Chichester: Wiley-Blackwell.

Reinboth, M., Duda, J. L., and Ntoumanis, N. (2004) 'Dimensions of coaching behaviour, need satisfaction, and the psychological and physical welfare of young athletes', *Motivation and Emotion*, 28, 297–313.

Reischmann, H., and Jost, N. (2004) 'Andragogy: History, meaning, context, function'. Retrieved from http://wwww.andragogy.net, 9 September 2004.

Rhind, D. J. A., and Jowett, S. (2010) 'Relationship maintenance strategies in the coach–athlete relationship: The development of the COMPASS model, *Journal of Applied Sport Psychology*, 22, 106–121.

Richardson, A. (1969) *Mental Imagery*, New York: Springer.

Rief, S. F. (2008) *The ADD/ADHD checklist: A practical reference for parents and teachers*, San Francisco, CA: Jossey-Bass.

Rieke, M., Hammermeister, J., and Chase, M. (2008) 'Servant leadership in sport: A new paradigm for effective coach behaviour', *International Journal of Sports Science & Coaching*, 2, 227–239.

Rizzo, T.L., Bishop, P., and Tobar, D. (1997) 'Attitudes of soccer coaches toward youth players with mild mental retardation: A pilot study', *Adapted Physical Activity Quarterly*, 14, 238.

Robin, N., Domonique, L., Tousasaint, L., Blandin, Y., Guillot, A., and LeHer, M. (2007) 'Effects of motor imagery training on service returns accuracy in tennis: The role of image ability', *International Journal of Sport and Exercise Psychology*, 2, 175–186.

Rodgers, W., Hall, C. R., and Buckholtz, E. (1991) 'The effect of an imagery training programme on imagery ability, imagery use, and figure skating performance', *Journal of Applied Sport Psychology*, 3, 109–125.

Rosenberg, M. (1979) *Conceiving the self*, New York: Basic Books.

Rosenfeld, L. B., Richman, J. M., and Hardy, C. J. (1989) 'Examining social support networks among athletes: Description and relationship to stress', *The Sport Psychologist*, 3, 23–33.

Rosenfeld, L. B., and Richman, J. M. (1997) 'Developing effective social support: Team building and the social support process', *Journal of Applied Sport Psychology*, 9, 133–153.

Rotella, R. J. (1985) 'The psychological care of the injured athlete', in L. Bunker, R. J. Rotella, and A. S. Reilly (eds), *Sport psychology: Psychological considerations in maximizing sport performance*, Ithaca, NY: Movement, pp. 273–287.

Ryan, R. M., and Deci, E. L. (2007) ' Active human nature: Self-determination theory and the promotion and maintenance of sport, exercise, and health', in M. S. Hagger and N. L. D. Chatzisarantis (eds), *Intrinsic motivation and self-determination in exercise and sport*, Champaign, IL: Human Kinetics, pp. 1–20.

Ryska, T. A., Yin, Z., Cooley, D., and Ginn, R. (1999) 'Developing team cohesion: A comparison of cognitive-behavioural strategies of U.S. and Australian Sport Coaches', *The Journal of Psychology*, 133, 523–539.

Sackett, R. S. (1934) 'The influences of symbolic rehearsal upon the retention of a maze habit', *Journal of General Psychology*, 13, 113–128.

Scanlan, T. K., and Lewthwaite, R. (1986) 'Social psychological aspects of competition for male youth sport participants: IV. Predictors of enjoyment', *Journal of Sport Psychology*, 8, 25–35.

Scanlan, T. K., Carpenter, P. J., Lobel, M., and Simons, J. P. (1993) 'Sources of enjoyment for youth sport athletes', *Pediatric Exercise Science*, 5, 275–285.

Schack, T., Whitmarsh, B., Pike, R., and Redden, C. (2005) 'Coach–athlete relationship', in J. Taylor and G. S. Wilson (eds), *Applying sport psychology: Four perspectives*, Champaign, IL: Human Kinetics, pp. 137–150.

Schmidt, R. A., and Bjork, R. A. (1992) 'New conceptualisations of practice: Common principles in three paradigms suggest new concepts for training', *Psychological Science*, 3, 207–217.

Schmidt, R. A., and Lee, T. D. (2005) *Motor control and learning*, (4th edn), Champaign, IL: Human Kinetics.

Seligman, M. E. P. (2006) *Learned optimism: How to change your mind and your life*, New York: Vintage Books.

Sheard, M., and Golby, J. (2006) 'Effect of a psychological skills training program on swimming performance and positive psychological development', *International Journal of Sport and Exercise Psychology*, 4, 149–169.

Sheldon, K. A., and Watson, A. (2011) 'Coach's autonomy support is especially important for varsity compared to club and recreational athletes', *International Journal of Sports Science and Coaching*, 6, 109–123.

Shilts, M. K., Horowitz, M., and Townsend, M. S. (2004) 'An innovative approach to goal setting for adolescents: Guided goal setting', *Journal of Nutritional Education and Behaviour,* 36, 155–156.

Shumaker, S. A., and Brownell, A. (1984) 'Toward a theory of social support: Closing conceptual gaps', *Journal of Social Issues,* 40, 11–36.

Siegenthaler, K. L., and Gonzalez, G. L. (1997) 'Youth sports as serious leisure: A critique', *Journal of Sport and Social Issues,* 21, 298–314.

Singer, R. N., and Janelle, C. M. (1999) 'Determining sport expertise: From genes to supremes', *International Journal of Sport Psychology,* 30, 117–150.

Singh, N. N., Singh, A. N., Lancioni, G. E., Singh, J., Winton, A. S. W., and Adkins, A. D. (2010) 'Mindfulness training for parents and their children with ADHD increases the children's compliance', *Journal of Child and Family Studies,* 19, 157–166.

Smith, A. M. (1996) 'Psychological impact of injuries in athletes' *Sports Medicine,* 22, 391–405.

Smith, C., and Strick, L. (2010) *'Learning disabilities: A to Z',* New York: Free Press.

Smith, D. (1992) 'The coach as sport psychologist: An alternative view', *Journal of Applied Sport Psychology,* 2, 56–62.

Smith, D., Wright, A., Allsopp, A., and Westhead, H. (2007) 'It's all in the mind: PETTLEP-based imagery and sports performance', *Journal of Applied Sport Psychology,* 19, 80–92.

Smith, H. W. (1994) *The 10 natural laws of successful time and life management: Proven strategies for increased productivity and inner peace,* New York: Warner.

Smith, M., and Cushion, C. J. (2006) 'An investigation of the in-game behaviours of professional, top-level youth soccer coaches, *Journal of Sports Sciences,* 24, 355–366.

Smith, R. E. (1980) 'A cognitive-affective approach to stress management training for athletes', in C. H. Nadeau, W. R. Halliwell, K. M. Newell, and G. C. Roberts (eds), *Psychology of motor behaviour and sport,* Champaign, IL: Human Kinetics, pp. 54–72.

Smith, R. E., and Smoll, F. L. (1990) 'Self-esteem and children's reactions to youth sport coaching behaviours: A field study of self enhancement processes', *Developmental Psychology,* 26, 987–1003.

Smith, R. E., and Smoll, F. L. (1996) *Way to go, coach! A scientifically-proven approach to coaching effectiveness,* Portola Valley, CA: Warde.

Smith, R. E., and Smoll, F. L. (1997) 'Coaching the coaches: Youth sports as a scientific and applied behavioural setting', *Current Directions in Psychological Science,* 6, 16–21.

Smith, R. E., Zane, N. W. S., Smoll, F. L., and Coppel, D. B. (1983) 'Behavioural assessment in youth sports: Coaching behaviours and children's attitudes', *Medicine and Science in Sports and Exercise,* 15, 208–214.

Smoll, F. L., and Smith, R. E. (2006) 'Enhancing coach-athlete relationships: Cognitive behavioural principles and procedures', in J. Dosil (ed.), *The sport psychologist's handbook: A guide for sport-specific performance enhancement,* Chichester: John Wiley & Sons Ltd, pp. 19–38.

Smoll, F. L., Smith, R. E., Barnett, N. P., and Everett, J. J. (1993) 'Enhancement of children's self-esteem through social support training for youth sport coaches', *Journal of Applied Psychology,* 4, 602–610.

Spaniol, J., Voss, A., Bowen, H. J., and Grady, C. L. (2011) 'Motivational incentives modulate age differences in visual perception', *Psychology and Aging,* 26, 932–939.

Sport England, (2007) *What we do and how we do it: Sport England's role and links to the Youth Sport Trust and UK Sport,* London: Sport England.

Sport England, (2010) *Active people survey (APS) results for football: Period: APS2 (Oct 07/Oct 08) to APS4 (Oct 09/Oct10),* London: Sport England.

Sport England (2011) *3x30 Sports Participation Indicator,* London: Sport England.

Sport Scotland (2008) *Sports participation in Scotland 2008: Research Digest no. 110,* London: Sport Scotland.

Stebbings, J., Taylor, I. M., and Spray, C. (2011) 'Antecedents of perceived coach autonomy supportive and controlling behaviours: Coach psychological need satisfaction and well-being, *Journal of Sport & Exercise Psychology,* 33, 255–272.

Stein, J. F., Richardson, A. J., and Fowler, M. S. (2000) 'Monocular occlusion can improve binocular control and reading in dyslexics', *Brain,* 123, 164–170.

Stowe, C. M. (2000) *How to reach and teach children and teens with dyslexia,* San Francisco, CA: Jossey-Bass.

Stryer, B. K., Tofler, I. R., and Lapchick, R. (1998) 'A developmental overview of child and youth sports in society', *Sports Psychiatry,* 7, 697–711.

Sulzer-Azaroff, B., and Mayer, G. R. (1991) *Behaviour analysis for lasting change,* Fort Worth, TX: Holt, Rinehart, and Winston.

Taylor, J., and Schneider, B. A. (1992) 'The sport-clinical intake protocol: A comprehensive interviewing instrument for applied sport psychology', *Professional Psychology: Research and Practice,* 23, 318–325.

Taylor, S. E., and Brown, J. D. (1988) 'Illusions and well-being: A social psychological perspective on mental health', *Psychological Bulletin,* 103, 193–210.

Taylor, J., and Taylor, S. (1997) *Psychological approaches to sports injury rehabilitation,* New York: Aspen Publication.

Taylor, K. E., and Walter, J. (2003) 'Occupation choices of adults with and without symptoms of dyslexia', *Dyslexia,* 9, 177–185.

Tennen, H., and Affleck, G. (1993) 'The puzzles of self-esteem: A clinical perspective', in R. F. Baumeister (ed.), *The puzzle of low self regard. Plenum series in social/clinical psychology,* New York: Plenum, pp. 241–262.

Terry, P. C., Keohane, L., and Lane, H. J. (1996) 'Development and validation of a shortened verison of the Profile of Mood States suitable for use with young athletes', *Journal of Sports Sciences,* 14, 49.

Theeboom, M., De Knop, P., and Weiss, M. R. (1995) 'Motivational climate, psychological responses, and motor skill development in children's sport: a field-based intervention study', *Journal of Sport & Exercise Psychology,* 17, 294–311.

Thelwell, R. C., Such, B. A., Weston, N. J. V., Such, J. D., and Greenlees, I. A. (2010) 'Developing mental toughness: Perceptions of elite female gymnasts', *International Journal of Sport and Exercise Psychology,* 8, 170–188.

Tracy, A. J., and Erkut, S. (2002) 'Gender and race patterns in the pathways from sports participation to self', *Sociological Perspectives,* 45, 445–466.

Treasure, D. (1993) 'A social-cognitive approach to understanding children's achievement behaviour, cognitions, and affect in competitive sport', Unpublished doctoral dissertation, University of Illinois.

Treasure, D. (2001) 'Enhancing young people's motivation in youth sport: An achievement goal approach', in G. C. Roberts (ed.), *Advances in motivation in sport and exercise,* Champaign, IL: Human Kinetics, pp. 79–100.

Udry, E. (1997) 'Coping and social support among injured athletes following surgery', *Journal of Sport & Exercise Psychology,* 19, 71–90.

Udry, E., Gould, D., Bridges, D., and Tuffey, S. (1997) 'People helping people? Examining the social ties of athletes coping with burnout and injury stress', *Journal of Sport & Exercise Psychology,* 19, 368–395.

U.S. Department of Education (2007) *Digest of education statistics,* retrieved on 19 January 2012 from http//nces.edu.gov/programs/digest/d07/tables/dt07_047.asp

Vallerand, R. J. (2001) 'A hierarchical model of intrinsic and extrinsic motivation for sport and exercise', in G. C. Roberts (ed.), *Advances in motivation in sport and exercise,* Champaign, IL: Human Kinetics, pp. 263–320.

Vallerand, R. J. (2007) 'A hierarchical model of intrinsic and extrinsic motivation for sport and physical activity', in M. S. Hagger and N. L. D. Chatzisarantis (eds), *Intrinsic motivation and self-determination in exercise and sport,* Champaign, IL: Human Kinetics, pp. 255–279.

Vallerand, R.J., Colavecchio, P.G., and Pelletier, L.G. (1988) 'Psychological momentum and performance inferences: A preliminary test of the antecedents-consequences psychological momentum model', *Journal of Sport & Exercise Psychology,* 10, 92–108.

Vargas-Tonsing, T. M., and Guan, J. (2007) 'Athletes' preferences for informational and emotional pre-game speech content', *International Journal of Sports Science & Coaching,* 2, 171–180.

Vargas-Tonsing, T. M., Myers, N. D., and Feltz, D. L. (2004) 'Coaches' and athletes' perceptions of efficacy enhancing techniques', *The Sport Psychologist,* 18, 397–414.

Vealey, R. S. (1986) 'Conceptualisation of sport-confidence and competitive orientation: Preliminary investigation and instrument development', *Journal of Sport Psychology,* 8, 221–246.

Vealey, R. S. (2001) 'Understanding and enhancing self-confidence in athletes', in R. Singer, H. Hausenblas, and C. Janelle (eds), *Handbook of sport psychology,* New York: Wiley, pp. 550–565.

Vealey, R. S., and Chase, M. A. (2008) 'Self-confidence in sport', in T. S. Horn (ed.), *Advances in sport psychology,* Champaign, IL: Human Kinetics, pp. 65–98.

Vealey, R. S. and Knight, B. J. (2002) *Multidimensional sport-confidence: A conceptual and psychometric extension,* Tuscan, AZ: Association for the Advancement of Applied Sport Psychology.

Walters, S. R., Schluter, P. J., Oldham, A., Thomson, R. W., and Payne, D. (2012) 'The sideline behaviour of coaches at children's team sports games', *Psychology of Sport & Exercise,* 13, 208–205.

Wandzilak, T., Ansorge, C. J., and Potter, G. (1988) 'Comparison between selected practice and game behaviors of youth sport soccer coaches', *Journal of Sport Behavior,* 11, 78–88.

Weinberg, R., and Butt, J. (2011) 'Building mental toughness', in D. Gucciardi and S. Gordon (eds), *Mental toughness in sport: Developments in research and theory,* London: Routledge, pp. 212–229.

Weinberg, R., Yukelson, D., and Jackson, A. (1980) 'Effect of public versus private efficacy expectations on competitive performance', *Journal of Sport Psychology,* 2, 340–349.

Weinstein, R. S. (1989) 'Perceptions of classroom processes and student motivation', in C. Ames and R. Ames (eds), *Research on motivation in education,* San Diego, CA: Academic Press, pp. 187–221.

Weiss, M. R. (1995) 'Children in sport: An educational model', in S. M. Murphy (ed.), *Sport psychology interventions,* Champaign, IL: Human Kinetics, pp. 39–69.

Weiss, M. R., and Amorose, A. J. (2008) 'Motivational orientations and sport behaviour', in T. S. Horn (ed.), *Advances in sport psychology,* Champaign, IL: Human Kinetics, pp. 115–155.

Weiss, M. R., Amorose, A. J., and Wilko, A. M. (2009) 'Coaching behaviours, motivational climate, and psychosocial outcomes among female adolescent athletes', *Paediatric Exercise Science*, 21, 475–492.

Weiss, M. R., and Williams, L. (2004) 'The *why* of youth sport involvement: A developmental perspective on motivational processes', in M. R. Weiss (ed.), *Developmental sport and exercise psychology: a lifespan perspective*, Morgantown, WV: Fitness Information Technology, pp. 223–268.

Weldon, E., and Weingart. L. R. (1988) 'A theory of group goals and group performance'. Paper presented at the annual meeting of the Academy of Management, Anaheim, CA, 7th to 9th August.

Weston, N. J. V, Greenlees, I. A., and Thelwell, R. C. (2011) 'The impact of a performance profiling intervention on athletes' intrinsic motivation', *Research Quarterly for Exercise and Sport*, 82, 151–155.

Westre, K. R., and Weiss, M. R. (1991) 'The relationship between perceived coaching behaviours and group cohesion in high school football teams', *The Sport Psychologist*, 5, 41–54.

Widmeyer, W. N., and Ducharme, K. (1997) 'Team building through team goal setting', *Journal of Applied Sport Psychology*, 9, 97–113.

Williams, A. M., and Hodges, N. J. (2005) 'Practice, instruction and skill acquisition: Challenging tradition', *Journal of Sports Sciences*, 23, 637–650.

Williams, J. M., and Roepke, N. (1993) 'Psychology of injury and injury rehabilitation', in R. N. Singer, M. Murphy, and K. Tennant (eds), *Handbook of research on sport psychology*, New York: Macmillan, pp. 815–839.

Wilson, R. C., Sullivan, P. J., Myers, N. D., and Feltz, D. L. (2004) 'Sources of sport confidence of master athletes', *Journal of Sport & Exercise Psychology*, 26, 369–384.

Woodman, T., and Hardy, L. (2003) 'The relative impact of cognitive anxiety and self confidence upon sport performance: A meta-analysis', *Journal of Sports Sciences*, 21, 443–457.

Wrisberg, C. A., and Pein, R. L. (2002) 'Note on learners' control of the frequency of model presentation during skill acquisition', *Perceptual and Motor Skills*, 94, 738–794.

Wu, W. F. W., and Magill, R. A. (2011) 'Allowing learners to choose: Self-controlled practice schedules for learning multiple movement patterns', *Research Quarterly for Exercise and Sport*, 82, 449–457.

Wulf, G., and Lewthwaite, R. (2009) 'Attentional and motivational influences on motor performance and learning', in A. Mornell (ed.), *Art in motion: Musical and athletic motor learning and performance*, Frankfurt: Peter Lang, pp. 95–117.

Wulf, G., and Lewthwaite, R. (2010) 'Effortless motor learning? An external focus of attention enhances movement effectiveness and efficiency', in B. Bruya (ed.), *Effortless attention: A new perspective in the cognitive science of attention and action*, Cambridge, MA: MIT Press, pp. 75–101.

Wulf, G., and Shea, C. H. (2004) 'Understanding the role of augmented feedback: The good, the bad, and the ugly', in A. M. Williams and N. J. Hodges, (eds), *Skill acquisition in sport: Research, theory and practice*, London: Routledge, pp. 121–144.

Wulf, G., and Toole, T. (1999) 'Physical assistance devices in complex motor skill learning: Benefits of a self-controlled practice schedule', *Research Quarterly for Exercise and Sport*, 70, 265–272.

Wulf, G., Chiviacowsky, S., and Lewthwaite, R. (2010) 'Normative feedback effects on learning a timing task', *Research Quarterly for Exercise and Sport*, 81, 425–431.

Zaff, J. F., Moore, K. A., Papillo, A. R., and Williams, S. (2003) 'Implications of extracurricular activity participation during adolescence on positive outcomes', *Journal of Adolescent Research,* 18, 599–630.

Zentall, S. S., and Zentall, T. R. (1983) 'Optimal stimulation: A model of disordered activity and performance in normal and deviant children', *Psychological Bulletin,* 94, 446–471.

Zourbanos, N., Harzigeorgiadis, A., and Theodorakis, Y. (2007) 'A preliminary investigation of the relationship between athletes' self-talk and coaches' behaviour and statements', *International Journal of Sports Science & Coaching,* 1, 57–66.

Zourbanos, N., Harzigeorgiadis, A., Tsiakaras, S. C., Chroni, S., and Theodorakis, Y. (2010) 'A multimethod examination of the relationship between coaching behaviour and athletes inherent self-talk', *Journal of Sport & Exercise Psychology,* 32, 764–785.

Zourbanos, N., Harzigeorgiadis, A., Goudas, M., Papaioannou, A., Chroni, S., and Theodorakis, Y. (2011) 'The social side of self-talk: Relationships between perceptions of support received from the coach and athletes' self-talk', *Psychology of Sport and Exercise,* 12, 407–414.

Index